THE SECRET

THE SECRET

*The Strange Marriage of
Annabella Milbanke and Lord Byron*

Ashley Hay

AURUM PRESS

First published in Great Britain
2001 by Aurum Press Ltd
25 Bedford Avenue, London WC1B 3AT

A catalogue record for this book is available from the British Library.

ISBN 1 85410 783 6

1 3 5 7 9 10 8 6 4 2
2001 2003 2005 2004 2002

Cover design by Alex Snellgrove and Roger Hammond
Cover illustration of Annabella Milbanke by
George Hayter, 1812, © the Earl of Lytton.

Printed in Great Britain by MPG Books Ltd, Bodmin, Cornwall

for Sophie Cole and Ross Warren

CONTENTS

List of Illustrations

'Fame is the sum total of all the misunderstandings
that can gather around one name.'

Rilke

'To have read and reached out for all that comes
to hand about Byron, to have enjoyed to the full
the fun of making him up, of imagining how he
spoke, looked, dressed ... all this is nothing but a
random game ... it is making up a whole ...
but only such a whole as we could live in ourselves,
and imagine as the living place of others.'

Virginia Woolf

'I harm nobody – I make love with but one
woman at a time and as quietly as possible, and
they lie through thick and thin and invent
every kind of absurdity.'

Lord Byron

There were three people in the room. The man leaned against the fireplace. A woman sat on a sofa; another stood in the doorway. A man, his sister, his wife. Lord Byron, Augusta Leigh, Lady Annabella Byron. Outside, the light was cold and yellow from the middle of winter, January, 1816. Outside, Piccadilly Terrace – one of London's stylish streets – held deep shadows and heavy silence. Inside, these people watched each other, waited for someone to speak. The moment froze, and then Byron, smiling, quoted *Macbeth*: 'When shall we three meet again?'

From the doorway, his wife peered at him the way she always peered at him, as if he was a page of tightly-packed writing to comb and decipher. 'The least word,' Byron had complained, 'or alteration of tone – and you know I rattle on through thick and thin – has some inference drawn from it.' She stared at him, and she said: 'In heaven, I trust.' They had been married just over a year. Their daughter, Ada, a month old, was asleep upstairs.

His sister sat looking from one to the other. The silence settled.

It had come to this: name a date, Byron had said to his wife, as soon as possible after the birth of the child. Name a date to travel north, two days in a carriage through the dead of winter, to your parents' house. The Byrons hadn't paid the rent on their grand London house – another year's £700 was due soon –

and Byron had been juggling debts all year, with the bailiffs circling, moving in, moving out, threatening. He would give up the house. He would send his wife into the country. He would sort it all out. He would follow her. They would start the new year fresh.

She had come to tell him that she would leave the next day. She did not tell him, though, that when she left his house she would be leaving him. Fifty-four weeks of marriage, and she was walking away from it. For two weeks he wouldn't know that this had happened, sitting in the big, empty house, going to sessions at the House of Lords, planning to fix a date when he would join her – while she began to write statements and consult lawyers and collect depositions and the great London rumour mill swung into action.

She left him that night, she said, in an agony of tears.

They would not speak to each other again.

I

THE BEGINNING

'The sun may shine upon a bit of broken glass till it
glitters like a diamond, but then if you take it up,
you will only cut your fingers.'

Lady Caroline Lamb

This story began in another room in another
jaundiced winter in another part of England;
another argument in another year. It was 1812.
It was February, Lady Byron was still Miss Annabella
Milbanke, and she was arguing with her mother.

This was where it began.

The space between Annabella and Lady Judith
Milbanke was bruised with the words they had jabbed
back and forth at each other. Annabella wanted to go to
London – she had a friend there, who was sick and was
probably going to die at any minute. She wanted to go.
She wanted to see her. She wanted to be with her.

Against which her mother pointed out that her
father was ill, and she should stay home. As simple as
that.

I thought, said Annabella, that I was to be allowed

to do these things, make these journeys.

Your father, said her mother, has been ill all winter.

In another story the argument might have had a great denouement, a brilliant single line thrown down by one or the other, clinching the matter. But in this room, in this argument, Annabella walked away, went to her desk, and began to write a letter which a servant would carry through the house to her mother. Her handwriting was level, particular, uniform: it defied any reader to mistake anything that was written, or to weasel something other out from between the lines. Her sentences, on the other hand, were miasmically long. The nineteen-year-old Annabella dealt in distinctions and definitions as clear as the difference between black ink and a white page.

It wasn't that she didn't want to discuss these things with her mother, she wrote, nor that she was at all uncomfortable talking about them. It was simply that, on paper, she could 'collect her sentiments' so much more clearly. She could set down – without the pesky interruption of an argument – precisely what she wanted to say. Which was that she wanted to go to London and didn't see why she shouldn't. Her friend was ill, could very well be dying – or dead, wrote Annabella – and it wasn't that she hadn't considered this death a possibility. She had. She did, often.

The problem was that, when she didn't have the invalid in front of her, when she couldn't see *how* she was and *what* the doctors were prescribing for her and pre-dicting for her, she made up the most terrible scenarios of pain and suffering and fatality. Much worse than the thoughts she entertained when she could see her friend's pain and knew quite candidly that she would die.

'I can truly say from experience,' she wrote to her mother, on the other side of the house, 'that though I have often thought of her dying *when she has been with me*, I never from that idea experienced anything so painful as the present total uncertainty with regard to the progress of her malady and the propriety of measures pursued.' This was why, she insisted, she had to drive two days down England to London, against the wishes of her parents, and without them to accompany her.

She won the argument – she almost always won her arguments – and she went, packed into a carriage with frocks and books and all the other paraphernalia of a single young lady at the beginning of the Regency. She promised to write home whenever, she said, she could 'conveniently epistolise'. The carriage arrived in London, pulled up outside the house where she would stay under a friend's chaperoning eye, and Annabella unpacked herself into the spare room and found herself, like this, at the end of February, with a glimmer of spring and the social season of 1812 about to start.

The London 'season' corresponded roughly with the time that Parliament was in session, and the time when there were no animals or birds to be pursued across the countryside. It closed, officially, on August 12, when the grouse season opened. It was a glancing, abbreviated world, restricted by a series of incontrovertible codes about who could say what to whom, in what order, when, and for how long. Friendships and conversations had little chance to move beyond the three-minute grabs of conversation that people were allowed at balls and the fifteen–minute calls that women made to each other on fine London mornings. There was hardly enough time to move beyond a comment on the weather, an inquiry about which function your hostess would be at that night, and a comment on the pleasure it would be to see her there. Its purpose was the speedy transformation of girls in their late teens from children sequestered with governesses into young ladies capable of navigating the etiquette of dinner parties, dances, conversations and a presentation to the monarch at St James' Palace. Capable of achieving, moreover, the ultimate goal of acquiring a husband. And this quest for matrimonial success was made easier by the fact that everyone with the right sort of pedigree was corralled into one confined space in London between at least Easter and late summer, proceeding through the same gamut of social occasions. If someone smiled sweetly at you on Wednesday evening, you were bound to run into them again by the following Tuesday. In the face of this, young ladies had, at the most, two or three seasons to secure a husband or be considered failures.

This would be Annabella's third season. And she seemed completely uninterested in finding a husband. Young gentlemen came and went – some even proposed to her. But she had no vocabulary for the common pastimes of flirting, of attraction and desire. She held herself above these things, with far more grave issues at hand. 'Your Annabella,' the mother of one of her suitors said, 'is so odd a girl: she is good, amiable and sensible, but cold, prudent and reflecting.'

And Annabella was, after all, in town to watch the gradual demise of an invalid friend. Yet here was the thing: Annabella's friend was found not to be so near to death's door after all (the friend would, in fact, still be approaching its portal some thirty years later). But Annabella did not go home. Nor, when she did conveniently epistolise to her parents, did she mask the fact that she had thrown herself, head-first and unrestrainedly, into the whirl of the city's activity. Went to a ball,' she wrote astonished in her journal, 'and stayed until dawn!!'

Which was all highly unusual. Somehow, Annabella had stepped out of being the person she usually was. The woman who would stay at a party all night was completely at odds with the earnest, dutiful, religious and slightly humourless person that Annabella was at the best of times. She took herself seriously. She took her religion seriously. She took what she perceived as her infallibility seriously. While she might acknowledge that she loved the compliments and the 'buttering speeches' of its flattery, she dismissed the social whirl of the capital city, disdainful, as 'scenes of dissipation'.

But she did organise, fashionable, to have her portrait painted – 'twenty guineas,' she wrote to her mother, and 'I can't get myself done decently for anything less.' It was the thing to do; it was one of the things you could do to fill in the gaping slices of time that cut the days of unoccupied aristocracy. She sat, sure that the painter would never capture her likeness since she was so 'disfigured by shyness' every time he picked up his brush. But there she was, her hair half piled up and cascading around her shoulders, her head back, her cheeks shining and rosy like a rubbed apple, her hand casual against the edge of her shoulder, and

smiling – maybe she was even laughing – all the rich-
ness of the silks in her dress painted so lush and opulent
that they looked edible. It was true, she joked with her
father, that she had simply never looked as good: 'I am
quite the fashion this year. Mankind bow before me,
and the women think me somebody.'

She looked, on her canvas, like somebody it would
be possible to fall in love with.

And eligible bachelors did send their mothers and
sisters to call on her, or left small libraries of calling cards
for her themselves. She was a young woman with a
good set of what were called 'expectations' – an heiress
to a fortune and a title in her own right. She was attending dinners, she was attending balls, she was going to the
theatre, and she was calling on her aunt, the leading
Whig hostess of the day, Lady Melbourne. As Lady
Melbourne's niece, Annabella had a way into the highest aristocratic circles of London society – but two
things generally kept her on its periphery. First, there
was an old animosity between Lady Melbourne (her
father's sister) and Judith Milbanke (her mother), which
meant the two families were never close. Second, with
all her huffing disapproval of those 'scenes of dissipation', Annabella's friends were drawn from circles of
like-minded people – aristocrats themselves, certainly,
but the ones who, like her, always gave the impression
that they'd rather have their nose in a tract. Religious
men. Confirmed spinsters. People who, like Annabella,
sought out the gossip of the beautiful people only
so they could disapprove of lost morality, erring souls
and irresponsibly spontaneous behaviour. This was
Annabella's natural milieu, not the whirling and glamorous parties but the people who sat apart from them,

shaking their head. Annabella, taken off to the Lord
Mayor's Ball, commented on neither the frocks nor the
dancing nor the fun everyone was having. Her letters
about it dissected and disapproved of its vanities.

But this year, in her slightly different being, Annabella was, for the first time, several steps further into
that fashionable society. For one thing, she was spending much more time with the fashionable women
married to her cousins, Lady Melbourne's sons:
Mrs George Lamb and the wife of Lady Melbourne's
favourite son William, Lady Caroline Lamb. It was
Mrs George Lamb whom Annabella really warmed
to – saying that she was 'too kind-hearted to be *quite
fashionable*', which was high praise from her. She liked
her so much that she altered the definition of the
people who might properly chaperone her so that she
could go to parties with both Mrs Lamb and a clear
conscience. Of Lady Melbourne's other daughter-in-
law, Caroline, Annabella was more suspicious and
wrote disparagingly of the lisping way she spoke as
sounding like the baa-ing and bleating of a lamb.

After a dinner with Caroline in early March,
though, Annabella conceded that 'when she was silly,
she was really *unmeaning*, not artificial'. Backhanded,
she announced Caroline as 'clever in everything that is
not within the province of common sense', and said –
scathing – that her *attempted* quotations from *Julius
Caesar* almost certainly came from seeing the play *per-
formed*, rather than having read the original.

But Caroline seemed to respect Annabella's morals
and foibles: she invited her to one of her parties and
warned her ('with more consideration than I should
have expected from her') that a lady who had been

divorced and remarried would be present. There was a danger, you see, in meeting such a profligate and fallen woman. Annabella decided, on the tightrope between morality and enjoyment, that she could attend but that she must certainly decline an introduction to this notorious lady if one was offered. She was sure, she said, that her parents would not object to her being at a party with *anyone* Lady Caroline chose to invite as a guest: 'no one will regard me as corrupted by being *in the room*.'

And it seemed to her, through that heady season, that her cousins could hardly host a gathering without inviting her. She was swept into their conversations about the latest in politics and international affairs, the latest anecdote about the newly-appointed Regent (King George III had only just been stripped of his powers as monarch on account of his madness) with whom Lady Caroline's extended family all socialised, and the latest in literature. By virtue of wangling an advance copy, Lady Caroline even had the distinction of being one of the first people to read the absolute hit of the season: *Childe Harold's Pilgrimage*, by a young peer called Lord Byron. She had finished it in a gulp and sent him one of his first fan-letters: 'I have read your book and think it very beautiful. You deserve to be and you shall be happy.' *Childe Harold* was heavy with pining, unrequited passages and 'the turns taken by the passions of women':

> Oh! Many a time and oft, had Harold loved,
> Or dreamed he loved, since rapture is a dream ...
> Dear to a heart where nought was left so dear!
> Though to my hopeless days forever lost,
> In dreams deny me not to see thee here ...

Caroline begged him not to throw away his talent in gloom, in regretting the past. She begged him 'above all', to live in England, his 'own country, which will be proud of you and which requires your exertion'. She offered him all of her jewels, as if he was a revolutionary who only wanted funds to raise an army and storm – something.

Caroline had even met Lord Byron: he had presented her with a rose and a carnation and said – pointed and charming – that he had heard Her Ladyship liked all that was new and fashionable, for an instant. She had looked at him and, in that instant, set him down famously as 'mad, bad and dangerous to know'.

After at least a week of listening to conversations about this new and fashionable poem, Annabella began to read *Childe Harold* herself on March 22. Copying some passages from it to send to her father, she wrote literary criticism, not fan-letters. It held, she conceded, 'many passages in the best style of poetry', but 'he is rather too much a *mannerist*, that is, he wants variety in the turns of his expressions. He excels,' she said, 'in the delineation of deep feeling, and in reflections relative to human nature.'

Every life has those moments that shine, illuminated as if a gig-lamp had been strung up in the arch of the sky, with the light puddling into one place, onto one person, one time, all bright and beautiful. These months shimmered for Annabella. In the first weeks of the season of 1812, her journal, her letters, overflowed with the people she had seen, the conversation she had heard. Stepping outside of herself, Annabella Milbanke had found a levity, an approximation of other people's social ease. She was still the same person, but the reflection of Melbourne House and the opulence of Caroline Lamb's attentions had put her in rooms with whole new sets of people. Looking like someone who could be loved.

Which was why it was disastrous when Caroline invited Annabella to a morning party at Melbourne House on March 25, where forty or fifty of her most intimate friends would practise their quadrilles and waltzing 'from twelve in the morning till near dinnertime, all young, gay and noisy'.

Disastrous that Annabella got out of bed, and chose her frock, and had her hair dressed, and ate her breakfast, and got into her carriage, and went through London's streets and into Whitehall, arrived at Melbourne House, and walked up the great stairway to Lady Caroline's rooms, and settled herself – sedate – on a sofa in line with the doorway. Disastrous that as anyone arrived, Annabella Milbanke was the first person they saw. Disastrous, too, that Lady Caroline – intent on assembling the best soirées, overflowing with people, and intent on keeping all that was new and fashionable close to her – invited Lord Byron. That he arrived after Annabella. That he came up the stairs, clutching at the rope handrail strung up especially for him to smooth his clubfooted climb, and stumbled and muttered darkly to his friend, the Irish poet Thomas Moore that this was a bad omen. And kept going.

Annabella, on her sofa, was sitting by herself. There were people, there was music, there was conversation, there was dancing. And there was a man coming up the stairs.

The rich, thick brown of his hair appeared over the threshold. The high, smooth white forehead that some went so far as to describe as alabaster. The fine, almost manicured eyebrows, the eyes down as he concentrated on his steps, on his feet, on his climb: eyes whose gaze made women's breath catch in their throats. The rest of his face by degrees – an elegant nose that looked like it had been borrowed from a Greek statue, the deep ridge of the philtrum running from his nostrils down to the perfect bow of his soft, pink top lip. The chin, rounded and firm. The long, long neck made longer by the open-necked shirts he wore (his valet couldn't tie a cravat to save himself): it was reminiscent of a swan's neck, all long and white and elegant. His broad shoulders. His toned and slimmed body. And the fine, fine whiteness of his trousers – their fabric so delicate, nankeen or silk, that he could only get one wear out of each pair – pulled down sharp over his shoes to reduce his clubfoot to the hint of a limp, the edge of a rumour.

Lord Byron arrived, looked into the room, and – most disastrous of all – saw Annabella Milbanke sitting alone, and marked her down. Remembered her. Then went on into the melee to find his hostess, Lady Caroline Lamb. It was Caroline he was there to see. Caroline – London's 'most correct waltzer' – stepped out of her dance. Lord Byron and his clubfoot could not dance, would not dance, and had forbidden her to waltz. She smiled at him.

In all the excitement around him and his poem, there was a sense that a party hung frozen until he arrived. Women, on seeing him, had been known to swoon. Literally. Annabella Milbanke sat firm. She watched him. She watched him talk to Lady Caroline Lamb. She watched him talk with other people, run his eye across the gathering – a smile on him, she said, that couldn't mask the 'violence of his scorn'. A mouth that 'constantly betrays the acrimony of his spirit'. She watched him watch the rest of the room and she reckoned that he dismissed it all as human absurdity. His features, she would admit, were quite fine – 'his upper lip drawn towards the nose with an expression of impatient disgust and his eye,' she noted, 'restlessly thoughtful.' It was murmured, low and dangerous, that Byron was an infidel: Annabella watched him and thought it 'probable from the general character of his mind'.

She did register other people: one young woman was 'incomprehensible', and another was 'sensible amidst this contagious folly'. But it was Byron her eye followed. It was Byron whom she carried with her through the rest of the day, through dinner with one of her mother's friends (who told her stories about the poet that she thought indicated his feelings were 'dreadfully perverted') and back into her own bedroom where she sat with her journal, with the beginnings of a letter to her mother, and wrote up those gig-lamped moments from her day. Her diary overflowed with his shape.

If Annabella Milbanke had been anyone other than Annabella Milbanke – if she really had been a person who went to parties, stayed till dawn, threw her head back in paintings and generally had fun – then none of this would have been either extraordinary or dangerous. It's hardly a remarkable thing that someone spends their morning watching a famous person and spends their evening writing letters about it, filling pages in their journal.

But Annabella did not see herself as someone like this. She was, after all, the person who had come to London in the first place not for its entertainments and delights, but to sit by the bedside of an invalid friend. She had been, further back, a little girl who didn't fill her imaginary worlds with pirates or princes or fire-breathing dragons, but with imaginary bishops, after whom she trotted, patting comfort onto the febrile foreheads of the imaginary suffering and dying. She was someone who drew the edges of herself in the heavy ink of capital-lettered Duty. Who had decided – at the knowledgeable age of twelve – that life was about turning away from all the things that were enjoyable to concentrate on all the things that were 'irksome'. Life was not about celebrity and frivolity. Life was certainly not about going to parties and staying till dawn. Life was not about anything so inconsequential as crushes or flirtations. It was about Religion. It was about the Salvation of Souls. It was about unimpeachable morality and standards that were immutably black or white, wrong or right. Annabella had not only pondered whether it was right to sit in a room with a woman who had been divorced and remarried. She had also wondered whether it was better to leave a party on the eve of Good Friday as the clock ran up to midnight, rather than breaking the sanctity of the religious day. Better then, she had decided, not to attend at all.

Parties and preoccupations were distractions from one's path: on the eve of her first presentation into London society, two years before, she had been almost distraught. 'What is to become of me when the trials of affliction shall fall on me, with the terrible capacity I now feel of being miserable?' she had wondered. 'In the constant exercise of the duties of my Religion, let me find firmness and resignation, in promoting the happiness of others let me seek the only source of pleasure that can hereafter be connected with Memory.'

She had gone through the seasons of 1810 and 1811 with 'happifying parties' and meetings with the Persian ambassador. She had gone to the opera, too, although she wrote home that she 'would rather not do, as it is a considerable fatigue to me who do not take pleasure in flirting or listening to squalling'.

She always behaved as if she was Above It All. And, in 1812, she found herself so far above Lord Byron that she could round off her evening's writing with a page of rhyme about how uninterested she was in him:

> ... Reforming Byron, with his magic sway,
> Compels all hearts to love him and obey –
> ... Is Human nature to be cast anew,
> And modelled to your Idol's Image true?
> Then grant me, Jove, to wear some other shape,
> And be an anything, except an Ape.

After all, as she commented to her mother from her extraordinarily great height, 'I cannot worship talents unconnected with the love of man, nor be captivated by that Genius which is barren in blessings.'

The woman on the sofa, the woman in the painting,

the woman it looked possible to love may well have been an Annabella Milbanke with something loosened, eased, abandoned in her. But she was Annabella Milbanke nonetheless.

I I

THIS LIFE

'[Byron] says himself that his poems are of that sort
which will, like everything of the kind in these days,
pass away, and give place to the ancient reading, but
that he esteems himself fortunate in getting all that
can now be got by such a passing reputation, for
which there are so many competitors ...'

John Cam Hobhouse

Lord Byron was born with a clubfoot and the prosaic name of George Gordon in January 1788 to
an abandoned mother in a rented upstairs room
off London's Oxford Street. His father was somewhere
else in London dodging creditors and there were at least
three unlikely deaths between the new Byron and a
peerage. His mother had carted him up to the godfor-
saken and windswept extremity of Aberdeen, where her
family came from and where she thought Byron's father
wouldn't think to look for her or what little was left of
her money. Byron's half-sister Augusta – from his father's
first marriage – was growing up in the aristocratic care
and opulent world of her maternal grandmother.

It was in Scotland that his mother heard, almost accidentally, that the Nottingham Byrons were dying without having taken the precaution of producing heirs, and that her little boy was moving closer to a baronetcy. When the fifth lord died in 1798, George Gordon was taken into his headmaster's study, given a sip of sherry and a bit of cake and hailed as a peer. When he was announced in his class the next day as Georgeus Dominus de Byron, he burst into tears. His mother, entertaining the rosiest idea of her boy's future even though the fifth lord had left so much debt that she had to sell most of her furniture to pay for his funeral, packed up what was left and moved halfway down England to the crumbling Byron home, Newstead Abbey, just out of Nottingham on the edge of Sherwood Forest.

Byron went off to be schooled at Harrow – which he hated until he was about to leave, and then at Trinity College, Cambridge – which he hated until he was about to leave. He bought a bear for a pet (the University had a rule against dogs) and frolicked with it in his plunge pool during the holidays. Chubby, he sparred and swam and played cricket in seven waistcoats and an overcoat at the height of summer and had himself buried up to his neck in piles of manure in a successful attempt to lose weight. He wrote to his older half-sister sporadically, until they fought and stopped speaking – either over an uncle's opinion of Byron, or over the guarantee for one of his many loans – in 1809. He wrote a book of mediocre poetry and a scathing satire of those who criticised it, which caused something of a flurry.

Unable to find anyone to sponsor his first appearance

at the House of Lords when he turned twenty-one, he appeared hurriedly, embarrassed, and alone. And then, with more knowledge of London's rings of prostitution than the Classics and in debt to most of the leading usurers of the day, he was awarded his MA in 1809 and set off on a Grand Tour of Portugal, Spain, Greece and Turkey with his best friend, John Cam Hobhouse.

Away from England for two years, he wrote extravagant and exotic accounts of his physical and sexual feats that put away forever the image of him as anything other than Byron the svelte and dashing romantic hero. He carved his name into a great quantity of ancient Greek temples and monuments, protested Lord Elgin's removal of some marbles from the Athenian Acropolis, bathed in the Kastalian spring at Delphi (said to be propitious for anyone with literary aspirations), seduced so many women and souvenired so many locks of hair that he could have become a wig-maker, and swam the Hellespont. He wrote, in his spare time, a couple of hundred stanzas of the thing he called *Childe Harold's Pilgrimage*.

On the prow of his ship, coming home to Sheerness in July, 1811 with 'an ague and the clap and the piles all at once', he itemised 'Four or Five reasons in favour of a Change':

1st   At twenty three the best of life is over and its bitters double.

2ndly   I have seen mankind in various Countries and find them equally despicable, if anything the Balance is rather in favour of the Turks.

3rdly   I am sick at heart ...

4thly   A man who is lame of one leg is in a state of bodily inferiority which increases with the years and must render his old age more peevish and intolerable. Besides in another existence I expect to have *two* if not *four* legs by way of compensation.

5thly   I grow selfish & misanthropical, something like the 'jolly Miller'. 'I care for nobody no not I and Nobody cares for me'.

6thly   My affairs at home and abroad are gloomy enough.

7thly   I have outlived all my appetites and most of my vanities aye even the vanity of authorship.

It was a dreary thing to be twenty-three, your big adventure over, and nothing to look forward to. Lord Byron, being a lord, was marked down for a dull life, trying to keep himself amused – as a gentleman he didn't need a profession, as long as he could keep up some sort of style of life without, vulgar, displaying any means of support. His ancestors had spent their lives in either a welter of hedonism or sailing off to unknown parts of the world for the Royal Navy. (Captain Cook had named Australia's eastern-most point, Cape Byron, after Byron's high-seas-exploring grandfather, Foul-weather Jack.) The former was certainly the more appealing of the two.

He arrived in London with luggage that included four Athenian skulls, a phial of poison, the manuscript for his poem, and several live tortoises. This poem – a heady mix of travelogue, philosophising, and reminiscences about lost and unrequited love – cut a swathe through London's highest circles.

An extraordinary fortnight, from the moment he made his maiden speech to an enthusiastic House of Lords (aligning himself with the most radical of the left-wing Whigs) on February 27 to the moment he woke, on the morning of March 9, 1812 – the morning after the publication of *Childe Harold* – and, as he put it, 'found himself famous'. The sales were extraordinary too: an expensive quarto first edition sold out almost immediately, and the poem was reprinted in a cheaper octavo format. It was estimated that the first ten editions, representing between 15,000 and 20,000 copies, were sold across four years. The street in which its author was lodging was jammed with carriages pushing through to deliver invitations to this formerly uninteresting young peer.

There had never been, people murmured, such an immense and instant sensation in London, and your party was not a party unless you could convince the poet to make an appearance at it. Men read themselves into his days of distant travel and dangerous adventure; women read themselves into his descriptions of amorous encounters. (Some wrote offering themselves – their hearts – to him.) Byron's trusty friend Hobhouse said that he lied to keep people from guessing the true identity of these beloved women. Byron said that there had been nothing further from his mind than creating a character that mirrored himself in any way, and kept quiet about the fact that he had originally planned to call the thing *Childe Biron's Pilgrimage*.

The ordinary name 'George Gordon' disappeared forever, and Byron became a chimera of all of London's fantasies and desires. Word about him – speculation, rumour, gossip – filled London's mouths, which the week before had nothing but the war in Spain and the madness of King George III to toss between them. 'In short,' it was observed, Byron was 'the only topic of conversation.' He was the one thing people wanted to know about, and he learned early the trick of dropping a suggestion, an insinuation, of something he might have done into the middle of a crowded salon, and watching it roll out, changing and growing and taking on a life of its own, through all his listeners: 'the fact is,' he said later, 'I always say whatever comes into my head, and very often say things to provoke people to whom I am talking.' It was, after all, the Regency: it was fashionable for men to dot their love letters with rosewater so that it looked like the paper was spotted with their tears. The Prince Regent, too, had made it 'the fashion' to lie, to boast of every vice: 'men about town were ashamed of being thought virtuous and bragged of their profligacy,' one of those men remembered. Byron, he said, '"gave his worst thoughts the worst of words". I and others have done the same thing.' The difference was, he said, 'Byron's words were not lost, but noted and circulated – ours forgotten.'

'I could not get away from Lord Byron when once he began talking to me,' Lady Caroline Lamb's mother told a friend of hers. 'He was part of the time very pleasant and talking of other things – but he did tell me some things so terrifying and so extraordinary!!'

In the instant of becoming the darling of 1812 London, he became someone about whom it was possible to say anything. Part of him revelled in it: that he had dressed prostitutes up as boys and tried to pass them off as his brother; that he had bought himself a mistress for £100 and was on the verge of marrying her, before he turned twenty-one.

There were his amorous poems to 'Thyrza' too – all unrequited, and all tragic after 'Thyrza's' untimely death. One woman wrote that she recognised herself in the description (despite the fact that she was alive and Thyrza was dead), offering her heart up to her 'dearest darling boy'. And then those rumours about a friendship at Cambridge, a 'pure love': what was the boy's name? Edleston? A chorister? Wasn't there some silly statement Byron had made about wanting to set up a house with him? A soft poem written to commemorate a cornelian brooch such as the one Byron had been given by his young boy friend? Was *he* Thyrza? Whoever 'Thyrza' had been, sometimes there seemed to be more rumours about the mystery's identity than there were women (or men) to take up the part.

But there should have been no reason to suspect that this would impact on Annabella Milbanke, with her loud and often-proclaimed distaste for fashionable society and its darlings – a mindset more likely in an elderly spinster aunt – and no interest in the world of flirting, of coquettish behaviour, or of seduction. Still, even Annabella had to confess to her mother, as she sat writing about her first sighting of Byron, that while she would not seek an introduction to him, she would not turn one down if it came her way.

Lord Byron, 1813

III

THE SEASON

'Indeed, I rather look upon Love altogether
as a hostile transaction – very necessary to make – or
to break – matches and keep the world a-going – but
by no means a sinecure to the parties concerned.'

Lord Byron

Annabella may have held it as essential to herself that she would not become an apeish follower of the cult of Lord Byron, but she spent a good part of her time across the next weeks wheedling information about him out of people. That he had argued with his sister. That he could be profoundly generous (she collected several examples of this – kindness to old servants, loans given with no expectation of their being repaid). That he was certainly an atheist. She built a compendium of knowledge about him, story by story, and by the time she saw him again – three weeks later, in early April – she no longer spoke of the parlous nature of his soul, nor the perversion of his feelings. By then she said that she had 'met with much evidence of his goodness'. He was 'the very comet of the year', and she watched him 'shine with all his customary glory'.

By then, too, it was no longer that she wanted to stand back – unapelike – from the other women 'yelping around Lord Byron' (as her father put it). Rather, she found herself cornered by an unwanted suitor and his loathsome conversation, and was 'without leisure to concert an attack' on the poet. She saw that Lord Byron, whom she had so recently labelled as sarcastic and scornful, was actually shy and retiring. By the time she finally spoke to him, on April 14, he was 'without exception of young or old more agreeable in conversation than any person I ever knew'.

Nothing less.

Of course there was nothing unusual in the number of times she mentioned his name – everyone was talking about Byron. Of course there was nothing peculiar in the anecdotes and stories she was collecting about him – everyone had their own sliver of information to add, to latch themselves vicarious onto a tit-bit of his fame. Of course there was nothing resembling interest or sentiment in the fact that she filled her letters and her journal with him – everyone who had seen him was virtually obliged to tell everyone else what he was like. These have always been the mechanics of celebrity.

And so there would have been nothing unusual in anyone falling in love with Byron – he was synonymous with the idea: he was designed for it, glamorous and mysterious and oozing charisma. And he had, according to Samuel Taylor Coleridge, nothing less than a voice that was 'angelic – or demon-like: it was the voice with which the serpent had tempted Eve'.

Annabella failed to mention this the first time they

spoke, although she did say that he addressed her with great respect, and that he was very handsome, and that he had the superior manners of 'Nature's Gentlemen'. Also – offhand – that he 'wants the calm benevolence which could only touch my heart'. The next day she decided that he was 'sincerely repentant for all the evil he has done, though he has not resolution (without aid) to adopt a new course of conduct and feeling'. She thought of him, she confessed, as 'a very good, very bad man'. She seemed to think of little else.

Lord Byron, at a masquerade party, leaned forward and felt the roughness of his monk's costume rub against his leg where the soft silk of his trousers would usually have brushed. Love comes on, he said, love comes on for some people, we know not why, and for others not at all.

There is no way to pin it down, the attraction, the magnetism of what one person says – the way that they say it – over any number of other people saying the same thing. This piece of a sentence, you think: perhaps it implied this – and by the morning it *did* imply that. Not even imply: it stated it directly. Lord Byron mentioned to Miss Annabella Milbanke, in their first conversation, another poet whom she had supported and championed, and who had died. Byron, the poet of the moment, had heard of someone handling posthumous publication of that poet's work. He wanted to warn Annabella of this gentleman's impropriety. Was there a significance in his mentioning that? Byron was identifying Annabella as a lady known for her interest in poets and – furthermore – a lady who could be treated as an intellectual equal and warned about the behaviour of another man in business. Was that something she should pay particular attention to? Easy to find the threads and coincidences that string facts together to create an inevitability.

Spring skipped on. Annabella spoke to Byron, whipped off the letters to her parents about his ascension over anyone who ever had or would have a conversation with her, and believed that she was as far as ever from anything so irrelevant as attraction. It can't be said that she lied to herself about this, because it wasn't something sinisterly or maliciously suppressed. It just wasn't part of her perception of herself: she was Above Desire – and Lord Byron was Desire incarnate. She was always at parties, at dinners, at conversations, though – and how often, it seemed, Lord Byron was there too. She reported conversations with him about whether it was necessary for a poet to have felt something to be able to make his readers feel the same thing – he said it wasn't. She wrote Byron's selection of the best English novels in her journal – he nominated *Caleb Williams* and the novels of Miss Burney; Annabella agreed with her cousin William Lamb's attack on Miss Burney's work. Everyone nodded over the inclusion of *The Vicar of Wakefield*. In the end, she had so many conversations with him that she stopped transcribing them for her parents – she didn't have the time, she said.

People noticed Annabella and Byron: the mother of one of her suitors wrote that she saw Lord Byron making up to Annabella 'a little; but she don't seem to admire him except as a poet, nor he her, except for a wife.' And Judith Milbanke, too, wondered precisely what sort of relationship her daughter was headed for with this most notorious of men. Annabella told her, 'I consider it as an act of humanity and a Christian duty not to deny him any *temporary* satisfaction he can derive from my acquaintance, though I shall not seek to encrease it.'

'He is not,' she said – lofty and dangerous – 'a dangerous person to me.'

Lady Melbourne, Annabella's aunt, was also watching what was going on. And Lady Melbourne herself was in an extremely interesting position. One of the aristocracy's most powerful women, she was in her sixties and stood slightly back from all the fluster and activity of the season. There were three figures, though, who occupied her attention this year. The first was her pesky daughter-in-law, Lady Caroline Lamb, the wife of her son William. Caroline was a sprite, was ethereal, was Ariel – all light vivacity and spontaneous enthusiasm, if you were one of her admirers. The truth, she held, was what you believed at that moment, and she thought most of the social codes of the day were daft. Brazen, she would offer someone her hand on only their second meeting. She would have herself carried into dinner parties naked and covered with a silver salver. She would ask people, direct, whatever it was she wanted to know. An unheard-of liberty. People who were not her admirers went so far as to search their hands for the mark of Beelzebub if she shook it.

Lady Melbourne's famous position on adultery was that one did one's duty and provided an heir, and then one could do as one pleased but *always* (and she could not stress enough the importance of this) with attention to public appearances and decorum. Caroline, in 1812, had gone beyond her previous improprieties of befriending flagrantly unfaithful women or enjoying surreptitious flirtations with a man who gave her a yappy dog. The yappy dog affair had confined itself to this code, but her latest indiscretion was just that: indiscreet. Lady Caroline Lamb was having an affair with Byron. She publicly boasted that they were invited to parties as a couple. Worse, she was seen pacing around gardens, openly and obviously waiting for him and − outrageous − hanging in through his carriage window, talking to him. That infamous label she had tacked onto Byron − 'mad, bad and dangerous to know' − was actually quite a good description of herself. There were, as Lady Melbourne knew, limits.

The second figure who occupied her was Byron himself. As the man who was cuckolding her favourite son, she should have wanted nothing short of his destruction. But, inconveniently, she was fond of him. He made her laugh. He flirted with her. It was perfectly obvious why Caroline threw herself at him: he looked divinely mysterious, limping and brooding all over the place with that pale skin, those eyes, those soft lips. And he brought Lady Melbourne his confidences, told her his secrets − almost cast her as a mother-figure − while he seduced her wretched daughter-in-law and assured Lady Melbourne that he, too, wanted nothing more than to end the affair. As the Prince Regent himself commented, taking the mother of your lover's husband as a confidante was an inconceivable state of affairs, but Lady Melbourne was entertained by Byron and, to be blunt, she liked him a lot more than she liked Caroline: 'once you told me you did not understand friendship,' she wrote to him, 'I told you I would teach it to you, and so I will, if you do not allow C to take you quite away.' But whatever friendship she fancied for herself and Lord Byron, his affair with Caroline had to end. And, for her son's sake, it had to end with Caroline standing publicly and dutifully by her husband.

The third figure, then, was her earnest and relatively dense niece, Annabella Milbanke, present at so many of London's finest functions and yet apparently ignorant of Byron's affair with Caroline. About the only person in London who was. If she was unsure of whether it was acceptable to be under the same roof as a divorced woman, she would have had no doubts about avoiding the conversation of a philandering gentleman. Perhaps people didn't include her in their gossip.

Or perhaps she, like the poet Samuel Rogers, had watched Byron and Caroline and decided that there was 'nothing criminal' between them. She said later that she had been assured by Lady Melbourne that, although Caroline had 'thrown herself at his feet', Lord Byron had resisted her and remained honourable. Caroline, for her part, clearly thought her slightly provincial cousin was worth paying more attention to this year. She arranged to show Byron some of Annabella's own poetry, and to pass some of his comments on them back to Annabella. For whatever reasons. Whatever motives.

Annabella was less serious about her poems than she was about either religion or maths, but she was still pretty serious about them. People always told her she was good at things – actually, people usually told her she was *perfect* at things. She had her own boasts too:

proficient at maths at six, she said, or sometimes she said it was four. But Lord Byron must certainly take her, and her talents, very seriously – she may have told herself – if he offered to critique her verse. That had to be a mark of profound interest, beyond the interest her future fortune usually whipped up in eligible young men. Far more gratifying.

He read them – a little practice, he suggested through Caroline, would 'very soon induce the facility of expressions'. And, 'she certainly is an extraordinary girl, who would imagine so much strength and variety of thought under that placid countenance?' But to Caroline herself he said that he 'desired no better acquaintance' with Annabella: she was 'too good for a fallen spirit to know' and he should 'like her better if she were less perfect'.

Lady Melbourne stood outside the three lines of this volatile triangle, watching. And Annabella made jokes for her mother about having to go and 'exert my eloquence to prove to Lady Melbourne that there is no danger in my meeting Lord Byron'.

It was Lady Caroline Lamb, though, who confronted Annabella about her interest in him first.

I V

THE 1812 OVERTURE

'I have no very high opinion of your sex, but
when I do see a woman superior not only to all
her own but to most of ours, I worship her in
proportion as I despise the rest.'

Lord Byron

I t's an aggravating fact that no one ever has the fore-
sight to write down absolutely everything they said
or thought or did, precisely and contemporane-
ously, with an eye to the various well-intentioned or
muck-raking biographers who will plod along years
later, trying to make sense of those sporadically shining
spots of life. Annabella Milbanke, for one, was not kind
enough to leave a complete transcript of an interview
she had with Lady Caroline Lamb in the first days of
May, 1812. Instead, with a pen lathered up with obfus-
cation, she wrote merely that she had seen Caroline
and 'undeceived her by a painful acknowledgement'.

Neither Caroline nor Annabella went back to
explain what this meant. Perhaps Caroline had

confronted her about her absorption in Lord Byron and she had confessed to it, confessed that she thought him the one man she might step down from her pinnacle for. Or that she had known all along of his affair with Lady Caroline, and flatly dismissed him on the basis of the immorality he played in so casually. Or that she had to tell Caroline that another suitor (who went on to become governor-general of India and would have made a lovely husband) had indeed proposed, and that she had turned him down. Or that he had not – or would not – propose.

Whatever they talked about, Annabella's journal – so weighed down with words at the beginning of the year – never elaborated on that one short conversation, and soon after petered out altogether into fragments and snatches. Their brevity made them sound like code. She had her twentieth birthday. Her parents finally came down to London. The prime minister, Spenser Perceval, was shot and killed in the foyer of the Houses of Parliament. And another young lady said that Lord Byron had told *her* that he wished someone would tell Annabella not to trouble him with any more of her little poems.

While Caroline had withheld some of Byron's remarks on Annabella and her poetry, she herself sent Annabella pages and pages of letter: foolscap sheets apologising to her for not being a better friend, and warning her to stay above all the tarnishments and treacheries of fashionable society. Sheets thick with advice: the people to avoid, the people to suspect, the people to mistrust. She wrote about Annabella's over-arching goodness and perfection and the ways she might be trampled by the evil of the world and those vile men who pretended and misled with their impostures as fallen angels 'who are ever too happy to twine themselves round the young Saplings they can reach. But if they are falling,' Caroline warned, 'you cannot save them – depend on that.' The danger to your purity, she told her cousin, will not come from 'Balls, routs, Coxcombs and Gossips, but beware of what may come across you in the shapes of Genius, superior abilities, Heroic sentiments, affected innocence. Look to their conduct,' she warned, 'and do not attend to their prating.'

She drew, in all but name, a clear, sharp portrait of Byron, with the warning implied as heavy as red ink underneath the lines: this man, this dangerous man – stay away. To Byron she said, certain, that Annabella was on the eve of receiving a proposal from another man – had probably already received it – would certainly accept it. Definitely, Caroline purred in reassuring unison with the wife of Lady Melbourne's other son – Miss Milbanke's heart was definitely engaged.

Annabella saw him occasionally – here he said something satirical about one of her very close friends; there she thought (it seemed a belated thing to realise) that he had a 'propensity towards coquetry'; somewhere else, she discussed the poet Thomas Campbell with him. Towards the end of the season, they were actually seated next to each other at a supper party and Byron did not talk to Annabella at all, pouring his words entirely towards Lady Melbourne on his other side. She heard him, though, as he thanked God that he had not a friend in the world. She was, she said, shot through by a kind of chill: she felt herself dismissed by his melodramatic claim. The duty she marked herself out by became a little more honed: it was the duty to be his friend and to save Lord Byron's soul. 'When I returned home to solitude,' she recalled of that night two years later, 'I wept over the recollection ... and prayed that you might receive consolation from a friend below, as well as from a friend above.'

To alleviate a soul: this was the greatest thing that Annabella Milbanke thought she could wish for someone – especially with the idea of *loving* someone, of *desiring* them, not in her way of thinking at all. Who knew what sort of relationship – if any – she would have with this man she collected stories about, had slivers of conversation with? But she decided she could stand beyond that and say, as she saw him flinch at the mention of religion in a lecture, that she *knew* why he flinched, and that she would devote herself to somehow engendering the happiness in him that would still that twitch. Other women offered their hearts and their bodies. Annabella Milbanke offered to retrieve Lord Byron's floundering soul – with or without his knowledge or his co-operation. 'You know how easily the noblest heart may be perverted by unkindness,' she commented to her mother, 'perhaps the most easily a *noble* heart, because it is more susceptible to ungenerous indignities.'

At the same time, she became convinced that Byron was about to announce his engagement to someone else – to the young lady, in fact, whom he had told he wanted to see no more of Annabella's poems. All the light, all the spark, went out of her and out of her effervescent summer: she told her aunt of this imminent announcement so definitely that Lady Melbourne took the idea to Byron as a fact, not a rumour, and he was at a loss to explain its origins or its vehemence.

Annabella thought, then, that Byron paid less attention to her – but he had been assured she was going to marry someone else. Byron, too, thought that Annabella paid less attention to him – but her mother had just arrived in the city, and he assumed that Annabella had finally been warned that his was an inappropriate friendship for a young lady to court. The energy it took to be someone who could stay at a party until dawn collapsed into the fatigue of a bad mood. Annabella packed up her books and her dresses and her journals and her mementos and waited for her parents to take her to their house in Richmond, just out of London. She waited for the time to pass, for the winter to come, for her parents to decide it was time to go home, for the year to turn. She never mentioned Lord Byron – there was more distance between them than if he had taken himself back to the East. She had no time to think of such a person. No reason to waste her time writing about him in her journal.

Byron had also left London, having tried to shake free from Caroline Lamb, who had been incapable of leaving him alone: she broke into his rooms when he was with another woman, ran away from home threatening to take the first ship out of Portsmouth to anywhere, anywhere. She expected daily – she hissed at him – to hear that he was to be married. If she had stayed with him, she said, he would have 'made me make the bed for his new favourites'. She sent him, as a little keepsake, a clipping of her pubic hair – asking for a lock of hair in return. If it was to be clipped from the same part of his body, though, she asked that he be careful with the points of the scissors.

He was now safely out of the city, in the swirling, relaxing hot springs of Cheltenham and at his letter-writing best when he was in the middle of a compromising situation. 'It is true from early habit, one must make love mechanically as one swims,' he wrote brightly to Lady Melbourne as Caroline Lamb was dispatched across the Irish Sea for a holiday with her husband, and his roving eye picked out an Italian diva for his next mistress. 'I was once very fond of both, but now as I never swim unless I tumble into the water, I don't make love till almost obliged.' Still, although it was all so tiresome, he had gone to the trouble of drawing up a list of women he was tempted to romance – the diva was just one of the possibilities.

The season was winding up, more and more people filing out of London to begin their round of visits to each other's country houses, to relax in the restitutional waters of England's spas. Fashionable gentlemen, like Byron, had trekked out to Newgate to watch the Prime Minister's assassin hang. As with every year, there was a sense that the playtime was over, and even someone as taken up with the easy hedonism of fame as Byron began to think about what he should do next. He had debts. He was plagued by Caroline, still bombarding him with letters from Ireland, while her mother pleaded with Lady Melbourne not to lose her hold over Lord Byron, for fear he would cross the Irish Sea as well and resuscitate the whole mess. 'Pray don't' lose your hold, Byron repeated to Lady Melbourne, as if he already had one foot out and was only held back by her restraining arm. He went on to tell her that – notwithstanding all the public shenanigans he and Caroline had filled up the months with – she was entirely wrong in guessing where his true affections lay.

'There was and is one whom I wished to marry,' he said, adding that his affair with Caroline had 'intervened … the woman I mean is Miss Milbanke.' He knew little of her, he confessed, and didn't have the slightest reason in the world for thinking she might fancy him, but 'I never saw a woman whom I *esteemed* so much. But that chance is gone,' he finished dramatically, 'and there's an end.'

Lady Melbourne, who had just lived through the tumultuous season of Byron and Caroline all indecorous and all over the place, asked if this could possibly be true, if he was sure of himself. No, said Byron, 'but *you* are, which I take to be a much better thing.' Miss Milbanke was clever, amiable, and had a respectable pedigree. Any *love*, he said, would be done with in a week: 'Besides, marriage goes on better with esteem and confidence than romance.' If it was to happen at all, he levelled, 'positively it must be in three weeks'.

Lady Melbourne assured him that he had been misled about Annabella's attachment to or proposal from any other eligible man in London, but he thought then that 'she deserves a better heart than mine'. Still, a wife was the only answer, the only 'rational outlet' from the mess of Caroline. 'What shall I do?' he cried, certainly with his hand thrown to his forehead: 'Shall I *advertise*?' And then, before anything else could happen, another letter came from Caroline and Byron exploded: '*At this moment*, another *express* from Ireland!!! more scenes! … I see nothing but marriage and a *speedy one* can save me; if your Niece is attainable I should prefer her – if not – the very first woman who does not look as if she would spit in my face.' As the Milbankes prepared to leave London for Richmond, Lady Melbourne sent for Annabella.

It was October 8, 1812. Between March 25 and mid-July Lord Byron and Annabella Milbanke had seen each other perhaps fifteen times, and had had – at a very generous estimate – ten conversations with each other, however many they may have had about each other. And Lady Melbourne wondered if Annabella might be open to a proposal.

No matter how much she had thought about him or talked about him, it must have come as something of a surprise. An offer of marriage, from the most seductive and notorious of London's bachelors. Entirely out of the blue. This was the proposal that all of London had anticipated, the proposal that every woman who swooned over Lord Byron would have imagined receiving. Hardly romantic, for a poet, to send such a request through your aunt. It was an inconceivable thing.

Those illuminated moments – you convince yourself that, if you ran a line across them, they would mark out the totality of a situation rather than showing up the fragments and shards that you have exalted above the mess of everything else. But, as Virginia Woolf once pointed out, life isn't a series of gig-lamps. It's one blur of luminosity that surrounds people from beginning to end. The flashes of those brilliant moments are just a distraction from the layers and shadows and contradictions that jam into every other piece of time. They ignore all the other things that happen, that are important, that are done, when two people are not in the same place. Which, in the case of Byron and Anna-bella, was pretty much all the time.

Still, if you ran a line across Byron's first glimpse of Annabella, which he noted and marked down (that young woman sitting off to the side, more simply dressed than the others), and all that she assembled of him before their first conversation – and the pleasant-ness of that first conversation in an environment entirely geared towards brokering marriages – then all you would see yourself heading for was a happy ending. This woman had, after all, committed herself to his soul. Everyone smiling. Music swelling. Lovely.

Byron leaned back and smiled: music – he could not believe that anyone could be indifferent to music ...

While Annabella sat up a little straighter and asked, music? She had no love of music, she said, and there was some music (she could not make this point too forcefully) that was simply repugnant to her nature 'and sometimes quite terrible to me – I mean terrible from the sensation of extreme fatigue in hearing *some* kinds of music, or indeed *any* for a continuance.'

It was a shame, but a disagreement about music would be the least of it.

Annabella, in Richmond, squared up that ubiquitous stack of notepaper on which she collected her senti-ments. The most she had thought of this man – she had assured everyone of this – was that he should find guid-ance in her friendship below and God above. All this had been whittled down to the most worldly of over-tures, the request that she become Lady Byron.

When you have as strong a sense of your own infal-libility as Annabella Milbanke had, you must believe entirely in the rightness of every decision you make. It is an idea of infallibility that does not even admit to changing your mind: a course taken once is a course that must always be taken. If, for instance, you're going to marry someone – and you don't know or can't bring yourself to say that you love them, or desire them, or harbour any other trivial emotion towards them – then you must have the most clarified and self-sacrificing reasons for doing it. You cannot be doing it for your own happiness, your own good or – most definitely – your own pleasure. As Annabella herself said more than a year later, 'on the whole, I think myself formed for domestic ties, but I cannot seek them on the principle of either Self-Love or Expediency.'

She must not be misunderstood: the very idea of a romantic marriage was entirely removed from the goal she had assigned herself. This was what it was to be Annabella. Her other suitors – those luckless men who had left their cards, and their female relatives, to try and win her over – had never been worth more to her than a single line or an overblown anecdote for her father: one gentleman was dismissed sharply as 'bandy-legged, very tall and ungraceful'. Worse, his mother was found to be '*a Bligh*'. Someone else's mother was sent to deliver 'an oration on the merits of her children, particularly William my suitor, whom one of my smiles would encourage to propose, but I am very niggardly of my glances.' She didn't seem to be planning on marrying anyone. Unlike almost any other single lady among such a welter of men, she had made a point of inviting to the one dinner party she gave during the season only men 'who cannot think I am in love with them'.

And now she sat with that trusty pile of paper, just as she had done when she needed to convince her mother that she was *right* to want to go to London in the first place, and she began to draw Lord Byron's character. It was a fortunate thing that she believed you could know someone as well in the first five minutes of your acquaintance with them as you would know them over a lifetime – because in the greater scheme of things, she didn't have much more than about five minutes direct and personal knowledge of the man who wanted her to be his wife.

Drawing a character, stretching out merits and flaws, was something by which Annabella set much store. It was a skill of dissection that she prided herself on: even in the height of her heady summer, she had knocked out a series of character sketches – first the positives, then the negatives – of the women she was closest to. And she had shaped them as judgementally as if she had the final word on their entry to Heaven or Hell.

Passions, she wrote of Byron, had enveloped his intellect 'in the obscurity of temporal delusion unenlightened by the *Faith* of an immortal existence ... there is a chivalrous generosity in his ideas of love and friendship,' she decided, 'and selfishness is totally absent from his character.' He hated bitterly, she thought, and then as soon as he had hated, he swung through to repentant humanity: 'his mind is continually making the most sudden transitions – from good to evil, and evil to good. A state of such perpetual tumult must be attended with the misery of restless inconsistency.'

She pinned Byron down with a handful of conversations, the edges of everything everyone else had said – sixteen rounds of drawing room gossip – and drew these out into a whole person. She drew him – a person, she concluded, unsuited to bring her domestic happiness – and she turned him down.

She excused herself politely, though, saying to Lady Melbourne that 'from my limited observations of his conduct, I was predisposed to believe your strong testimony in his favour, and I willingly attribute it more to the defects of my feelings than of his character that I am not inclined to return his attachment.' She included, for her aunt's information, her character sketch of Byron.

Annabella Milbanke, that woman in the corner, dressed so meekly that he had mistaken her for some fine lady's companion, and she turned him down. The very man of the moment.

She wrote up a list of all the characteristics she did require in a husband, which she sent to London a week later. Lady Melbourne, reading this complement to the character sketch, commented, acid, that Annabella would be lucky to find anyone at all who could match a list of requirements that long. None of this, much of that, and certainly a man with 'consistent principles of Duty governing strong and generous feelings, and reducing them under the command of Reason'. Annabella was never irritated, she said, except when others were, which made 'good temper in my companions very necessary to my peace'. She was never sulky, she said, but her spirits were 'easily depressed, particularly by seeing anybody unhappy'. Finally, she said, there must be absolutely no hint of insanity in his family.

Annabella knew at least one thing: she could not lay the shape of Lord Byron over the shape of the man she thought she would marry. Well, commented her aunt, 'a man possessed of such a Character as you have drawn would marry you from reason, and not from Love – which *you*,' inaccurately, 'will not say is what you would wish or like.'

Lady Melbourne produced all the letters that Lord Byron had written to her that mentioned Annabella, and passed them over for her niece to read. 'They appear to me expressive not only of the sincerest but of the deepest attachment,' Annabella commented to a friend. 'Were there no other objection,' she went on, 'his *theoretical* idea of my perfection which could not be fulfilled by the trial, would suffice to make me decline a connection that must end in his disappointment. I confess that this, and the Irreligious nature of his principles are my sole objections, but you know that I regard the latter too strongly to sacrifice it to the love of Man.' Presumably she did not see his charming statement that if she turned him down he would marry the first woman who didn't spit on him.

Annabella said she left any 'future intercourse' between them entirely up to him. And that, said Lord Byron on receiving her rejection, 'must take its chance – I mean the *acquaintance*, for it will never be anything more, depend upon it, even if she *revoked*. I have still the same opinion, but I never was *enamoured* and as I very soon shall be in some other quarter, *cossi finiva*.'

Cossi finiva. Thus it ends.

Annabella took her checklist for a husband, and went home. Alone.

The only woman proposed to by that notorious lover, Lord Byron.

The only woman who turned him down.

One of the last truly sensible decisions she made.

It was October, 1812.

V

ABSENCE AND THE HEART

'I congratulate A[nnabella] and myself on our
mutual escape. That would have been but a cold
collation, and I prefer hot suppers.'

Lord Byron

Then there was silence.

Put yourself in this position. All your life the thing you have imagined for yourself is a kind of religious happiness, an extension of all those bishops you invented when you were little. Annabella must have talked about this, must have at least intimated it: one of her beaux wrote that he thought she was the sort of person who may never find domestic happiness, but that she seemed to know this about herself and was happy to accept it. Against whatever buttressed this in Annabella came her off-balance interest in Lord Byron. She got through explaining to herself and to her aunt why she would not marry this man she had spent the better part of six months thinking about, and everything went back to normal.

But she couldn't shake his shape from her thoughts.

He had said that he would not be embarrassed to meet Miss Milbanke socially after she rejected him, and at some point Annabella began to stretch towards that moment in the next season, 1813, when she would see him again. He was, after all, a superlative conversationalist.

London, though, was a different place in the new year. For one thing, there was a new literary lion in 1813 – it was not Lord Byron whom people craned and queued to see. It was the author Madame de Staël, and people teetered on chairs to catch a glimpse of her, although there was nowhere near the amount of swooning involved. And the new literary hit of the year was nothing as exotic or pacey as *Childe Harold's Pilgrimage*: it was a realistic novel written by an anonymous spinster, called *Pride and Prejudice*. Annabella thought it the most 'probable fiction' she had ever read. 'No drownings, nor conflagrations, nor runaway horses, nor lapdogs and parrots, nor chambermaids and milliners, nor rencontres and disguises. It is not,' she conceded, 'a cosying book.' But it did stand as something believable against the extremities that they said went on in the echelons of London society – as if such things were true. As if the Prince of Wales had had a secret wife. As if Lady Caroline Lamb would pawn her jewellery to get a hackney coach to Kensington, planning to run away to the coast and take the first available ship to anywhere. These things would be impossible in Annabella's conception of the world.

Of course, Lord Byron could be seen clearly in Mr Darcy – that dark and abrupt man with such a wealth of generosity at his centre. Annabella had, you will remember, spent much of her time, in the previous

year, in collecting stories of his philanthropy to set
against the awful things London wanted to believe of
him. And then, of course, there was the embarrassment,
the offence, at the completely unexpected proposal
Elizabeth Bennett received from Mr Darcy. Who knew
about Annabella's own unexpected proposal? There had
been no fanfare. No gossip. Lady Melbourne, of course.
And Annabella's friend, who had been told about the
properness and esteem in the letters from Byron that
Annabella had been shown. But did she even tell her
mother?

Strange and confronting, then: she read on to the
end of the book – the second, accepted proposal. Now,
for it to be acceptable for Elizabeth Bennett to marry
Mr Darcy, in the last pages of *Pride and Prejudice*, then
Mr Darcy himself must have reformed. Mr Darcy must
have taken on all that Lizzie said to him when she
refused to marry him, must have become the man that
she saw he could be. So that now it was right for her
to marry him, and to appreciate the changes that he
had made. In marrying him, Elizabeth Bennett could
keep her husband on that path of reform.

'The interest is very strong,' Annabella commented,
'especially for Mr Darcy.'

Annabella waited, in the middle of her 1813 round of
dinners and conversations and soirées, to see Lord
Byron. Who did not come. Was not there. Was occupied in the first half of the year in another affair with
another married lady, and still – would it never end –
avoiding the pestiferous attentions of that madwoman
Caroline Lamb, who burnt him in effigy and bit
through glasses when she saw him with other women.

People arrived at gatherings, and were not him, even though he had told Lady Melbourne that he would be 'very happy to encounter A[nnabella] in such a manner as to convince her that I feel no *pique* nor diminution of the respect I have always felt for her'.

She wondered sometimes about meeting him. Perhaps unexpectedly, in a doorway. His hand would go out to her – perhaps his touch would be cold. She went over this encounter again and again – by the end of her life she believed that it had taken place. She did, one morning, come into an assembly – it was early July – and see Lord Byron leaning over a woman on a sofa. Laughing. All attentive. It was his sister, she heard, the Hon. Mrs Augusta Leigh. Annabella had heard, as all London had heard, that they had fought many years ago. That they had made it up, and had seen each other again only within that week. Annabella stood and watched as Byron leaned, warm, conversational, over his sister. He didn't look up. He didn't see Annabella. He didn't notice her. He had said he wouldn't be embarrassed to meet her. This was not what she had had in mind.

From a distance of almost 200 years, there is still something enormous in Annabella Milbanke mentioning in a letter to her aunt, casual and nine months after Lord Byron's proposal, that she had heard he was accused of mistreating the man who planned to buy his ancestral home, that she wished him to be informed of this scurrilous report so that he could contradict it and that – an aside – she wished to be remembered to him. She had heard that he was planning to leave England again. She wanted him to take her assurances that, despite the awkwardness of his proposal the year before, she would always wish him the greatest happiness. 'As I shall not have an opportunity of seeing him again,' Annabella justified herself to her aunt, '... I shall always have pleasure in hearing that he is happy, and if my esteem can afford him any satisfaction, he may rely on my not adopting the opinions of those who wrong him.' Would her aunt pass this message to him?

Byron was terse, dismissive: Lady Melbourne could defend him however she pleased, he said, and only to amuse herself. He sent his best compliments to Miss Milbanke. He had nothing else to say. Lady Melbourne sent her own reply back to Annabella and must have defended Byron exemplarily. Because a month later, there was a letter from Miss Milbanke herself, lying with his post.

In the world of 1813, a woman could not visit a man alone – unless on a point of business. There were strict codes to govern who was introduced to whom, when someone could speak to someone else, what could be said, what could only be implied. There were messy contradictions between the flimsy, damped-down clothing women wore, and the disinterested propriety they were supposed to observe. There were double standards layered between how you should appear to behave in your marriage and what you could actually do. Illegitimate children were discreetly swallowed into the most respectable families without the law commenting on questions of inheritance or provision, while petty-sounding evasion of the hair-powder tax was still, as Lady Caroline Lamb's mother had found, an indictable offence.

Into the middle of this minefield of restriction and

contradictory convention waded Annabella Milbanke and her desire not to let Lord Byron entirely out of her sight. Unconventional, almost downright brazen, she opened a correspondence with him. That desk in Durham again, that notepaper squared to 'collect her sentiments', and she headed up a sheet with the daring address: Lord Byron, London. Lady Melbourne had assured her of the pleasure Lord Byron felt on being remembered by her, Annabella explained, and she took this as an invitation from him to write to him herself.

You have to feel the immensity of this.

It was a long letter. It was a revealing letter. She filled pages with her own character sketch. Byron had remarked on her serenity, she wrote, but she wanted him to know that she was no stranger to care; she wanted him to know that she could feel as deeply as he felt and this – she thought – would be the best basis of the 'unreserved friendship' she wanted to establish between them. 'It is my nature,' she wrote blatant, 'to feel long, deeply, and secretly and' – most telling – 'the strongest affections of my heart are without hope.'

Whatever she believed about the purity of her motives in writing to the bachelor Lord Byron, she took this one step to make sure that there was no impropriety in it. She invented a suitor – an unrequited love who held her heart 'without hope' – and made it completely appropriate and *safe* for her to write to Byron. Who had, she interpreted from the message he had sent through Lady Melbourne, 'expressed a determination to render your conduct conformable to my wishes, as if your attachment had been returned. I now claim that promise,' she said. And then, declamatory: 'I have the right of a constant and considerable zeal for your happiness' – and she launched into a sermon about the things he should do and think to make himself happier in this tricky, temporal life. Do good. Feel benevolence. Etcetera.

Passionate letters came for Lord Byron all the time, but they were for the poet not the man, and ended up stored in tin trunks in his publisher's office labelled 'Anonymous Effusions'. Their writers offered themselves squarely to the poet, dripping intimate with all that his words had made them feel. Promising him the world, albeit often anonymously. But this letter wasn't for the poet, and nor was it anonymous. Byron suddenly seemed so prescient to have commented the year before that there was a surprising amount of emotion under Annabella's placid countenance.

'You will not reject my admonitions as the result of cold calculation,' she felt sure, 'when you know that I *can* suffer as you have suffered.' And she assured him that she sent this extraordinary letter with the full knowledge of and approval from her parents. But please, she barbed, don't mention it to Lady Melbourne, who is so unused to seeing plain intentions.

His words were careful when he replied – nothing of the fast slap of his letters to her aunt – but still he sent her huge opening lines. 'I must be candid with you on the score of friendship,' he confessed from his sister's house in Cambridgeshire. 'It is a feeling towards you with which I cannot trust myself – I doubt whether I could help loving you.' But this was all playful: he didn't seem to have any serious intention of winning Annabella back from her unrequited love, nor did he seem keen to establish a correspondence between them. It was a single reply, sent off polite. And in it, he mused, too, that Lady Melbourne may have been a little premature in making an overture to Annabella for him the previous year. In a single smooth sentence he dismissed her concerns about people's gossip: 'if you hear ill of me, it is probably not untrue, though perhaps exaggerated.'

This was one of the truest things he ever said about himself. Which is the way of letters: reeking with an illusion of perfect honesty and confession, they let each writer put the best and most positive spin on themselves – and slip revelations of truth in between seemingly harmless comments.

His flourishing writing across the outside of the sheet of paper – Miss Annabella Milbanke, Seaham. She replied the day she heard from him, back-pedalling: she could not forgive herself for intruding from an 'impulse of ill-judged kindness. That I may not encrease the error' – the pathos of it – 'farewell. I will not regret the friendship which you deem impossible,' she wrote, 'for the loss is *mine*, as the comfort would have been *mine* …' So noble. So flattering. If there was one thing Lord Byron loved it was an audience: he had his reply to her in the next post, saying that certainly it was not his wish to correspond with her. And then filling a page. He caught himself on the last line – charming: 'I perceive that I *begin* my letter with saying, "I do not wish to draw you into a correspondence", and *end* by almost soliciting it – admirably consistent! But it is human nature, and you will forgive it – if not, you can punish.'

A piece of paper has in its rectangle both safety and licence. Annabella lobbed the rules of engagement back into Byron's court: 'act then towards me as best accords with the state of your mind,' she suggested. 'I said the comfort would be *mine*, for the idea – it is a vain dream – of alleviating the bitterness of your despondency if only by the wish to do so, would give me real comfort ...'

'It is my happiness,' she claimed after a fortnight of this volley of letters, 'to feel that in some degree I live for others.'

Whether Byron thought of this as another one of those feminine 'anonymous effusions' – this time offering him a soul instead of the usual heart – or whether he read it remembering all his fondness for that Miss Milbanke and how much he had admired and esteemed her the year before, he was drawn in. After all, was there a man who would not swoon or soften to think that the pure heart of a pure woman was taken up by wishing to alleviate his – particularly *his* – despondency? That such a gentle creature had the piteously small dream of doing this, and the grandiosely large belief that even her very wish to do this might in some way achieve it? There is no smoother elixir for the soul than such well-poured and large concern.

It was a tantalising correspondence, but neither had to worry that it was flirtatious. Annabella had the armour of her imagined heart's desire, which was Byron's protection too. They could tell themselves, then, that they were to be the rarest of animals in Regency England: two unmarried and well-prospected people who would simply correspond. Platonic. But had Annabella asked that Byron not *mention* the correspondence to Lady Melbourne? Not *mention* it to Lady Melbourne? He simply passed these letters on to her and received, in exchange, the list of characteristics

Annabella had drawn up for her Ideal Husband. Which he said he could make neither head nor tail of. 'She seems to have been spoiled,' he said, 'not as only children usually are – but systematically Clarissa Harlowed into an awkward correctness – with a dependence on her own infallibility which will or may lead her into some egregious blunder.'

More abiding truth, casually put down. He wrote next to Annabella that, yes, he would write to her 'occasionally, and you shall answer at your leisure and discretion'. Keeping himself uncommitted, but inviting her to keep up what he jokingly told Lady Melbourne was this illicit correspondence, between the greatest of St Ursula's thousand virgins and the most notorious of London's roues. Not, he clarified, that Annabella wrote anything that could not cheerfully be shouted through the streets by the town crier.

This illicit correspondence. Annabella, whether she knew it or not, was romancing Lord Byron: she was drawing him on and in. And Byron – no matter what he thought he was doing – was replying, was responding, was participating. At the same time, having replied to them earnestly and politely, he was passing Annabella's letters over to Lady Melbourne that the two of them could giggle over her sentences, her piety, her pedestalled morality.

To Annabella, in her confined world of history and geometry books, her mother, her father, and the odd reverend or spinster for conversation, he wrote: 'the great object of life' – perhaps he imagined himself in the pit of one of the halls at Cambridge, delivering a signature lecture – 'is sensation – to feel that we exist –

even though in pain − it is this "craving void" which drives us to Gaming, to Battle, to Travel − to intemperate but keenly felt pursuits.' An open definition for Lord Byron, and one of the clearest explanations he ever gave of why he did what he did.

Annabella was more one for a calm walk along the seashore, against which this treatise on activity was intriguing. She wanted to hear more. If she could just get him to think of her as his confessor, then the litany of those 'sensations' that he could pour out and be relieved of must be almost never-ending. '"As your friend I will bear with your faults,"' she assured him, 'and my patience for them is more than you can exhaust.' She had no idea what she was getting herself into. He had more faults than Annabella could have dreamed of, and a delightful propensity to make up others, to keep the tally high. It amused the drawing rooms of London − who could believe and be scandalised by and forget about any number of outrages in the course of a single evening. But now he was setting himself down in black and white to a woman who took every word he said seriously and − more dramatic − was running a ledger on the ultimate salvation of his soul. 'You may be *gay*,' she levelled at him, 'but you have not convinced me that you are *content*.' Certainly, she said, she did not approve of all this restless sensation business.

'My dear friend − for such you will permit me to call you,' he wrote back endearingly. 'You don't like my "restless doctrines" − I should be very sorry if *you* did − but *I* can't *stagnate* nevertheless.' And to wheedle further into her soul, he remarked too casual, 'you write remarkably well − which you won't like to hear so I shall say no more about it.'

It was a kind thing to say: Annabella wrote remarkably dense and laboured. Annabella wrote self-importance. 'If you are fatigued by the too great seriousness of my thoughts,' she countered, 'you must excuse it at this time as the unavoidable consequence of sorrow which I do not indulge. My most valued friend Miss Mont-gomery' – she who had been at death's door at the opening of 1812 – 'is going abroad by medical advice, which renders her return extremely precarious.' She wrote simultaneously – and cheerfully – to her aunt that she had read Byron's latest poem, *The Giaour* (unpronounceable name, commented Byron), an Ori-ental tale about the liberation of a woman who was bound in a sack to be drowned for promiscuity. Gossip suggested that Byron himself had been either the knave sleeping with her in the first place, or the brave gallant who saved her in the second. It ran through six editions in its first four months on sale.

It would have been more removed from feeling than even Annabella wanted to be to have stood resilient against all Byron's words – his poetry, for instance, read differently now that she had his letters, his voice in them, in her mind. Sometimes, one of them would realise that their correspondence – their *friendship*, if it was – was something extraordinary. And would write something more blatant, more heartfelt. There was strange see-sawing. Byron – practically flirting – would throw out something big, soft, declamatory, and Annabella would glaze over with a reply about religion or morality, or duty. Or Annabella would run a slightly riskier or more engaging suggestion through a para-graph, and Byron would recommend a book she should read. It was as if there was a hard length of something between them so that as one stepped forward the other always had to step back and keep the gap uniform. But beyond their letters to each other, it was possible to say larger things – no matter how flippantly they were put down. Byron's descriptions of love in *The Giaour*, for instance, 'almost make me in love' Annabella told her aunt, while she wrote to Byron about being sad at her friend's leaving. And she could go further: 'I consider his acquaintance as so desirable that I would incur the risk of being called a Flirt for the sake of enjoying it, providing,' she backed down, 'I may do so without detriment to himself – for you know that his welfare has been as much the object of my consideration as if it were connected with my own.'

So she is melancholy when she writes to me, Byron mused to Lady Melbourne, and gay when she writes to you at the same time – 'little demure Nonjuror'. It was the sort of emotional opportunism he was bound to admire.

He went to stay with a friend whose wife he thought he might seduce and let his letter-writing to Miss Milbanke slip. Of Annabella, he wrote to Lady Melbourne that their correspondence had 'ceased on both sides' – without confessing that it was his slackness that had ended it. He was thinking of new poems. He was playing with the idea of a new affair – there might even be a duel, he thought at one stage. And all that made letter-writing seem a futile kind of effort. (The new affair was itself a platonic thing in the end: the lady gave him a poodle that he liked, and he slipped her a few covert love-letters and kisses in the billiard room. That was the extent of it.)

Annabella – who had had at least enough letters to think she could rely on them continuing – tapped her fingers in Durham for more than a month, walking down to the blacksmith's cottage to collect her mail, coming home with nothing from Byron. And then she wrote, exact and firm: 'I am not exacting an answer. I only request to be informed whenever my communications become unacceptable that I may discontinue, and when you *partially* disapprove them pray tell me, that I may perceive my error.'

A letter came within a week. A letter full of invitation – he even declared himself happy to hear anything she wanted to say about religion, 'or any subject – if anybody could do me much *good* – probably you might'. Nothing about the poodle or the billiard table that had taken up his attention, although he did write about the mathematics that Annabella always put up as her greatest occupation. It wasn't really his field, he confessed. He could go along with it so far, but then 'if by any sort of process I could convert 2 and 2 into *five*, it would give me much greater pleasure.' He had heard, too, that she had turned down another man – a rumour left over from 1812 – and commented wryly that she made 'sad havock among "us youth" ... And this the suicide season,' he admonished, devilishly.

He was back. She had his attention again. She wondered whether his new knowledge of all she was had put him off her. 'Perhaps,' she suggested, 'I *have* occasionally forgotten the humility which should have regulated my opinions.' And she waxed lyrical about the delight with which she anticipated seeing him in the next year's season: '*I* shall not be distressed if the design to captivate should be imputed to *me*,' she promised, along with the usual rattle about her parents who knew, of course, and approved – even more so – of this vaguely risque correspondence she kept up. Positively coquettish, for the woman who turned her suitors into jokes about their mothers and the number of calling cards they left.

There was such an ease in these letters. This friendship she had with him, the access she had to him – there was nothing quite like it in her life. Annabella had the very words and ideas and workings of someone's soul. He sent himself, folded into sheets of paper, stuck down with a glob of wax – his seal pressed in hard – his peer's signature as the postage on the front.

'You wrong yourself very much,' he calmed her, 'in supposing that "the charm" has been broken by our nearer acquaintance – on ye contrary, that very intercourse convinces me of the value of what I have lost – or rather never found.' Balming flattery – but he stepped down from it immediately: 'I will not deny that the circumstances have occurred to render it more supportable.' He didn't tell her what these circumstances were – who the new woman who occupied him was. He expected, he said, that Annabella would think him very capricious, and he even admitted – and this should have been spotlit – that he 'could not exist without some object of attachment'. And along with this insinuation that he no longer pined for her, he dropped the comfort that the *only* woman he had *ever* seriously considered as a wife (whom she knew to be herself) had disappointed him by having 'disposed of her heart already'. This odd friendship, he wrote in his own (sporadic) journal, 'without a spark of love on either side'. And he listed her indisputable merits:

> She is a very superior woman, and very little
> spoiled, which is strange in an heiress – a girl of
> 20 – a peeress that is to be in her own right – an
> only child, and a *savante*, who has always had her
> own way. She is a poetess, a mathematician – a
> metaphysician, and yet, withal, very kind, gener-
> ous and gentle, with very little pretension. Any
> other head would have been turned with half her
> acquisitions, and a tenth of her advantages.

This was Byron's Annabella Milbanke. Not a spark of
love. And he confessed to her aunt that half the reason
he had wanted to marry Annabella (his 'Princess of Par-
allelograms' he called her) in the first place 'was the
vision of our *family party*'.

Apart from letters to Lady Melbourne and her niece,
he had rattled through the first draft of *The Bride of
Abydos* in eight days at the beginning of November.
Another Oriental tale, this one was about an affair
between cousins: he originally thought of making the
lovers 'rather too much akin to one another', before
editing out their 'consanguinity' to 'confine them to
cousinship'. Five editions sold out in a year. He
launched, almost immediately after *The Bride*'s publication, into *The Corsair* (a piratical tale about a girl called
Medora), and had it knocked out in four days. It sold,
unprecedented, 10,000 copies on its first *day* of publication. Readers, insatiable, could not get enough.
Byron, the poet, was invincible: 'I was more pleased
with the fame my *Corsair* had than with that of any of
my other books,' he said. 'For the very reason because
it did shine, and in boudoirs. Who does not write to
please the women?'

He giggled through the winter with Lady Melbourne and spent Christmas and New Year with his sister and her children, while Annabella – ill in bed through its long, grey days – had to write, despondent, that it would not be possible for her to see Byron in the spring, as she had been looking forward to. She could not inform him of this, she said, without serious disappointment: she would not be in London. And she made the first plunge of a dagger into her phantom lover: 'You have thought we perfectly understood each other ...' she began. She wanted to set the record straight.

Upright at her desk, she weighed each single word before she set it down, her sentences weaving elliptical to clarify themselves. She must not be misconstrued by him, and he must no longer believe that her heart, her affections, belonged to someone else. Wisdom, she launched in, is 'not less necessary than Will for an absolute adherence to Veracity. How I may in a degree have forsaken *that* – and under the influence of an ardent zeal for Sincerity – is an explanation that cannot benefit either of us. Should any disadvantage arise from the original fault, it must be only where it is deserved. Let this then suffice – for I cannot by total silence acquiesce in that, which, if supported when its delusion is known to myself, would become deception.' She told herself, as she told him, that this was all motivated by her inability to tell a lie. But it was, in effect, a declaration of availability.

Byron, not surprisingly, frowned, bewildered. 'There is one sentence,' he said – far too mild, 'that I do not understand.' And he wrote what a small man he would have been had he despised another man simply for his good fortune in winning Annabella's heart. 'The moment I sunk into your friend,' he assured her, 'I tried to regard you in no other light – our affections are not in our own power ...' And before she could reply, he had written again: 'pray take care of yourself – consider how many are interested in your health and welfare – and reconcile us to your absence by telling us that you are better for it.' Counting himself in the community of her admirers but not taking up her hint about being single, being free.

How blatantly should she tell him that there was no other suitor? How blatant did Annabella ever manage to be? 'I will comment as explicitly as I can on the passage which you wish me to elucidate,' she began circuitously. And she wound around the idea that circumstances had changed, that it was impossible for her to even dream of hope with her mystery man, and that she had sometimes regretted 'that lost chance of Domestic happiness'. She wanted Byron to know that she was attached to no one else – but she also wanted to make sure (she assured herself) that he wasn't languishing for her. As close as she would get to asking him if he was. She invoked the propriety of her parents' approval – again: 'I have not formed any friendship on which they reflect with more satisfaction than on ours ...'

Byron hosed down any idea that he was languishing. That interest, he assured her, 'was not in any great peril of revival before – but it is now more completely "numbered with the things that were" and never can be again.' Nothing more crushing. Especially combined with Byron's next melodramatic claims about himself: he was feverish, he was on the brink of something terrible 'which will probably crush me at last – and cut our correspondence short with everything else …'

She took the bait: it was hardly fair, she protested, to imply that some terrible disaster was about to crash around his ears and then leave her in suspense about it. It was not, she said, 'considerate towards one who so anxiously desires your welfare. You can *only* wrong me by doubting that – by refusing me a participation in your cares.' And she told him then that she could not seek 'domestic ties … on the principle of either Self-Love or Expediency'. They were back into a rapid-fire exchange – four letters in a week.

No one writes letters and expects to be pinned in perpetuity to the words they set down. 'You can *only* wrong me by refusing me a participation in your cares': this sentence of Annabella's was as huge a truth, subtly slipped in, as Byron's comment that the terrible things people said about him were usually based in truth – but blown out by exaggeration. And each must have wondered where this correspondence would lead to: people met to assess each other for marriage. Before they were married, they had the company of reliable companions or university mates. Once married, some of them made friends with other men, other women. But there wasn't much scope for a friendship between an unmarried (and desirable) young man and an unmarried (and potentially rich) young woman. Regency London, at least, was not designed to consider such a possibility.

And still the letters continued.

By March of 1814, Byron was back to addressing her as his dear friend, talking amicably about the religion that she cherished and writing soft words for her in the smallness of late night, 'wishing that you may awake to the most agreeable day-dreams which the pure in heart desire and deserve'. He had heard, too, that it was said in the city that Miss Milbanke had refused him for a second time. He assured her that he would much rather hear wrongful rumours that he was *refused* by her than *accepted* by anyone else. Sweet charm. He had been thinking, pragmatic, about marriage and the strangeness that there was 'something very soften-ing in the preserve of a woman, some strange influence … which I cannot account for'. He even had a couple of women in mind as potential Lady Byrons – neither of which, of course, was Miss Milbanke. He still thought her off-limits.

'I still hope the best for you,' Annabella said, much more succinct than usual, 'and whencesoever it may come, though not through *my* means, it will add to *my* happiness.'

'A letter from *Bella*,' he commented to his journal. 'I shall be in love with her again if I don't take care.'

A pet-name for her. And 'in love'. And 'again'.

It was an otherwise ordinary day in Annabella Mil-banke's life when Byron's next letter arrived in her hand, halfway through March, and she read, extraordi-nary, how much he wished to see her. A proposal coming out of the blue from a man she hardly knew would have been one thing. But now, if Lord Byron came, there would be some presumption of inti-macy.

'You do not know how much I wish to see you,' he wrote, 'for there are many things *said* in a moment – but tedious upon the tablets – not that I should intrude upon your confidence any thing (at least I hope not) you should *not* hear.'

Parents needed to be consulted. Official invitations needed to be extended. There was no chance that Byron could simply pop in for a chat. It all had to be much bigger than that – and was it what he had really said?

Annabella took a deep breath. It took her about a month to persuade her parents that this was an acceptable thing to do, while he visited his sister – about to give birth to her fourth child. Finally, she sent down a cautious reply. 'I have been prevented once or twice when I was going to write to you,' she said without explanation. Then, 'am I mistaken in imagining you are disposed to visit? I agree with you that the pen is unsatisfactory in discussing interesting topics, and I could not object to converse with you on any.'

A visit by Lord Byron to Miss Milbanke would signify only one thing to the marriage-centric world.

Well, Byron prevaricated, maybe he would visit, or maybe he would finally leave the country. He had taken new rooms – bachelor's rooms – at the Albany in London, and taken a couple of cosy runs up to the country to see his sister. Perhaps, he mused, he would get as far as Yorkshire – possibly even Scotland. She would have heard, he assumed, about Napoleon going off into exile and the Empress's refusal to follow him. This, said Byron, laying out the behaviour he at least expected of a consort, was not acceptable: 'men will always fall away from men – but it may generally be observed that no change of fortune – no degradation of rank or even character will detach a woman who has truly loved – unless there has been some provocation or misconduct towards herself on the part of the man – or she has preferred another for whom her affection will endure the same.'

He should have had it worked in cross-stitch for her.

She did want to see him – even if she said it would be for the entertainment and education of his conversation – and she took one of those steps forward (always matched by his step back) when she wrote: 'I *wish* to see you, and am happy to think I shall not wish in vain.' She assured him that, safe in her family home, there would be no influx of visitors, and he would not be made a lion.

But Byron didn't know, anymore, if he wished to see her. You tell me what I should do, he appealed to Lady Melbourne: 'I am not now in love with her – but I can't at all foresee that I should not be so if it came "a warm June" … I do admire her as a very superior woman,' he confessed, 'a little encumbered with virtue.' He knew, he said to Annabella's aunt, that if he married, he'd have to stop playing around everywhere else (Annabella didn't know it, but he'd hardly been without a lover between the day she turned him down and the day he said he wanted to see her). But then he trusted that whoever ended up being his wife would have it in her power to ensure this. 'My heart,' he said, 'always alights on the nearest *perch* – if it is withdrawn, it goes God knows where – but one must like something.'

Which was the antithesis of Annabella Milbanke's determination that one needn't like anything (or, more correctly, anyone) in that way at all. The soul: remember the soul.

It was well into that invoked June – warm or not – before he bothered to write to her again, although she wrote to him more than once in the meantime, reminding him both of his hazy plan to visit and his unpaid 'epistolary debts'. 'Pray write to me,' she said simply at last, 'for I have been rendered uneasy by your long silence, and you cannot wish to make me so.'

He blustered, he apologised. He didn't tell her that he had been shooting confusion back and forth with her aunt. No, she had been away from Seaham, he said, and he hadn't wanted to write while she wasn't there. And he had been trying to set a date for a visit, and couldn't. He signed himself, for the first time, 'very affectly. and truly yrs'.

She wrote, to her 'dear Lord Byron', that his letter had made her very happy. He would come: she would see him. And so there were things she wanted him to know of her. She knew, for example, that she often appeared formal and cold – both in herself and in her letters – and she wanted him to know that, to him at least, she never wanted to appear that way. Last year, she thought, he may have misunderstood her behaviour, and she was 'as anxious then as since to make my real feelings known to you'.

Silence. Byron was swanning in London, taking his sister to masquerade balls and dealing with new onslaughts from Caroline Lamb. Another month. Annabella enclosed her father's formal invitation for Lord Byron to visit Seaham with her own condition: before they met they had to establish – absolutely clear – how they thought of each other. This was, she felt, 'too essential to be sacrificed by either to false delicacy'. She talked about affection, and about her peace with herself and with her God: 'if you love me,' she wrote out of nowhere, 'make it your first object as it is the first object to me.'

Byron had just finished writing *Lara*, the last Oriental epic (published with comparatively little fluster in early August), and was now frolicking by the sea with his sister, her children, and an old friend from university. He wrote one reply and threw it in the fire, sure that he had misunderstood her and would just be muddling things more. He frowned over Annabella's letter again.

'Write to me openly and *harshly* if you please,' he offered at last, 'if there is anything you wish to know or say.' She was the last person in the world, he said, that he ever wanted to misunderstand. They seemed so close to being in the same place at the same time – emotionally and geographically – except for one thing: 'I have not so far lost all self-command,' wrote Byron, proving entirely that he had, 'to require repetition that you are attached to another.'

She was back to square one: he was closer to coming and still thought she wanted to marry someone else.

Annabella, had she been anyone else and come this far along the track of inveigling a correspondence with Lord Byron by first convincing him she was off-limits as a possible amour, and then deciding that she didn't want to be, might simply have dashed off a letter declaring: was he blind? Of course it was him that she had wanted to marry all along. What had he been thinking? But instead, after a year of this ping-pong between them – all that she laid out for Byron to know of her, all that he sent back to add to her compendium of him – she still only wanted to be certain that Byron was *not* going to fall in love with her *again*. This, at least, was how she phrased it: 'when I last wrote I feared from some reconsiderations that you might still be in danger of feeling more than friendship towards me ...

'My doubt then – and I ask a solution – is whether you are in *any* danger of that attachment to me which might interfere with your peace of mind.' She turned the knife again in the heart of her invented lover, writing that she was 'very far from being indifferent to him and shall probably always continue the very sincere and unembarrassed kindness of which he is the deserving object.' But, in clear, stark black and white she said of her phantom: 'nothing could now induce me to marry him.'

She waited for Byron's reply, and a lilting sentence came fast, within a week: 'I did – do – and always shall love you – and as this feeling is not exactly an act of will – I know no remedy.' He was in no position, he knew, to ask why she did not love him. And he didn't want anything from her that came from pity instead of affection. There it was.

Annabella flattered? Annabella gracious? She turned it into something she could sermonise about – that she had refused him simply because 'a comparative view of your character and my own' must make it clear that 'they are ill-adapted to each other'. She had, she said, 'objections ... you do not appear to be the person whom *I* ought to select as my guide, my support, my example on earth with a view still to Immortality.'

She had asked him for one clear statement of how he felt about her – and he had replied. She gave her own reply back: these objections. Stated in these words. This simply. This clearly. On August 13, 1814. He said I love you – and she said yes, but –

They hovered there, at the height of what they said they felt for the other. And then it collapsed, again. He bounced a letter back, chirpy, saying that now that all that awkwardness and confession was out of the way, they could talk about something else. And it was hardly a dangerous intimacy, he cut, 'a few letters and still fewer interviews in the course of a year'.

Peaks and troughs: the letters built up and up to almost something – and then fell back into the nothingness of his suggestion of some Sismondi and Gibbon to complement her reading. He said he loved her; she said he shouldn't. They dropped into desultory exchanges and pleasantries, a bit of a dissection of Annabella's famed 'consistency' (she thought it flawed, he thought it formidable), and Byron's unsurprising discovery – after so long, after her implicit rejection of him again – that there was no way he could travel to Seaham that year. It looked like the correspondence would simply run on and on into volumes.

And then, less than a month beyond her August 13 remark about his personality and her immortality, the whole remarkable exchange clawed its way up to a definitive point. Lord Byron, clearly suffering short-term memory loss about the phrase 'ill-adapted', wrote to Miss Annabella Milbanke to enquire 'are the objections to which you alluded insuperable? – or is there any line or change of conduct which could possibly remove them?' Tell me who I should be. 'I neither wish you to pledge nor promise yourself to anything – but merely to learn a *possibility* which would not leave you the less a free agent.' Tell me if I may hope. 'It is not,' he confessed, 'without a struggle that I address you once more on this subject.'

This was – and you may not have noticed – what would be taken as Lord Byron's second proposal. All summer, his sister Augusta and his friends had been telling him that this was the only thing to do: a wife would mean a dowry to clear some of his mountainous debts. A wife, it was felt, would be the saving of him. Augusta had even been sounding out a friend of hers as a potential bride, but nothing had come of it. Finally Byron sat down and wrote his letter to Miss Milbanke. He handed it to his sister – 'a very pretty letter,' she commented. 'It is a pity it should not go.'

'Then it shall go,' said Byron. Easy.

He sat out on the steps of Newstead Abbey watching for the post every day until he received her reply.

When the letter reached Annabella, on September 14, 1814, it looked like any other from Lord Byron – the alphabet fast and various compared to Annabella's contained lettering, the punctuation all over the place and usually marked out by long dashes – wrapped in a sheet of paper. The address. Byron's signature. His seal. In it, she read, blatant and explicit, nothing less, nothing other, than another plea from him that she should become his wife.

There was no time, this time, for sitting and writing character sketches, for drawing lists of requirements, of pros, of cons. There was certainly no time for remembering that she had said they were 'ill-adapted' less than a month before. She replied – she accepted – on the same day. She had not seen him for more than a year, nor spoken with him for more than two. But the shape of the man drawn out by all those letters she had

cached away now lay neat and complete over the picture of the ideal spouse she had drawn up for Lady
Melbourne. Those few foolscap pages, the oblique
words of his proposal: somehow these stifled all the
objections she had held only a month before.

But what had Byron actually said? That he didn't
want her to promise herself to anything. That she
wasn't to consider herself anything less of a free agent.
That he merely wanted to know if her 'objections' were
'insuperable'. She may as well have been having herself
measured for her trousseau before the day was out. Her
self. Lady Byron. Her husband. Lord Byron.

Annabella didn't even know where he was. She
wrote one long letter: 'I am almost too agitated to
write ... I am and have long pledged myself to make
your happiness my first object in life. *If I can* make you
happy, I have no other consideration. I will *trust* to you
for all I should look up to – all I can love. The fear of
not realising your expectations is the only one I feel.
Convince me – it is all I wish – that my affection may
supply what is wanting in my character to form your
happiness ... this is a moment of joy which I have too
much despaired of ever realising,' and 'there has in reality been scarcely a change in my sentiments.' She sent
this cascade to London with her father's permission for
them to marry. But Byron was not there. She sent, on
the off-chance, about fifty words to Newstead, where
Byron read them on the same day that his gardener
found his dead mother's long-lost wedding ring: 'I
hope you will find in my other letter *all you wish*,' she
wrote.

He looked up and across the table at Augusta, at the
gardener standing holding that thin gold band: he said,

'it never rains but it pours.' But he didn't write to Annabella until her long, long letter had reached him, redirected from his bachelor's rooms on Piccadilly. 'Your letter,' he said on Sunday, September 18, 1814, 'has given me a new existence. It was unexpected, I need not say welcome – but *that* is a poor word to express my present feelings.' He wrote nothing about coming to her, seeing her, setting a date. He wrote that certainly it was in her power to 'render me happy – you have made me so already'.

It was a particularly flat letter.

To Lady Melbourne he wrote simply, 'Miss Milbanke has accepted me.' And then on Monday he doubted even that and wrote Annabella a second letter: 'the fact is I am even now apprehensive of having misunderstood you and of appearing presumptuous when I am only happy ...'

She had been perfectly sure that he was proposing – but Byron was suddenly uncertain that she had accepted him. He thought perhaps he had made a precipitate fool of himself, assuming that she had just agreed to marry him. But the next day, Tuesday, everything was certain. He even mentioned the magic word in 'my third letter in three days'. He signed it, he said, 'with every sentiment of respect – and – may I add the word? – *love* – ever yours.'

V I

NOVEMBER 2, 1814

'There could not be a worse preparation for
marriage than Byron's preceding life. He had never
known any domestic connexions, no regularity of a
home, none of that deference to women and that
respect for their good qualities which a youth passed
among female relatives inspires. The women he had
been intimate with were all of the worst kind; even
what he called love having been squandered on
worthless and corrupt persons ...'

Thomas Moore

People had been placing bets on Byron's marriage
for years: he had had to pay 50 guineas to one
friend as soon as he announced himself engaged.
The newspapers couldn't believe that, if the Regency's
Casanova was marrying, he would marry Miss Milbanke. So wonderful, someone murmured, of that
'sensible, cautious prig of a girl to venture upon such a
Heap of Poems, Crimes and Rivals'.

Judith Milbanke showed Annabella her own letters
from 1812. She was astonished by what she read – what

she had thought about Byron, what she had written about him, the number of times he had graced her pages. I always thought, Judith Milbanke commented flatly to Lady Melbourne (who had sent her congratulations), that Byron was the only one who interested her, and I was right. These lovers, she said, who seem to delight in perplexing themselves and each other ... she didn't understand them.

Everyone wrote congratulations: 'all our relatives,' said Byron, 'are congratulating away to right and left in a most fatiguing manner.' Byron's friend Hobhouse (miffed because he had thought Byron was organising to travel to Italy with *him* when all the time he was proposing to Miss Milbanke) sent a brief letter. Annabella gushed that 'one believes every word Mr Hobhouse writes, because there is not a word too much.'

Annabella's friends wrote – but not words about love, or her happiness with the man she would spend her life with. Instead there was confidence 'built on your sense of religion, which will enable you to find Peace and Consolation in the fulfilment of your Duties, even should my hopes, my prayers for your Worldly Happiness prove vain! But I am sanguine,' wrote this unenthusiastic correspondent, 'for I know the motives of your acceptance – they are pure.' 'I know you too well,' said another, 'to fear your having been dazzled and captivated by the mere brilliancy of genius or that you have fixed your expectations of future happiness on so frail a foundation.' Lady Caroline Lamb wrote too – but to Byron, wishing him all the happiness and the blessings of God for his marriage, while commenting cattily to his publisher that he was bound to fail with a woman who went to church, understood mathematics and had a bad figure.

But Byron's sister wrote to his betrothed, and she and Annabella were immediately voracious correspondents. Augusta confessed how frustrated she was whenever she tried to talk about Byron's goodness and kindness she saw a room full of people smirk, sceptical. It was a great thing, she gushed, to be able to write to someone who loved him as she did. This wasn't hagiography: among her words of adoration were comments about the allowances that must be made for her brother's behaviour. About certain methods of handling him, of laughing him out of suspicions and moods – none of which tallied with the Byron who had arrived for Annabella to read and to learn in the pages of his own letters. Then, said Augusta, there were his financial worries.

'If I could possibly express how deservedly dear my Brother is to me,' wrote Augusta to Annabella, 'you might in some degree imagine the joy I have felt in the anticipation of an event which promises to secure his happiness.'

'I received a letter from your sister – *mine*,' said Annabella to Byron, 'so cordially kind that I cannot say how much I thank her.'

'It gives me much pleasure to hear that Augusta has written to you,' said Byron to Annabella. 'She is the least selfish and gentlest creature in being, and more attached to me than any one in existence can be.'

Augusta, Annabella, Byron. Each claiming the other: none of them can have had the slightest idea how taut that triad would remain through the rest of their lives.

The correspondence ran on between Byron and Annabella – still in two different places – more things revealed, discussed, clarified. More knowledge to paste onto the two-dimensional image each had of the other. Annabella began, overwhelming, a whole week after she had accepted Byron: 'Since I made myself yours, I have had a happiness, deep as it promises to be durable – not a moment of doubt ... I have been very foolish,' she said of all the time she had spent telling him he should not love her, 'and if you had not been wiser, we might both still have been without hope.' Rewriting how things had been. Establishing the courtship they would hold common. And she laid bare the phantom lover she had created. She had known, she confessed, that Byron could 'excite affection', but she had doubted – in that clear-lit October, two years before, when Lady Melbourne delivered his first proposal – 'if your character, as I then misconceived it from false accounts, could *support* that affection in one who *loves* only where she can *honour.*'

Note this down: this is what I expect you to do.

'Lest mine should become engaged to you,' she went on, 'I sought an object for them ... [a man] who so far from showing affection to me, had bestowed it elsewhere.' The phantom suitor exposed: 'had I not conjured it into being, my impulse to write to you would probably not have prevailed against principles that forbad the measure.'

This is how I have won you.

Byron made no comment about this (although he told Hobhouse all about it, who later commented, pointed, that Lady Byron 'would not stick at a trick' to win Byron as her husband: 'I know, from her having told Byron that she was in love with another man in order to hook him'). He sent back pages of himself instead: the first time he had seen her, how unworthy he was of her from that very moment, and 'Dearest Annabella – allow me for the first time to use that expression ... do not grow tired of hearing me repeat seemingly by rote but really by *heart* how faithfully I am your most attached and unalterable ...'

For her, now, he would rewrite his past two years: recollections, explanations, how he had dreamed of her across that time. 'Forgive my weaknesses,' he wrote. 'Love what you can of me and mine – and I will be – I am whatever you please to make me ... you should be not only my Love – but my first friend, my adviser, my reprover – when necessary – that my head should at times be as much indebted to your counsels as my heart is to your regard. In difficulty or danger I would not call upon you to share it or extricate me – I would not throw upon you the weight of my griefs or my perils – but I would ask you if I had done well or ill – and upon your answer would materially depend my estimation of my conduct. I write to you as if you were already my wife – "the wife of my bosom" as assuredly you are – for it does not contain a thought which I can separate from you.'

It was all going so well. If only he would set a date when he would arrive in person at Seaham, rather than in letters. She waited through September, through October. Still he did not come. Lawyers' business, he said, and depositions to be made, and a visit to a phrenologist, who pronounced on the basis of Byron's skull that 'my good and evil are at perpetual war – pray heaven,' he wrote, 'the last don't come off victorious.'

'If you were here,' Annabella wrote plaintive, '*what* Anxiety would remain? Till you are here we shall all feel *some.*'

Finally, on November 2, 1814, he arrived. She looked well. She must have wondered how he would look, downstairs, peeling off his travelling cloak and walking away from the mess of his luggage and his books, his writing desk and his servants. She had been reading: she stood up, smoothed the front of her dress, felt her hands stick even though it was wintery, blew out her candles. 'I never like to *make scenes,*' she had assured him while she waited for him, 'even on the most favourable opportunities.'

This was her biggest moment of certainty – 'calm,' she felt, 'with that perfect self-possession which had not suffered any interruption since the time that I accepted the offer of marriage.' A husband. To wake up and listen to his breath in the night. Homes and dinners and visits and children. New names – new titles. She stood on the brink of all this.

As she opened the door she saw him start and straighten himself, as though he had been about to move – to cross the room, or lean forward and study something on the shelves, or on the table. He leaned back against the mantelpiece. The room was silent. He stood, perfectly still, and he watched her. In her mind, he should be striding – awkward with rushing. But he stood. Fiddling, she noted, with his watch-chain – which she took as unpardonable vanity rather than nervousness. Augusta had told Annabella he was so shy with new people – he had written that to her himself. And, as he had confessed to Hobhouse, 'the character of the wooer in this regular way does not sit easy upon me.'

She looked at him long enough to think he was 'coarser, more sullied since we last met – it was like a deathchill.' Which was hardly a good start. She thought he was reluctant to move towards her; but he was just self-conscious about his limp, the way he had to walk to compensate for that deformed foot, that withered leg, especially in front of strangers. So there it was too: he thought of her as a stranger.

It was a farcical room: him completely frozen and her weaving a perilous path through the furniture, a sense of perpetual motion. He held his hand out to her, and looked at her with that infamous gaze that brought women's hearts into their mouths, made them faint, made them speechless. He kissed her hand. Silence. He said, at last, 'It's a long time since we met.'

She was completely dumbstruck. Her reply, as she described it herself, was 'hardly articulate. I felt over-powered by the situation, and asking if he had seen my parents, I made an excuse to leave the room, in order to call them – but they had met him at the door.' She crossed the room again, reversing the too-fast motion she had come in with, and pulled the door hard behind her. He watched it slam. This frantic rushing at him, and then just-as-frantic retreat. He slumped, still frozen against the flickering of the fire when the door opened again, and she brought her parents in. They talked about theatre, about London. They talked about his journey. And they muddled through their first evening under the same roof.

She was up early the next morning, thinking that he might be waiting for her in the library. She sat. She waited. She waited 'till near twelve, and then finding that I had symptoms of head-ache, I determined to take a walk, supposing that Byron must have left his room by the time of my return.'

Here stood Lord Byron and Annabella Milbanke, used to communicating in the very safe, two-dimensional space of a foolscap page. Used to saying things which would take at least two days to reach the other person, never seeing their immediate reaction. They tried to work out how to talk to each other. To work out what they knew about each other, or if – perhaps more honest – they knew each other at all. Each must have read the other's letters like a primer. He would say this; she would say that. There would be long conversations about religion, about his poetry, thought Annabella. 'Seriously, if she imagines that I particularly delight in canvassing the creed of St Athanasius – or prattling of rhyme,' wrote Byron to Lady Melbourne. Both clinging to the pernicious idea that, by agreeing to marry someone, you were immediately cocooned in a kind of intimate knowledge of them that, two minutes before, you couldn't have had. Cocooned in an ease of what to say, or of how to be, simply, together.

The problem lay in what fell outside the boundaries of those pages. Like Byron telling Lady Melbourne, after two days in Annabella's house, that he couldn't 'yet tell whether we are to be happy or not – I have every disposition to do her all possible justice,' he wrote grand, 'but I fear she won't govern me, and if she don't it will not do at all.' Like Annabella declaring, months earlier, 'it is not the Poet' she was interested in: 'it is the immortal Soul lost or saved!' Their secrets.

They circled. Annabella coaxed Lord Byron outside

to walk with her, along the beach, through quiet country lanes – although she didn't understand why he froze
or ran awkward into the shrubbery, whenever someone
approached. He thought of his limp as the biggest part
of himself. He kept up his commentary for Lady Melbourne: there was more feeling under Annabella's cool
exterior than might be suspected. And then, too, his
discovery that Annabella was 'quite *caressable* into kindness and good humour'. She began to talk: he began to
kiss. Her *passions*, he told her aunt, are 'stronger than
we supposed … she herself cannot be aware of this.'
Lady Melbourne, Byron's greatest female friend, as he
told Annabella: there was nothing that he would not
tell her – and he clearly saw no reason why he should
not continue dissecting and discussing Annabella.

'Do you know,' he whispered to Lady Melbourne
after just over a week, 'I have great doubts if this will
be a marriage now. Her disposition is the very reverse
of *our* imaginings – she is overrun with fine feelings –
scruples about herself and *her* disposition (I suppose in
fact she means mine) and to crown all is taken ill once
every three days with I know not what.' Some days, he
said, the two of them were too alike. Some days, too
unalike. He couldn't say that her temper was *bad* – 'but
very self-tormenting – and anxious – and romantic'. In
short, he said plainly, it is impossible to foresee how this
will end.

Still there was no date set for the wedding.

Annabella, too, seemed uncertain of what was
going to – or should – happen. Sometimes he kissed
her; sometimes he seemed further away in the same
room than he had been when they corresponded from
different ends of the country. The only thing, then,

was to be direct. Upfront. To go to him and to stand in front of him and ask him whether he wanted to call the marriage off. That, she thought, was what she should do.

It should have occurred to her, as the words took their shape in the air, that this was something which, once said, could never be unsaid.

He was almost apoplectic. To him, she was all sureness and certainty – that formidable consistency. Whatever concerns, whatever reservations, whatever evasions he had, he had not thought they were part of her. She was the one fixed point around which the rest of the world could crumble while she, even in her own conception of herself, stood straight, dependable, and above all supportive. He fell back onto the sofa as though she has struck him with the stinging flat of her hand. For too long a moment, there were no words to get the room past this point. She didn't even reach out: there was nothing in Annabella to let her imagine that she could walk across the room and touch him. The silence held.

He rocked back and forth. He said, over and over, you don't know what you've done, you don't know what you've done. She thought: I am *sure* he must love me.

Time began to flow again: small, tentative words. It was decided – neither said by which – that Byron would leave her parents' house. Neither explained what had happened to her parents (although Byron described it to Lady Melbourne as a scene along the lines of something Caroline Lamb would get away with – and neglected to mention that the histrionics were his, not Annabella's). To be together and not be married was, as

Byron said, a kind of thing like purgatory. All that desire – and suddenly a danger that Annabella was no longer going to be above anything. Lord Byron drove away from Seaham, a fortnight after he had arrived. He had brought no engagement gift and, despite Annabella's mother already going over cake recipes, he had named no date either for the wedding or for his return.

Annabella was, she wrote as their letters began again, in a 'dim eclipse … my own dearest there is not a moment when I would not give my foolish head to see you.' While he let three days lag before he said, 'to yourself, Dearest, if I were to write forever I could only come to one conclusion which I may as well make now and that is that I ever am most entirely and unalterably your attached, B.' She knew nothing of his life in London: single men's rooms in the Albany and gentlemen's clubs.

You don't know what you've done.

She ached for him: 'I wish for you, want you Byron mine, more every hour.' While two gangs of lawyers tossed the details of a settlement forward and back – all delay and quarrel – as if there were no bride or groom involved, only two sets of account books and piles of unrepaid credit. Byron's sister, Augusta, wrote again of the weight of the worry that Byron carried with his business affairs. He offered to delay – Annabella said she could marry him if he hadn't a coin in the world. She offered to delay – he said he was getting a special licence from the Archbishop of Canterbury so they could be married wherever they liked, whenever they liked, and on the shortest possible notice. The wedding cake was already made, although Annabella had told her mother it would be better to wait and Byron had said he would 'try to be ready before it is baked'. And wasn't. He hoped, too, they might 'love each other all our lives as much as if we had never been married at all.' 'I have learned,' she said, 'that I cannot enjoy any-thing without you – these long blank days.' Still no date.

'With regard to our being under the same roof and *not* married,' Byron wrote, 'I think past experience has shewn us the awkwardness of that situation.'

'If we meet,' he wrote, 'let it be to marry.'

Annabella ignored the first word of this to concentrate on the last.

Lord Byron stood in the middle of his rooms in London, clutching at the hand of a young woman he had met twice, maybe three times. Her name wasn't even important: she would never be anyone other than the person who wrote down their encounter. Lord Byron clutched at her hand saying, I wish to God you had come sooner, and, we should have been so happy. If only I'd met you earlier.

Finally, though, he was coming through the snow on the other side of Christmas, John Cam Hobhouse with him to be his best man and to write, famously, that a lover was never in less haste. And Annabella ran to him, threw her arms around his neck, and then stood back admiring him while Hobhouse admired her and noted she had particularly fine ankles. It was the dead of winter, New Year's Eve. The man who had written his love, his esteem and his hopes had arrived. There was no reason to think she would not be happy.

On the first day of 1815 Lord Byron and Hobhouse rehearsed the wedding: Hobhouse played the bride. There were cushions for the couple to kneel on and the wedding cake was brought out to be cut and wished over and eaten. It was a small ceremony: the bride and groom, her parents, his best friend, and her old governess and companion, Mrs Clermont. The vicar, in a touch that must have appealed to Byron's enjoyment of high society's intricacies, was the illegitimate son of one of Annabella's relations. By noon January 2, 1815, it was all over. Miss Annabella Milbanke was Lady Byron. Lord Byron had a wife.

There was no shame, of course, in her running twice from the room during the ceremony, overcome by emotion, or in the great illumination of her face (so glaring that Hobhouse, usually prosaic, commented on her 'gazing with delight' on Byron). There was no shame, either, in Byron smiling sardonic at Hobhouse when he had to pledge all his goods to Annabella. Nor in his mistakenly calling her 'Miss Milbanke' again afterwards, instead of 'Lady Byron'. And there was no shame in Annabella answering Hobhouse's wishes for a life of happiness with perfect honesty and squareness: if she was not happy, she said, it would be her own fault.

As Hamlet observed once, nothing in the world is good or bad – only thinking makes it so.

The Hon. Augusta Leigh, 1816

VII

MARRIAGE

'Good breeding demanded that outward
conventions should not be violated, but asked few
questions as to what went on beneath the surface.
Scandals were glossed over by the decent
acquiescence of the wife or husband.'

Lady Airlie

Hobhouse, whose gift to the bride was a full set
of Byron's poems bound in yellow leather,
handed Annabella up into the carriage. He
wished her all the world of happiness, and stood with
her mother and father as the happy couple drove away.
Judith Milbanke was crying. The Durham bells were
pealing – they had pealed once before, premature, and
Byron had been as annoyed by that early tolling as he
was by this. Pestilent bells. The sound cut ribbons
through the air as the carriage rattled away through
winter to Halnaby, the isolated and empty house of
Annabella's father in Yorkshire where they would
spend their three-week honeymoon.

She had stood firm and resistant against all his

advances – other than those simple kisses, the smallest of caresses – during his uncomfortable engagement visit. Now she had married him, however that was supposed to make her feel, and there was nothing that was not permissible. You want to kiss this man, you want to call him by his first name, you want to wake up next to him in the middle of the night, watch him as he comes out of sleep in the morning? There is nothing that you cannot do. You can be beaten by him (so long as the stick is not thicker than his thumb), sold by him, imprisoned by him. You can touch him, feel him, bear his children. All this is possible.

Lord and Lady Byron in a carriage together, hours after their wedding ceremony, on their way to their honeymoon. He will turn to her, he will kiss her.

Except this didn't happen. What happened instead fractured the truth into a thousand and one possibilities. What he did – what happened from here on – was really at best a matter of conjecture.

What Annabella didn't know, or had never considered, was that there is never one version of reality that is absolute. Annabella Milbanke, saver of souls, dealt in absolutes. Black-white. Wrong-right. One version of how things were. That she manipulated things as much as the next person to make them fit that one version never crossed her mind. That there was a version of Lord Byron other than the one she knew – just one other version, mind you, rather than the myriad that existed – had simply never occurred to her. Up to this point, everything in Annabella's life had existed purely from Annabella's point of view. And that there was any other point of view was an impossible idea.

Lord Byron did not turn to her and kiss her. He did

something that the Lord Byron who had written to her, who had recommended books that she should read, who had taken on all her ecumenical ravings, who had said that he didn't know if he could help loving her, would never do. He turned to her, she said, and he began to spit the most vile and loathing accusations at her: what a fool she has been, what a dupe. That she deluded herself into thinking that she would be his salvation – ha! – he would more likely be her destruction. An outpouring of venom and of spite and of pure hatred, said Lady Byron: that was what she sat pressed against in a carriage driving away from her family home to her wedding night. And she arrived at Halnaby and a butler, more than fifty years later, remembered seeing her run up the stairs, crying – sobbing even – upset and looking nothing like a glowing bride at all.

There's only one problem with this: other accounts of that drive were completely different. In one version, Byron went so far as to say that he clambered into the carriage and found that his wife's maid was wedged in between him and his new bride. And another maid, more than fifty years later, remembered watching Lady Byron emerge at Halnaby and, smiling, walk up the stairs to the house, pausing to chat to all her father's tenants who had gathered to wish her well.

Two people locked into a small space together – a carriage, a marriage – see something immense, terrific happen. They will not see the same thing. Yet each will believe that they have seen the truth and that the other person must agree with them, or be lying.

Take your pick of versions: Lord Byron had Lady Byron on a sofa before dinner – out of the carriage, and onto another one of those sofas. Or Lord Byron was kept waiting until near two in the morning when his wife's maid finally came to say that she was in bed waiting for him. That it took his most complex and concerted scheme of seduction and entreating to get her to turn towards him, to even look at him or answer when he whispered her name. Or that, with his daggers and pistols beside the bed, as usual, he woke in the middle of the night to see the candlelight flickering through the red curtains that surrounded the bed. That he thought the room was on fire. That he shrieked at the bright glancing shadows: 'Good God, I am surely in Hell.' A quagmire of information.

Perhaps Annabella had never fully let herself believe that she would marry Byron – that it would actually ever happen. Perhaps Byron, too, had never expected that the marriage would take place. She looked at him and loved him, her husband: he looked at her and hated that she – that anyone – was to be his wife. There would be no way back from that point. They would never be two people looking in the same direction, because this difference lay at the base of every minute of their marriage. As they generated more and more versions of what had happened, to try to make sense of it.

All the rest of their lives.

Who knew what a honeymoon was supposed to be like? It was the middle of winter and Lord and Lady Byron were on their own – no company to call, no one else to pass the time with – in a cold, desolate house in the middle of nowhere. Other brides – like Lady Caroline Lamb, for instance – took their mothers on

Marriage

honeymoon with them. Or their sisters. Or a female
companion. These two were alone. Lady Byron went
into the room where her husband was writing and he
spat, peevish, do we have to be in the same place at the
same time *all* the time? Where else did she have to be?
Who else was there to be with? The weather outside
was all winter squalls and snow. Write to my sister, he
said, and invite her to come and join us. But Augusta
demurred: she had her children to look after, her house
to keep, her own husband to be with. She and
Annabella wrote to each other often: they still hadn't
met each other.

This was the time when Byron and Annabella were
supposed to tell each other their stories. This is who I
am, this is what I believe, this is what I want you to
know of me. Annabella's stories, though, fell down
between the cracks of her husband's. If she sat, curled
up by the fire, and told him about her childhood, about
the day when she was a little girl and hung back in the
kitchen to watch people's faces when they heard that
someone had died; if she giggled as she told him the
time she took a bet that she could walk blindfolded
from the road to the house and ended up knee-deep in
the duck pond; if she gave him those little pieces of
herself, they were lost. Because against these anecdotes,
Lord Byron told his new wife that he was as much a
fiend as that cousin of hers, Caroline Lamb, and that he
would wear down her heart like a perpetual drop of
water. He told her that he had two natural children. He
told her of his 'affair' with one of London's leading
ladies (that liaison that never progressed beyond the
presentation of a poodle and some letters). He told her

that there was no infallible system of right and wrong, and that the Muslims had just as valid a system of morals as those of the Archbishop of Canterbury. The differences, he told her, were more a matter of taste than of correctness. He told her that he had another wife living – 'you may find,' he said, 'that this is so.'

In the insipid yellow of another winter day, Byron followed his own train of thought to the corners of the room. He had played this game before in all the fashionable drawing rooms of London: suggest something about yourself, and watch it roll and grow and take hold in the imaginations of your audience. Except that now your audience is one woman, one earnest and hopeful woman, who believes that it is her mission to save your soul.

I am a fallen angel, I have this terrific destiny which I must fulfil. A fallen angel, he said, who has come to earth for the love of a human woman. Perhaps, he offered her, perhaps you are that woman. Perhaps I will write on it. In the blackness of the nights that followed he promised to tell her of something worse – much worse – than that platonic liaison with the poodle owner from the end of 1813. Anything more licentious than a peck on the cheek in an empty room would be monumental in comparison for Annabella, who thought of this incident with all the dread and horror of a fully blown sin. I will tell you in the morning, he said ... and then didn't. While she lay with her head against his chest and he told her that she deserved a softer pillow than his heart. 'Nobody understands me but Augusta,' he said to his new wife in their empty honeymoon house. 'I shall never love anybody as well as her.'

And he implied and hinted and brushed past the most amazing set of stories – confessing nothing to her directly although she was convinced, within two weeks of her marriage, that he was guilty of murder.

Byron wrote happily to friends that everything was going along swimmingly: 'I was married this day week,' he stated. 'The parson has pronounced it – Perry [an editor] has announced it – and the *Morning Post*, also, under the head of "Lord Byron's Marriage" – as if it were a fabrication, or the puff-direct of a new stay-maker.' He still thought marriage should be conducted more on the terms of a lease than an eternal contract, he said, although he'd be happy to renew the lease on Lady Byron – even if the terms were for ninety-nine years. Lady Byron remembered that he told her – worse, instructed her – to write letters to her friends telling them that she was happy. As they left Halnaby, after three weeks alone, Byron said, simple: 'I think you now know pretty well what subjects to avoid touching upon.'

Here's another problem. These memories of this terrible, fearful time, came not from the newly-married Annabella, but from Annabella a year distant – two – then ten or forty. And memories – like biographies, heavy with academic research or gold-embossed like historical novels, or just one person's version of what happened to someone else or themselves – are never absolute. Two people watching the same thing are bound to disagree about what they see. They will remember the moment one way at ten past eleven and another at five to four. They will give one account on Monday evening and a different one on Thursday morning. And the further they are from the moment itself, the more the moment will be coloured by what's happened in the interim. Perhaps, too, this honeymoon was what Annabella had anticipated, had even *wanted*, to trigger her plan to save Byron's soul. Her goodness: his evil. This was why she had loved him. What she had asked him to do was give her his sins, and she would bear them with him. All so simple to say.

It's a danger of biography, too, that it tries to make people as black and white as Lady Byron believed they were – while even she herself managed not to be. So many tellings of the Byrons' story end up roped in – one way or the other – by the necessity for Lady Byron to be one sort of woman or another. She herself seemed to have problems accepting that she could be more than one, and probably simultaneously. Which was to prove, in part, the root of the whole problem.

Back in her parents' home there were more people, and the air lightened. 'I have quite enough at home,' Byron assured his new aunt, Lady Melbourne, of his new-found fidelity, 'to prevent me from loving any one essentially for some time to come.' And he hunched over a sheet of paper with Annabella to play *bout-rimés*: one set up a line, the other made the rhyme. The two tracks of hand-writing that had gone between them, that had brought them to this point: Byron's dark and bold – Annabella's punctual italics.

> ... *My husband is the greatest goose alive.*
> **I feel that I have been a fool to wive.**
> *This weather makes our noses blue*
> **Bell – that but rhymes an epithet for you.**

It was their play. It was a joke. She wrote *alive*, and he could only shout and write something about **wive**. Each setting the other up – I can't believe you would write that – a game. But the sheet of paper was not thrown in the fire at the end of it. The sheet of paper was kept, filed away.

Byron, Lady Byron also wrote to Augusta, was to be seen playing at charades with his dressing gown on backwards, snatching the wig from his new mother-in-law's head. And playing *draughts*. Augusta couldn't quite believe such levity. But there's more, wrote Annabella to this sister she had not met: she found, she confessed, that 'the moon' did not interfere with her private passion for mischievousness. Time of the month – time of the night: nothing, Annabella said plain, interfered with her 'ruling passion for mischief'. And she won Byron over when he wanted to travel down to see Augusta on his own. Of course she must go with him.

They drove away from Seaham for the second time, no bells pealing. On the night before they reached Six Mile Bottom, near the Newmarket racecourse at Cambridge, in bed, Lord Byron turned to his wife.

'You say you married me to make me happy?'

Yes, yes she did.

'Then you do, you do make me happy.'

And it was another of those moments to tuck into a corner of yourself, a moment when everything in the world was possible and – on the arm of your new husband, the husband you love, the husband you tell yourself you are coming to know, to understand, to decipher – you could do anything. You will meet his sister – your own sister, as you have confidently, hungrily claimed her – and then this new family will be complete. The carriage pulls up at the front of her house. But your husband, her brother, doesn't help you down from your seat, doesn't wait for you to get out.

Byron was out of the carriage and in through the door, tearing through the downstairs room looking for his sister, his Augusta, the woman – he had told his new wife again and again – who understood him better than anyone else ever could or would. But she was upstairs. She made him wait. And Annabella came in by herself. Awkward. Thrown.

Augusta, flustered when she did appear, didn't kiss Annabella. Byron scolded her for this. And 'ain't I a reformed man?' he demanded of her, almost as soon as they were in the same room. She commented, small and cautious, on some observable differences. They looked alike, Byron and Augusta. They were half-siblings: the same father, but Augusta's mother was the elegant and aristocratic Lady Carmarthen, where Byron's mother was the slightly hysterical Catherine Gordon. They both had thick chestnut hair, a smooth, round, white face with a high forehead, and a pocking of shyness. The same laugh. Augusta was four or five years older than Byron: she already had four children by her husband, Colonel George Leigh, who was also her (and Byron's) cousin.

Augusta led Annabella upstairs to her room – all the house turned upside down and shifted to accommodate Byron and his new wife when Augusta couldn't find them a place to rent nearby. Augusta kissed Annabella then. And the two were friends. Were sisters. Augusta had written, already, that she believed her new sister-in-law had 'made yourself as completely Mistress of "the art of making B. happy" as some others would in 20 years.' These must surely be the happiest days of Lady Byron's life, so adored by the adored sister of her husband. Annabella watched her husband with two of his nieces, Georgiana (the eldest and his favourite), and Medora (born the previous April): he talked up his plans for Georgiana's education. He gazed at Medora fondly. Annabella caught the edge of his expression and said that she would like to have his portrait painted as he sat, like that, staring at his godchild. Byron lay on the sofa, demanded that Augusta and Annabella kiss him by turns.

Annabella wrote to her parents about the rest of the world, about Napoleon. In the afternoons, Augusta and she walked and walked through the countryside. Augusta had a manual of information for managing Byron: laugh him out of those self-important and melancholy moods he got into, laugh at the grandiose claims he made about what he had done, what he would be compelled to do, understand the full extent of his financial troubles, keep him away from brandy. There had been an incident at Seaham when Byron was overcome by smoke in his dressing-room – Annabella, the salving wife, had rushed in and revived him with a snifter of brandy, and it was no wonder (Augusta remarked dryly) that Byron had told her then that she was a good little wife. She stood warned not to repeat the gaffe.

She stood warmed in the effusion of Augusta's love for her brother and, by extension, for his new wife, while Augusta wrote to friends that this Lady Byron was all perfection, that she could not help but think that her brother had found the one person in the world who would be able to put up with his moods and his peculiarities: 'I have a sad trick of being struck dumb when I am most happy and pleased,' she confessed. 'I think I never saw or heard or read of a more perfect being in mortal mould.' 'The more I see of her,' she continued as her brother and new sister-in-law drove away at the end of March, 1815, 'the more I love and esteem her, and feel how grateful I am and ought to be for the blessing of such a wife for my dear, darling B.'

As long as you don't mind my words, he had said in the first days of their honeymoon ('expatiating,' explained Annabella, 'on his random way of talking'), we should get along very well.

Oh dear, said his sister, it's so like him to try to convince people he's terrible and disagreeable. His sister, who was so thrilled that her brother had a wife who didn't mind those outrageously affectionate words he poured onto her – when I think of my other brothers, if they said that no one loved them so well as me, well, she said, their wives would never stand for that. Dear Annabella, that she did. That she understood.

As they left to go to London, Annabella asked Augusta to visit them – in their grand, new £700-a-year house on Piccadilly – while Augusta waited to take up a position in the bedchamber of the Queen. And Annabella was pregnant.

It was something to come into London, to the Duchess of Devonshire's grand house, as its chatelaine – the wife of the country's premier poet. Annabella had always said that she, like Byron, shunned all the games and nuances of aristocratic society – 'I have never mixed with crowds but on principle,' she told him during their engagement. 'I *love* retirement – how much more shall I love it with the person who is dearest to me and the few associates whom he may select or approve.'

But then, it was something to arrive as Lady Byron on her husband's arm, to be immediately feted, immediately noticed. It was like that first season, when he became famous and she astonished herself by staying at parties till dawn: she was back in the thick of things. It was her turn to sit on a sofa and have Lord Byron lean – attentive, loving – over her. It was her turn.

This couple London was talking about, noticing – yet they left so few traces of themselves. There are gaps in biographies, and one chronology of Byron's life has a complete blank for a whole month of this first year of his marriage. It can offer up nothing about where he was or what he was doing. These months that came to mean so much, with so little put down to hold them at the time. But it is possible to look onto the watery surface of 1815 and see distinct points that have been dropped, like oil, onto the continuum of days.

There were only ten days in the house in Piccadilly, through the end of March and the beginning of April, when Byron and his wife are alone, 'and he was kind again, kinder … than I had almost ever seen him'. On the eleventh day, in the first weeks of April, Augusta arrived for an indefinite stay. Byron, refusing to be there to meet his sister, smashed a treasured watch Augusta had given him and went out into the town, hissing at Annabella that she was a fool to invite Augusta. You will find, he said, that it makes a difference to you *in all ways*. In all ways.

But Annabella was pleased to see her sister-in-law. Her sister. Byron could come and go and do as he pleased. And, for the first time in his life, he took a job – the manager of the Drury Lane Theatre. Negotiating tantrums with actresses, reading through mountains of scripts, running auditions, and attending performances in his own private box. He was out in the world. Lady Byron, on the other hand, was pregnant and grieving. Within six weeks of her arriving in London, her uncle had died. She had stayed by his bedside until Byron sent round a note ('Dearest, now that your mother is come, I won't have you worried any longer – more particularly in your present situation which is rendered very precarious by what you have already gone through. Pray – come home – ever thine'). She went into mourning.

And Byron kept his wife at home because, he said, he was worried about her health. She was in the first months of pregnancy. She had always been a bit of a hypochondriac – those mysterious illnesses he had noticed when he visited her before they were married. She wrote to her mother that she liked this unfashionable life of staying at home. She complained about it to Augusta. 'Lord and Lady Byron go out but little,' Augusta explained, 'in fact Lady Byron thinks – and I think – too little. But you know Byron must always be at one extreme or the other, she said, so perhaps this is the best of the two.' Still, Lady Byron walked in Green Park (almost wedging herself in the railings on her way out, which she thought the morning papers would have enjoyed publishing as an anecdote of the high life), and she went up to Henderson's Nursery off the Edgeware Road to buy flowers for the house, as Byron called in on a friend and kept her waiting cheerfully on the street while he finished his conversation. She received and returned some wedding calls, now a society hostess: flocks of well-wishing women, including Lady Melbourne, Lady Caroline Lamb and even an old, old flame of Byron's, Mrs Mary Chaworth-Musters.

And there were small moments that lodged somewhere, to pin down a fragment of the marriage: an American visitor came one day in the summer with a letter of introduction to Lord Byron, and had the great honour – as he put it – of spending time in conversation with Lord Byron's wife before she went out for a drive. And he watched, then, as Lord Byron took leave of Lady Byron and shook her hand as fondly, he said, as if they were to be parted for a month.

There were people who noticed these things.

There is a second portrait of Lady Byron. Circa 1815 by an unknown artist. There was no laughter in this one. No head thrown back and hair cascading voluptuous. No roundness in the cheeks to merit the nickname Byron had given her – 'Pip' or 'Pippin' – for a shiny, rosy apple. This was a small face, a waif, pointy, tentative. Hair all slicked down and flat – something almost callow in its subdued constraint. Lady Byron as she appeared to an artist in the first year of her marriage. A woman timid. A woman diminished. This woman would not lead the crusade to save a soul. This woman would be too meek. And Byron's soul did seem a long way from her reach. 'The manager', as she referred to him disparagingly as he took himself off to the Drury Lane. She complained that she hardly ever saw him now that he had this new occupation.

There were no more great Oriental poems from Byron in 1815: there was a set of things he called the *Hebrew Melodies* which were set to music. It sounded like a pleasant religious theme to come from the man with, as Caroline Lamb had commented, a wife who was punctual about going to church. But Byron snuck in some biblically irrelevant verses too – including one of his most famous meditations on an unidentified woman, 'She walks in beauty like the night'. The smart social set of Melbourne House believed that the 'she' was Lady Melbourne's *other* daughter-in-law, Mrs George Lamb. Someone else thought 'she' was his cousin's wife, who had appeared at a party in a ravishing black beaded dress. The composer felt sure they were meant for Lord Byron's dear sister.

Augusta's time in London, waiting for her rooms to be made ready in St James' Palace so that she could take up her position as a Lady of the Bedchamber to Queen Charlotte, the wife of the mad King, dragged through the months. She had brought her eldest daughter with her. Her husband came up from the country every so often to visit, and Augusta lived happy with her brother and sister-in-law. It was a bland time: Annabella's parents came to the capital and Annabella ate a dinner with them for her twenty-third birthday on May 17 – without Byron.

It would be impossible to pinpoint two days later – let alone almost two centuries later – the time at which a passing mood set in and hardened. All year, Byron worried about his financial situation. He was supposed to receive his first payment from Annabella's father in May and no money came. He complained, too, that Lady Milbanke was pestering and plaguing him about the sale of Newstead Abbey, and it was Augusta who defended the Milbankes, pointing out that they had their own financial concerns with the collapse of the Durham bank and the delay of their legacy from her uncle's death. He was drinking more and more brandy, and swinging manic with Annabella between playfulness and affection, and something pure and malignant that she marked down as aversion. For four days, she noted, he would not even speak to her, while Augusta tried to parry and lighten all these moods with a sensible sentence, a joke, a bit of encouragement. Byron pinned everything on the birth of his heir.

Annabella, sent to bed an hour before everyone else through spring and into summer, lay upstairs hearing her husband and his sister laughing while she was supposed to nurse her pregnancy to sleep. She thought, one night, that she should go into Byron's room, take up a dagger, and plunge it into Augusta's heart. Finally, in late June, she asked Augusta to leave. 'I conceived it a duty to my husband,' she explained to herself later, 'to remove a guest who, whatever the cause might be, seemed to encrease his ill dispositions.' Strip the house back to those first ten days – only herself, Byron, the idea of an heir. She would not have to lie in bed listening to Byron and his sister laugh as they came up the stairs. Hating the laughter. Hating them. Yet 'as soon as she had left us,' Annabella found, 'though for a few days I experienced the benefits I had expected from her absence, my heart reproached me.' Quite simply, Annabella missed her. She wrote to Augusta of how fondly Byron had been talking of her 'till he had half a mind to cry – and so had I. The conversation arose from his telling the contents of a Will that he has just made – as far as I can judge, quite what he ought to make … you should have the satisfaction of knowing that your children will afterwards have a provision … it appears to me very judicious.'

In August, Byron followed his sister back to her home at Six Mile Bottom. Her husband was supposed to receive a bequest, and Byron went to sort out the terms of the legacy. He went too, Annabella wrote at the time, because he had been '*very flat* indeed': 'I think the change will do him good,' she told her mother, 'for he was worried to death here by business.' His solicitor, Hanson, had advised Byron that he 'must not suffer himself to be concerned about these matters. Very easy to prescribe,' Annabella commented, 'but what few can practise as well as I can.' She wrote letters to her parents joking about her abandoned and *widowed* state, but she was – she said – 'glad' he had been able to get away from the city. What she remembered later, however, was that he had been 'perfectly ferocious towards me for four days' and that she was left 'without any human being to take care of me in my then very precarious situation'.

Augusta wrote to Annabella that Byron and she had sparred a little about whether Byron was allowed to drink brandy or not, but that she won the argument. She wrote, too, that she had got him to confess to 'all his naughty fits and sayings', and assured Annabella that Byron seemed 'as convinced as he ought to be [of your merits], and of whom he talks quite pathetically as the "best little Wife" in ye World'.

Annabella wrote yearning letters to Byron, her

'Darling Duck': she thought she heard him calling out her name, she said, and signed herself with his pet names for her: Pippin–pip–ip, and a sort of a gasp, –A–da. 'I think I hear you now, but I won't grow lemancholy.'

His letter to his 'dearest Pip' was signed 'yrs always most conjugally. B. A–da–'. Those gasping syllables again: their secret language. Secret names. He was home within a week.

They were beset by extremity. One afternoon, Annabella sat reading in an upstairs room. In the corner, a parrot squawked in a cage – part of Byron's substantial and ever-changing menagerie. It shrieked and guffawed, and it tried to bite at Annabella's fingers when she brushed them close to it. Byron came in. Annabella complained about the bird's behaviour. Byron picked it up, cage and all, and hurled it from the upstairs window. Annabella watched the one fluid motion of the cage sail through the air from her husband's hand, heard the bird's noise change its pitch as it fell, and wondered – in the instant of it falling – whether it was flapping its wings inside the cage, still trying to fly and to move itself upwards even while the metal that enclosed it fell to the earth. Where it sat, picking its feathers back into order on its perch, as it and the cage were carried inside and back up the stairs. She wrote it as a joke to her parents.

One night, in bed, he was sure he heard someone on the stairs. It was late in the year and Annabella was heavy with pregnancy. Byron was the man who always kept pistols and a dagger by his night table, sometimes even a rope ladder under the bed in case of fire. But, 'you go,' he said, you check what's there. And she hauled her big body out into the darkness, tired, heavy, prowling up and down the steps and hoping not that they would be empty and that she could set her husband's mind at ease, but rather that there would be an intruder there in the shadows, and that he would kill her. Dead. 'I should have rejoiced to die for him for whom I despaired to live.' Then she could have had some peace. This was the woman who had once said Byron could only hurt her by refusing to let her take her share of his burdens. Make me the fellow of your sufferings, she had written before they were married. She had had no idea what those sufferings involved.

There were layers of shadow all over the house. Things that people did not notice. Things that people did not comment on. None of the servants flinched when Byron shouted for his meal to always – *always* – be served in a different room to Annabella: for four or five months before she gave birth, he refused to eat with her. If there was one thing he could not stand, he fumed, it was to see a woman *eat*. It was only Annabella who sat, mortified. Everyone else continued as normal. There were people, too, who were not supposed to be noticed. A man came to stay: Byron didn't tell his wife who he was. A friend? No. A relative? No. She worked it out in the end: a bailiff. Lord Byron had been running up debts since even before his twenty-first birthday, convincing landladies and their daughters to stand guarantor for him when he was underage. And the debts sat, waiting, expanding, while he went out of England and travelled and came back, purported to have married an heiress, purported to have arranged the sale of Newstead, his ancestral home. But the sale of Newstead kept falling through: one buyer had handed over a deposit and never made good on any of the other payments. Put up for sale again in the middle of the year, it had been passed in. And Annabella's fortune was no closer to his hands – her uncle had died, but his money was not left to her as expected, but to her mother, to be passed down again on Judith's death. Her father was in such dire financial straits himself – 'as almost in Gaol as possible,' Annabella wrote – that Annabella spent the better part of August hunting out mortgages for both him and her husband. It was all very well that a peer, in 1815, could not be imprisoned for his debts – but his property could be possessed, his goods and chattels put up for auction in a common coffee house. Let them take even the beds, said Annabella stoically, I can just as well sleep on the floor. She was, after all, the woman who had said she would marry Byron if he hadn't a cent in the world. While Byron taunted himself into a kind of paralysis with 'the idea of Bailiffs in the house at the same time as the Midwife. For my part,' said Annabella, 'it would probably be the time when I should care least for them – but I care very much to see him in an agony.'

This was not how it should be, he knew that.

When it came down to it, a marriage was all about money. Perhaps the house could be closed – they hadn't paid the £700 rent for their first year yet. Byron thought he might have to sell his books. And for four nights, he ordered a separate bed from Annabella's. Perhaps Lady Byron could go to her parents' house to have the child: Byron, she told her mother, was in 'great anxiety about me and would have me go by myself – which I *will not*. As long as I am with him I am comparatively comfortable, and the anxiety of absence would far overbalance any little good that a change of air might do.' And if they did try to close their house, Annabella explained, the bailiffs would be on to them, taking their possessions as security. Her parents offered places for them to stay again and again. While Byron waited, and worried, and did not make a decision, and said that perhaps instead it would be better if Judith Milbanke came to London to be with her daughter. Annabella appreciated this suggestion – was grateful for it. Augusta would be with her too – Annabella had asked her to come back for the birth. And her old governess and companion, Mrs Clermont. And a nurse to stay for a few weeks. And the midwife. Strong women around her.

In the depths of winter, John Cam Hobhouse – the man Annabella thought so well of, the man who thought so well of Annabella's ankles – came home from his travels. He and Byron sat late into the night. There was a little sparring at home, Byron said, about money. His wife, he breathed exhausted, was perfection on earth, the best wife, but he had one piece of advice for Hobhouse: don't marry.

Things, Hobhouse wrote ominously in his bachelor's diary, do not go well there. He wrote of sitting with Byron into the night, hearing his confessions as he always had. But Byron did not make the full confessions to Hobhouse, his oldest friend, that he was making to his wife. It was to his wife that he poured out stories of the actress he had taken as a mistress, remarking on the difference between the bed he came from and the bed he would get into in Piccadilly late at night. Annabella would not sleep with him ('Lord Byron wished to go to bed to her,' Annabella's nurse said, 'but that she would not permit it'), and he must sleep with someone. He was Lord Byron, he was the great lover, he was the great seducer. He was the Casanova of the age. But still, his wife had said that she would take his confessions on, bear his sins, share any infirmity. His wife had said that even one transgression with another woman might be forgiven, might be borne. Now story after story cascaded onto her: take this on, take this on, take this all on. To cope with debt had never been as big, as hard, as impossible as it was now that he was married. The marriage was the problem: not Annabella, he tried to tell her, not you, not you – but the fact that I have a wife at all. Take that on as well.

Oh Augusta, Annabella wrote, will this ever change for me? She spent so much time, sitting at her writing desk, sending words up to her sister at Six Mile Bottom. Version after version of Byron laid out. She picked up the words he had written to her himself during their correspondence – his constant need for sensation – and she smashed them down into her own version: the 'ennui of a monotonous existence that drives the best hearted people to the most dangerous paths, and makes them often seem to act from bad motives when in fact they are only flying from internal suffering by an external stimulus. The love of tormenting,' she concluded, 'arises chiefly from this source.' She wrote a memorandum to herself that his sense of religion was strong, that his imagination was too exalted – when it could not do good on a vast scale, it gave up on the idea of it altogether. His imagination, she thought, dwells too much in the past or the future – never in the present, in the here and now where she sat, waiting for him. As his lawyers stalled the bailiffs again and again, Byron would leave the house, telling Annabella that he would 'at once abandon himself to every sort of desperation'. He would give himself up to every excess, every vice, every sensation – with or without the permission of his wife. He was, Annabella wrote to Augusta, 'all inexorable pride and hardness'. She wanted to save him, to liberate him. But the more she loved him, the more she bore, the more unbearable it was for him. He told her that if she behaved like most wives, got angry, picked fights, he could stand it much more easily than this calm. This forbearance. He told her that he believed she would keep loving him until he beat her. He told her that he had only wanted a wife who would be his friend. All right, said Annabella. She would 'renounce all personal feeling as his wife, and be his friend *only*'. She would step away from being his wife. Whatever he wanted. Whatever would make him happy.

And as my friend, Byron pushed, you would let me give myself up to women, to drinking, to travel, to sensation.

No – 'as such I never would sanction the vicious and self-destructive courses which he declared he was resolved to pursue.'

His exasperation cut through the room, through her, like a whip, while she took her own pride in the fact that it hit her, stung her, and that she did not flinch. Annabella, predicting the separation she said Byron had always predicted, was anxious on one point: to Augusta, 'will you still be my sister?'

On December 9, 1815, Lady Byron and the Hon. Augusta Leigh, went together to the house of Serjeant Heywood, an old friend of the Milbankes. While Augusta sat in the cold carriage, Annabella talked with him about the possibility of leaving her husband. She 'proposed the question,' she said, 'if I should not then leave the house. This too by the desire, or at least the full concurrence of Mrs Leigh – which of course I would not unnecessarily reveal to commit her with her brother.' She had been married for less than a year and she was looking for a way out. She had said that she would bear Byron's sins and confessions. After eleven months, she wanted to step clear from their weight.

The heir that Byron waited for was born the next day, with Annabella surrounded by her doctor, her sister-in-law, her nurse, her midwife, her companion. Her mother, ill, was kept away in a hotel in London. Byron downstairs – in the room directly beneath his labouring wife – filled the house with shattering noise, swiping the tops off soda bottles with a poker. Byron, who once announced that his feelings towards children were such that he always had the greatest respect for the character of Herod, who loved Augusta's children, had recast his will to provide for them, who could sit with Caroline Lamb's slow son cradled in his arms for hours. Byron, about to become a father, would have his heir to the title. Except that Annabella gave birth to a girl.

It was the end of the month before Byron mentioned his daughter in his letters. Mrs Clermont told Hobhouse that she had never seen a man so proud and fond of his child. Of course he would have preferred a boy, Augusta wrote, but he was thrilled with his daughter, who was named for her – Augusta Ada. The Ada, he explained to Hobhouse, was an old family name from the time of King John. He didn't mention that it was also the panting signature that he and his wife had used on letters to each other when he was away from home, away from her. Two days before Christmas, he finally received a thousand pounds of the £20,000 he was owed by Annabella's father for the marriage.

The year clicked over to 1816: the days clicked from New Year's Day into the rest of the normal days, normal weeks. Lord and Lady Byron had been married one year. Byron struggled with what he should do – no money, and now a child. Send Lady Byron up to her parents, he thought. Hear out the debate at the House of Lords, and wait for the poems that were about to be published – the historical *Siege of Corinth*, with its themes of betrayal and treachery from the eighteenth century, and *Parisina*, which dissected the incestuous love between a mother and her step-son. Annabella had acted as Byron's amanuensis for *Parisina*, sending it on to his publisher in her neat, uniform hand. The publisher had no idea of the theme, and recited it for his wife without scanning the verses first. 'I should not have read it to my wife,' he blustered to Byron, 'if my eye had not traced the delicate hand that transcribed it.' Annabella didn't know what she wrote down from the original, Byron patronised: she wouldn't even have realised there was anything about incest in the verses – she would 'write out anything I desired in all the ignorance of innocence'.

Now the poems would come out, and Byron could

then ride up to join his wife in the country. He could set a date to do that. Or he could leave England. Anything to be able to stop thinking about this mess.

While Lady Byron chattered on in letters to her parents, to her aunt Lady Melbourne: she had been churched at home; her daughter had nipped her as she fed; those two new poems on historical subjects (she couldn't, she wrote, pick which would be the more popular). Augusta, she gushed, had made her period of confinement so comfortable, 'which I never can forget, that I feel no inclination to break loose.'

There was a sense that there was no reality beyond them. Solipsistic, the world was contained by the Byrons' walls at 13 Piccadilly Terrace. Outside these was a great void where characters loitered and chatted to each other, waiting for their turn to come in through the door and perform their part. Outside, an enquiry was being held by the British parliament into the profession of mad doctors and the infamous institution at Bethlem. Reports came from its unknown chambers – inmates chained to hooks at such a height that they could never sit down; patients with their one piece of hessian clothing ripped around them, having to stand, hunched, naked. This was what it was to be mad.

There was a great deal of interest in madness: no less a person than George III, of course, was mad – England halfway through its years of Regency. The renowned *Edinburgh Medical Journal* had recently published an article on the causes, symptoms and treatments of hydrocephalus. And Annabella had gone through the article so carefully, reading over and over the pattern its words made. And she saw that they clearly described her husband, Lord Byron, as mad. She went through the house and found a bottle of laudanum and a book by the Marquis de Sade to prove it. She had taken the article with her when she called on her husband's own solicitor before she left London – who 'could not help remarking that he could account for all his Lordship's eccentricities in a more simple manner than by supposing him afflicted with hydrocephalus'. Those last weeks, she went around London to lawyers and experts, sharing with them her suspicions, her fears, for Byron's sanity. Do you fear for your safety, Lady Byron? one of them asked, as Augusta sat complicit and waited for Annabella in the carriage. No, no, said Annabella, firm: 'My eye can always put his down.' She had even written a statement for doctors about her husband's madness: his 'principal insane ideas are – that he *must* be wicked – is foredoomed to evil – and compelled by some irresistible power to follow this destiny, doing violence all the time to his feelings ... undoubtedly,' she assured her medical adviser, 'I am more than any one the subject of his irritation, because he deems himself (as he has said) a villain for marrying me on account of former circumstances – adding that the more I love him, and the better I am, the more accursed he is. When he uses me worst he seems most sensible that I do not deserve it – and speaks of me as the most perfect of human beings, with passionate affection – at times – at others he expresses loathing and hatred ...

'I am convinced,' she concluded, 'that my removal will compose him for a time – and I wish to defer any attempt at restraint till its effects are seen – but should they be such, ought I to suffer him to fulfil his intention of going abroad to the spot with which I know his most maddening feelings to be connected, without restraint, if I can impose it?' He wanted to go to Greece. And he had told her once, a long time before, that he expected to die in Greece. If he expected to die somewhere, Annabella reasoned, surely it was madness to want to go there. Surely it was her duty to prevent him from going.

By the first week of January, there were five or six bailiffs in the house. Lord Byron's agitated voice was heard through closed doors, from behind which Lady Byron would emerge, distraught. Finally he sent a note up to her, asking her to set a date for her departure: 'of my opinion upon that subject you are sufficiently in possession – and of the circumstances which have led to it – as also to my plans – or rather intentions – for the future.' The mansion on Piccadilly would be closed. Annabella's mother had written, again, inviting the whole family either to her house or to one of the houses on the estate: we have so much room here, she offered, and think how lovely it would be for us to have the three of you near – the whole family. Or Byron could go abroad (the preparations, said Lady Byron, were underway at the end of 1815); Lady Byron to her parents. Or both Byrons could travel north. Augusta had her position to Queen Charlotte at court. Byron made his decision. 1816 would be a better year.

Three people in a room. Byron. Augusta on the sofa. Annabella at the door.

He quoted *Macbeth*: 'When shall we three meet again?'

Lady Byron, framed by the doorway, replied, flat, absolute: 'in heaven I trust.'

On January 15, 1816, Lady Byron, her daughter and her maid, piled into a carriage to weave through the freezing grey streets of London, out through the country and two days north to Kirkby Mallory, her parents' home in Leicestershire. Coming down to the front door, she glimpsed Byron's room, his great mass of a dog spread out on the rug. For a moment, only a moment, she thought of going in, throwing herself at his feet with the dog, and staying with him in his house in London. But the moment passed, she walked on to the front door and the carriage. And she left. Although he didn't know it, although he would say until he died that he never knew why, they would never see each other again.

He had asked her, once before, just before the birth of their daughter, whether she chose to live with him anymore – she had cried and he had said, absently, well yes, I always mistime my questions. Those tears. But she had already consulted people about the possibility of leaving him. He didn't know that.

Two people, all lightness and potential, go into a marriage. They close themselves into it: few people see them – no one sees them always, sees everything. And then, stumbling and coughing and disoriented, one of them emerges from that dark space and can hardly articulate what has happened. And in all the time that it is not tamed by naming, by identification, it swells into the biggest and most horrific certainty. Whatever it really is, it springs from an unknown, unspecified point, in the unlit privacy of this marriage.

That was Lady Byron's secret.

She finished it off, sweeping out past her companion, Mrs Clermont, to the waiting carriage: should she return to Byron's house again, she said, she would never leave it alive.

Lady Byron, 1815

VIII

CONSTRUCTING
SEPARATION

'There is no reason why you should not
speak openly to me upon a subject already
sufficiently rife in the mouths and minds of what is
called "the World": – of the "fifty reports" it follows
that forty-nine must have more or less error
and exaggeration ...'

Lord Byron

The first two weeks Byron didn't even know that
Lady Byron had left him. Lawyers took her
consultations and her depositions. The great
machine of London tongues began to wag. Lord and
Lady Byron, all the suppositions and suggestions of
their marriage, were shattered into an infinity of possible scenarios. Lord Byron, so inconsiderate, cruel and
violent to his wife, they said. Lord Byron, always drunk
– and did you know he took his mistress back to his
own home? Lord Byron, traveller in the East – of
course they sodomised anything that moved there. But
he'd already started that when he was at school in

Harrow, buggered a couple of fellows there. Sodomised his wife too, did you know? Lord Byron, the greatest poet of the age.

And did you know about his sister?

Who knew what had really happened? No one. But everyone wanted to know.

Annabella was in limbo: to be with Byron, to not be with Byron – especially with her deep and abiding belief in the clarity of black and white, wrong and right, decisions made and decisions stuck to. But she didn't have to flounder for long. From the morning of January 15, 1816, when she left, it stretched a scant fortnight.

She had to wait, first of all, for a doctor to announce Byron mad. She was willing to care for him, she said, if he was to be an invalid. Of course she would nurse him then – it would be back to mopping imaginary brows in childhood games. And then, too, there were those moments of happiness with him, when he said something kind and she believed not just in its moment, but in a world of kindness stretching beyond it. If she gave him a son, perhaps there would be more of those moments. Although another part of her believed, too, that if he had a son, he would go abroad immediately. He had planned this, she believed, down to meeting that old amour – the one who gave him the poodle – in Paris. (The old amour had, in fact, written from Paris asking if it would be appropriate to name Byron as the godfather of her next child, and the old amour's husband had written asking if it was advisable to get involved with one Lady Caroline Lamb. Stay away, Byron warned, stay well away.)

Her first nights away from Piccadilly, Annabella

wrote soft letters to Byron: 'Dearest Duck', she began, and talked about what a good traveller their little daughter was. About him remembering all her 'medical prayers and injunctions', about him not giving himself up to 'the abominable trade of versifying' and about *Brandy*, which he shouldn't drink. Her parents, she wrote, were also looking forward to his arrival – 'such a *sitting*-room or *sulking*-room all to yourself,' she promised him. 'If I were not always looking about for B, I should be a great deal better already for the country air ... ever thy most loving, Pippin ... Pip–ip.'

At the same time, she wrote to Byron's cousin, staying with him in London: 'it would be most desirable for the Patient to be removed to this place,' she counselled, 'where he might pursue a medical regimen according to the London advice – with the additional advantages of air and exercise, which he cannot be induced to take in Town.' Her parents, she was confident, would 'devote their whole care and attention to the alleviation of his malady'.

She wrote – as always – to Augusta: her mother, she reassured her sister-in-law, could not feel more tenderly towards Byron if he were her own son.

This tiny knot of days.

Her parents' house was quiet: there was no one camped in a downstairs room, waiting to repossess the furniture, and she slept solid with no one beside her. She woke up, out of the black sleep of no dreams, and she wrote to Augusta that perhaps Byron could be convinced to come up to the country *'pour de raisons'* of sleeping with her. She had not, after all, fulfilled the duty of a wife that even as free-thinking a woman as Lady Melbourne said was paramount: she had not yet provided him with an heir. Could she be the same woman who left his house implying that to live with him again would be to die? The same woman who had offered, too, to make the return journey of two days at 'a moment's notice' if she was needed? Of course. Perhaps if his cousin could make some mention of this idea of the heir too, Annabella said to Augusta, and if she herself could 'touch that subject skilfully'? Byron, she recalled, had wanted their daughter weaned by February 10: perhaps it was his intention to begin sleeping with her again then.

Still, even now, there was a small puddle of belief that the story could have a happy ending. But it was also on this day that she was summoned by her parents to explain why a letter from one of her friends talked of Byron's 'outrages', of 'morbid passion', of 'distempered imagination'. She told them then the 'unhappy cause' of Byron's behaviour.

While her mother was almost immediately ordering carriages for the next day, pushing her arms into travelling coats to make the trip down to the city, Annabella wrote pages about Byron's insanity and the future of the marriage. He did this. He did that. He said he would 'give himself up' to either women or drinking, and drank brandy until he was drunk. In such 'paroxysms of rage or frenzy' (which Annabella – who had previously said that she was not afraid – now said were 'terrifying and dangerous'), he would 'commit many outrageous acts' like breaking or burning things he valued. He told her about his mistress and his visits to her, carelessly mentioning that Annabella may as well take a lover too – 'it was a matter of indifference to him & perhaps the easiest way to get rid of me would be by a Divorce.' She wrote about the things he had said to her during their honeymoon at Halnaby, a year earlier, about his behaviour being 'so alarming & cruel as disposed me several times to make my escape'.

All the things she had not said. All the things she kept out of her letters while she wrote about the parrot, the theatre, the smallnesses of London days. My husband said the strangest things. He had 'never *expressly* declared himself guilty of any *specific* crime – but his insinuations to that effect have been much more convincing than the most direct assertions.'

My husband made me think he was guilty of murder. My husband seemed sometimes to hate me. He mocked me for saying I wanted to marry into a family that had no insanity hidden skeletal in its cupboard: 'you have done very well indeed,' he sneered, and told her about a maternal grandfather who had killed himself and a cousin, too, who went mad and had set fire to a house. He drank. He drank. He had another woman. In the end, we didn't even eat our meals together. He would go days without talking to me. My husband always said the marriage must end. Bear this for me. I think my husband may be mad.

The words ran fluid and released over pages, through the year and up to his 'violence' during her confinement. She could, she said, 'bring three witnesses, if not more, who will swear to their belief that I was not safe in his house for some time before I quitted it.' It was her fourth day away from him.

She had heard by then the report – via Augusta – from the doctor. He came the afternoon of Annabella's

departure. He convinced Byron to request an examina-
tion (one couldn't examine a peer of the realm unless
he requested it). The doctor did not mention
Annabella's suspicions or the conversations he had had
with her. And the doctor – inconceivably – did not
agree with Annabella's diagnosis. This was not madness,
he reported to Augusta: this was torpidity of the liver.
You see the way one eye is squinted smaller than the
other? Byron confessed, too, to a raging thirst, insatiable
for months – like the night during Annabella's labour
when he knocked open bottle after bottle of soda
water, trying to quench its terrible parchedness. And
the doctor prescribed calomel pills, and no brandy, and
a quiet life, and some rest. In a short time, he suggested,
perhaps Byron might go up to the country. While
Byron sat back, discussed the state of his liver with
anyone who would listen, and bragged that the doctor
had dowsed his thirst in a mere three days. All this
information Augusta, deputising in Annabella's position, passed on.

Annabella is a good wife, Byron told anyone who
would listen – and desired that this be passed back to
Annabella herself: there was no other woman, he said,
with whom he could have lived for upwards of six
months.

Lady Caroline Lamb's sticking definition of Lord
Byron, the first time she saw him: mad, she said – mad,
bad and dangerous to know. But if Byron was not mad,
then how could his appalling behaviour through those
six, twelve, months be explained? If Byron was not
mad, then what could Annabella make of all the dark
and suspicious and hurtful – cuttingly hurtful – things
that he said to her during their marriage? What of the

drinking? What of the mistress? Was it better to wish your husband a lunatic, like the King or one of those chained men in Bedlam – or simply depraved? Leaving London, Annabella had said, 'if he is insane I will do everything possible to alleviate his disease but if he is not in a state to be put under care I will never return to his roof again.' Through the busy-ness of births and bailiffs, of visits to doctors and solicitors, that word running firm and correcting along Annabella's spine – duty – had been obscured. Its head reared, briefly, as Annabella considered Byron fathering an heir: that, after all, would simply be her doing her conjugal duty. Heaven forbid that she should be suggesting it because she wanted to be with him again …

It is a hard thing, in the moment of not knowing whether you should fight to hold someone or run away very quickly and never look back, to reconcile the information you have about them to fit both possibilities. On the one hand there was Annabella's sense of her own infallibility – that quality which Byron had long ago predicted would lead her into some great error – and her need to be right. If she decided to marry Lord Byron, as she had, it was because this was the right thing to do: it was right to believe that she should spend her life with him. This could not be the wrong decision. In fact, there was still no wrong decision: there was just a wrong Lord Byron. And this was Byron's doing – all Byron's doing. It was not at all to do with any expectations Annabella might have about what a marriage could be, what Byron could be. It had been her duty to marry him. In his own negligence, he had made it her duty to leave him.

For Annabella to have come round to considering the idea of leaving her husband required an immense change of heart about such socially dubious behaviour. Annabella was, after all, the young woman who had been uncertain if it was appropriate to be in the same room as a woman who had divorced her husband to marry another – who had worried at the dilemma in 1812 until she decided that to enter the room would be acceptable, as long as she avoided an introduction to this tarnished lady. To leave one's husband – and so notorious and sought-after a lover as well – after so short a time as a year: one must have a pantheon of incontrovertible reasons.

The issue of a marriage being formally (legally) ended was a complex and expensive thing in 1816: divorces would still be overseen entirely by the Church of England and Acts of Parliament for another forty years. A full divorce cost between £1,000 and £1,500 and was only rarely, very rarely, obtained by a woman. Annabella had to take these things into account. The more normal way of closing a marriage (less costly, and without the necessity of appearing before courts, where women couldn't testify anyway) was for the two parties to agree on a separation – to draw up another version of the financial arrangements made at the time of the marriage – and go their separate ways. All very civilised. All, in theory, very amicable. If Byron was not insane, this was Annabella's best means of leaving him.

Lady Judith Milbanke took her daughter's statement about that piteous sham of a marriage, she took her daughter's suffering and outrage and bewilderment, and she tucked them around her in the carriage as she sped fast down England to London. There was no sign anymore that she felt anything for Byron that she would feel for her own son. But 'she will break my heart,' Annabella wrote to her companion Mrs Clermont (to whose lodgings her mother was flying), 'if she takes up the thing in bitterness against him.'

There was that strange anticlimax that follows something immense being set in motion. The pages of her words cleared from her desk. Her baby woke, fed, cried, inconsequential. Annabella wondered if a child could suck its mother's emotions in with its milk, imagining those lows she called 'blue devils' swirling into Augusta Ada's tiny body. Her maid, who only a fortnight before had married Byron's valet, wondered when she would see her new husband again. Letter after letter came from Augusta: Byron had taken his pills and she had ordered him a fowl for dinner (she mentioned that they ate at separate times, but not with the sense of affront that Annabella had attached to this). Byron had a quiet night and she had seen him enjoying a broth of veal knuckle and some rice. Byron had been up drinking brandy until three in the morning with that reprobate friend of his, John Cam Hobhouse, who went home leaving the front door open onto Piccadilly and Augusta thought frankly it was a miracle that the whole house hadn't had its throats cut. (Hobhouse, Annabella now thought, 'under the mask of friendship was endeavouring Lord Byron's ruin, and had instigated,' she stretched further, '*more* than any one else, the conduct which has disunited us.' Hobhouse: Byron's faithful friend, who had been out of the country most of the year.) *And* he wants me to sit for a portrait, Augusta went on, and the painter will report it to Lady Caroline Lamb and her circle and it will be 'a fine affair in their imagination – your absence, and my stay'.

Annabella's emotions followed the peaks and troughs of a wave: one day she wrote, 'I must never see him again – I shall wish otherwise when I am less sane – but let me be preserved from it by every means.' Then, the next, she was sure that Byron 'loves me distractedly' and wrote pitiful, 'O! that I were in London, if in the coal-hole.' The malice, the systematic persecution of her peace, the insults that she had traced in Byron for her mother drained away and she said that her talk of 'that unremitting principle of Revenge' in her husband's behaviour 'was not a justifiable assertion – it is impossible to divine the principle. Nor can I think there has been any *design* or *cunning* in the business – far too much incoherency.' He had behaved badly, he had behaved appallingly. And what sort of wife would stand to be compared to the lusty charms of his mistress? But Annabella did not, on this day, think it was plotted deviousness.

And another side to the thought: what sort of wife would try to have her husband committed? Without even raising her fears with him? The sort who now said she only wrote kind, playful letters to him – her 'dearest duck' – on the basis of medical advice. There was no other feeling behind them but duty. And the kind, too, who said tellingly to her mother, 'I would willingly resign my judgement into anybody's hands and be found non-compos myself.'

Against these vacillations her mother counselled her to calm her mind, and to not 'see imaginary Bugbears when so many real ones exist ... Your agitation and unhappiness ... bring on apprehensions of evils which, bad as things are, *do not* or *ever can exist.*'

Through the curves of Annabella's emotions, Augusta wrote that Byron had heard his mother-in-law was in London and wondered what her business there was. 'By the bye Augusta,' he said, 'she is I suppose (or I fear) in a devil of a pucker with me.'

'Why?'

'Oh! Because I've not written or gone there.'

He asked me yesterday, Augusta went on, 'if I had given his love to you. I said, "no, you did not tell me." "Oh but you might say something civil to keep up the look of the thing."' The next day he heard from Mrs Clermont that his wife was not well and Augusta wrote that he seemed quite unhappy and had said to his sister, 'Poor thing! She worries herself about *it* all – I had better write to her.' And he asked after her again and asked Augusta if his wife wanted him.

Annabella, softer, wrote to her mother, that the separation '*for him* is best, and after all, that belief will go furthest to reconcile me to what is best *for me*. I do not see that it can advantage me in the world to deny these feelings. The more I love, the stronger causes must be supposed for such a measure.' Back to her duty. And against her mother's concerns about Augusta, she said her sister-in-law had been 'the truest of friends to me – and I hope you regard her and *seem* to regard her as such, for I very much fear that she may be supposed the cause of the separation by many, and it would be a cruel injustice.'

Then, as the next round of letters rushed up and down the country to and from Annabella – Byron apparently believing that, when the current round of debate was finished at the House of Lords, and when he could rouse himself to set a date for his journey, he would ride up and join his wife – Annabella decided that it was time for these vacillations to stop. While her mother sat in London with the man who would broker the separation, Lady Byron drafted in the most legalistic language she knew her certain authority for that separation to proceed. 'I being in a sound state of mind and body,' she led off – before deflecting the decision from herself altogether: the separation was a thing 'of the propriety of which none of the advisers seem to doubt. I therefore no longer consider that person as connected with me, or as the subject of consideration in any way but that of business. My last letter to you,' she wrote to her mother, 'was written in a wavering temper and contained some folly I believe.' (It was the letter in which Byron loved her 'distractedly', in which she gave her immense love for him as the reason for this immense step she took.) But, she said, no more of that. 'The *last* accounts seem to me to tend more strongly towards Insanity than any other,' she said of Augusta's letters, 'but in my opinion *that* ground will not do. Even *I* could not swear to a positive belief in it …'

Everything she had thought of him, everything she had held dear, everything that she knew or suspected of him, of what he did, of why he did it – all these things collapsed in the instant of these paragraphs. From now on, this statement resolved it, he would be built up in her mind with the same base of knowledge but as someone who hated her, someone who would hurt her. The same Annabella who collected information to build a Byron in that first season of knowing him took all the pieces she had and threw them down from the height of her most extreme emotion. Watched them shatter. And then, almost clinically, she began to put them together with no room, no glimmer, for warmth or hope or a happy ending. And with as many new pieces as she could find.

While, satisfyingly symmetrical, Byron decided on the date that he would ride north to be with his wife. Let it be Sunday the 4th of February, he said to his sister. While Annabella's new lawyer, Stephen Lushington, argued for a 'quiet readjustment' to be made, rather than anything huge, anything before the courts, anything public. If Lord Byron arrived at Kirkby he must not be allowed to remain alone in a room with his wife – otherwise he could sue in the courts for the reinstatement of his conjugal rights. And one other thing, said Lushington: he knew well the character of this actress Lord Byron had been sleeping with. Lady Byron's health, were she to return to her husband, would not be safe. At the suggestion of venereal disease, the possibility of Byron fathering a son disappeared forever.

In the streets of London, in the theatres, people already said of Lord Byron – of whom it was possible to say anything – that he was mad. But something tugged in Annabella – not yet, not quite yet, could she separate the idea of Lord Byron and love. Yes, she must separate from him. And yes, this was doing her duty. And she had a new duty to her parents to make up for it all (which was as close as she was likely to come to conceding that – unnatural – she made a mistake in marrying him in the first place). But still, but still –

> Under the circumstances of this awful and
> afflicting change I cannot yet think the last
> year of my life to have been *thrown away* on
> the person to whom it was devoted. He is
> habitually more impressed by objects in the
> past than the present – and his Imagination
> dwells more with Memory than Observation.
> If then I have been deserving of Love it will
> be awakened or produced when I am
> contemplated through the softening and yet
> deepening medium of Time – and the good
> which irritated when in action, will attach in
> retrospect … If I should be the means of
> creating one virtuous association, I rejoice to
> have suffered, and only wish I had left still
> better traces on Memory.

The selflessness of it. He would *remember* her and love
her. Even while she left him, she could still save his soul
by inspiring him, at some time in a hazy future, to
goodness. And the relationship, after all, had always
been about duty. She was above desire.

It's such a weighty thing to be required to be certain.
To be clear that you can say – always and honestly – yes,
this is absolutely the right thing to do. It is easier to bear
such a weight if you can convince the people around
you that you are certain, and that you are right. Because
then if you start to waver, they can push you back up,
reassure you, rally you. Easier, too, if you can keep finding more and more reasons to justify your certainty. Go
back to all those people who gave you your first layer
of information about Byron. All those people who have

known him in the meantime. And dredge every word they say for those justifications. Anyone you can implicate as working against you, any slight, any strangeness you can infer: use it to bulwark the infallible decision you have made.

Her father wrote to Lord Byron: circumstances just brought to his attention, he said, made it impossible for him to believe that a marriage could tend to Lord Byron's happiness. He proposed a separation between His Lordship and his daughter. Augusta intercepted the letter and sent it back. Was *this* what Annabella had wanted, while Augusta managed visits from doctors and invalid menus? While she managed the extremities of a Byron striding around in his peer's robes announcing himself as the greatest man in the world – and he didn't even except his defeated hero Napoleon? While she juggled visits from Annabella's mother and from Mrs Clermont and from Hobhouse and from Byron's cousin, and questions from Byron, and *still* found time every day to cover pages with domestic reports and reassurances for Annabella?

'For once in my life,' Augusta wrote, 'I have ventured to act according to my own judgment – not without 10,000 fears I assure you. But I do it *for the best* and I do hope at least it will not be productive of evil, as I only wish a *few days delay*...' Pause, she suggested, and hear all the latest information from your brace of advisers: your mother, the doctors, the lawyers, even Lady Melbourne, who has waded in to scold Byron for his behaviour towards you.

This branded Augusta as a traitor: she took her brother's part. Annabella's father left at once to deliver the letter a second time by hand, while Judith wrote venom to the treacherous Augusta Leigh: Annabella, her mother confidently predicted, would soon be dead from the trauma that Augusta's 'cruel and wicked brother' had put her through. The reasons Augusta gave for pause, spat Judith, would be the same in a week or a month or a year, and why should her daughter have to suffer living with a 'madman or a cruel savage – for one of the two he is'? Twenty-four hours later she was yet more convinced that her daughter 'will not long exist, so [Byron] may glory in the Success of his endeavours ... wonder not,' she said, 'that I write *strongly*, for who could see that Suffering Angel sinking under such *unmanly* and *despicable* treatment, and not feel? Ld Byron' – getting into her stride – 'is sending her Parents also with Sorrow to the Grave – let him *glory* also in *that* – and that he has three Lives to answer for at the great account, as much as if he had plunged his dagger in our hearts – indeed *that* would have been a short suffering compared to a *broken* heart ...'

The Suffering Angel had been out of London two weeks. The Suffering Angel convinced her mother that these letters should not be sent. The Suffering Angel, too, had been found by her maid on the floor of her room, hysterical, having *promised* to separate from Byron. Relieved that the letter had not reached him. That it could be snatched back. That there was still hope.

As if that was the way it had happened, Annabella scoffed when she found out about her maid's statement: I was merely pleased that the letter had not yet been delivered, she hissed, because there were certain changes I wanted to make to it. And, *hysterical* – indeed.

On February 2, 1816 – one year and one month

after his spare wedding ceremony – Lord Byron received a letter from his father-in-law. As much a bolt from the blue, by his reaction, as his first proposal to Annabella had been to her three and a half years before. Lady Byron had said that from almost the first moment of the marriage her husband had said he supposed – sometimes despondent, sometimes, she thought, quite jubilant – that it would end in separation. But Lord Byron was appalled, he was outraged – and he demanded his wife back. He wanted Annabella – and he could not, would not, believe that she did not want him. Lord Byron was not going to go quietly. Stephen Lushington's plans for that 'quiet adjustment' vanished.

There was, from this point, not even the merest possibility of turning back. The three months from the beginning of February 1816 marked a concentrated falling *out* of love as surely as the three months from Byron's proposal in September 1814 to his arrival for the wedding had marked the process of concentratedly falling *in*. She wrote to him – just once: she told him she had left his house 'under the persuasion of your having a complaint of so dangerous a nature, that any agitation might bring on a fatal crisis'. That possibility of fatality, she said, was the reason she had said nothing to him as she left although 'I had warned you, earnestly and affectionately, of the unhappy and irreparable consequences which must ensue from your conduct.' She could not, she said, 'attribute your state of mind, to any cause so much as that *total* dereliction of principle which, since our marriage, you have professed and gloried in.' And she finished, righteous: 'I have *consistently* fulfilled my duty as your wife. It was too dear to be abandoned till it became hopeless. Now my resolution cannot be changed.' It was as much explanation as he ever got. I thought you were going mad. I thought it was because you were married. I left you. I did my duty.

But from Byron's refusal to simply resign his wife and return to the life of a bachelor that he had always said he missed, there was an explosion of action and publicity. Activity, as the numbers of Annabella's advisers and lawyers and interested friends and confidantes swelled, and as Byron sat in his barrack-like house. Receiving occasional visits from Hobhouse, from his solicitor, from his cousin. And through it all, his sister. Of course, Judith Milbanke suggested suavely, Augusta must take her brother's part. After all, she stood to benefit quite considerably from his will, so she would hardly go against him, would she? Embarrassingly, one of England's leading advocates – who had already been advising the Milbankes for a fortnight – was found to have been on a retainer for Byron for several years. He withdrew, awkward.

Around Byron and Annabella, though, there was a strange pool of isolation: everything came into and went out from them, but they were forbidden – despite Byron's repeated requests and pleas – to see each other.

I X

THE SECRET

'I have often thought of writing a book to
be filled with all the charges brought against me in
England. It would make an interesting folio, with my
notes, and might serve posterity as a proof of the
charity, good nature and candour of Christian
England in the 19th century.'

Lord Byron

Annabella circumvented her own isolation by
deciding to go to London to see Stephen
Lushington in person. 'Happiness,' she wrote to
Augusta as she made this decision, 'no longer enters
into my views, it can never be restored and the greater
or less degree of my misery I must endure will depend
on the *principles* of my conduct, not on its *consequences*.
Now, independent of any advice whatever, I deem it
my duty to God to act as I am acting.' Against this,
against Duty, against God, Byron had no chance.
Lushington, though, advised against Annabella travelling to the city, dubious that she could be there and still
resist seeing her husband. He was such a gallant: you

could almost see the white horse he rode in on. There was something that she wanted to tell him, she said, in the utmost confidence, and in person. She arrived back in London five weeks after she had left, and spent a quiet evening with her lawyer. He had, for all that Judith Milbanke thought very highly of him, initially advised that a reconciliation might be the most prudent course of action. Annabella met him, alone, with all the sanctity of a confessional, in his office. She told him something. The secret. And a reconciliation became impossible.

Where before Annabella had begged that not a word of her troubles be broadcast, now there was no pretence that this was a private and family matter. And it was such a shame, Lady Melbourne said rather hypocritically, that it could not have been settled amicably rather than being 'brought before a tribunal like the World, where everything is discussed and represented with levity, indifference and derision and without regard to the pain it may give. Everything that passes between husband and wife,' she finished, 'ought to be sacred.' While another part of London buzzed with the rumour that Lord Byron had had an affair with Lady Melbourne at the same time that he was seducing her pretty young daughter-in-law, Lady Caroline Lamb. The aggravating thing was, no one knew whether *this* scandalous tit-bit of information was *the* scandalous bit of information that made it impossible for Lady Byron to return to her Lord. It seemed safe to say that whatever it was, it was a long way removed – and a lot more exciting – than the malevolence she originally charged him with.

First it was the claim of an affair with Lady

Melbourne. Then Hobhouse and Lushington – from opposing sides of the fence – heard that Lady Caroline Lamb was sending terrible stories about Byron into London: Hobhouse wrote in his diary that she accused him of _____. The mystery of that blank line: consensus said it represented sodomy, an offence still punishable by death – even between consenting, married adults. Dead cats were the missiles of choice to throw at its perpetrators as they were hanged. It was not just London that wanted to know what Lady Byron's accusations were. Much of Lord Byron's attention was focused on trying to find out exactly the same thing. He appealed to his father-in-law. He appealed to his wife. He sent Augusta to try to find out – and Lady Byron apologised and said she couldn't possibly tell Byron what the charge was: such a revelation would forfeit any advantage she might have if the case were to come to court.

He believed, said Byron, that she meant to charge him with cruelty, drunkenness and infidelity. He confessed, finally, his behaviour to Hobhouse, confirming the things Augusta and Byron's cousin had revealed to Hobhouse already: 'very great tyranny – menaces – furies – neglects, and even real injuries – such as telling his wife he was *living with another woman* and actually in *fact* turning her out of the house ... locking doors, showing pistols, pouring reproaches at her in bed.' And then the rumour of that blank line reached him, and Byron blustered that he was ruined, that no man could survive having such a thing even said about him, and that he would blow his brains out.

'There are reports abroad,' Augusta wrote despairingly to Annabella, 'too horrible to repeat ... every other sinks into nothing before this MOST horrid one. God alone knows what is to be the end of it all.' Augusta, the one person who, as even Lady Byron acknowledged, could attest to the situation in the house on Piccadilly for most of the year, took another treacherous step. No longer did she argue for Annabella to pause. Instead, she argued for reconciliation: 'I do think in my heart dearest A, that *your return* might be the *saving* and *reclaiming* of him. You could but give it a trial, and if he persisted in his ill-conduct you would be fully justified in *then* abandoning him. Your doing it now, I do think will be his *ruin*.' It was a moderate kind of line. It made sense. Only a year, even Hobhouse the bachelor dared to remind Lady Byron: wasn't a marriage worth a longer trial than that?

Dangerous, Augusta warned Annabella of the difficulties of a woman arguing a case in court: 'You may know more than I do of the charges you have to bring against him. Most likely, you are aware you will have to depose against him *yourself*, and that without witnesses your depositions will go for nothing – the same thing in regard to those who have only heard circumstances from you.' And there was one other thing she wanted to ask her sister-in-law: what had changed her mind about the cause of Byron's behaviour? You left here under the impression that he was insane more or less, said Augusta. Now you say subsequent accounts have convinced you that he is not. Augusta had stayed in Byron's house. She could think over all she had seen in the past months, all she had heard. She could not see how Annabella, who refused even to grant Byron a five-minute interview, could have this great certainty *now* of his sanity, of his composure.

Annabella did not reply: her lawyer, as Augusta wrote this long, pleading letter, had recommended that there be no contact between the two women.

God alone may have known what was to be the end of it all, but Augusta didn't seem to have had any idea that the next rumour Byron would be branded with was – as Hobhouse amazedly heard in late February – that 'a report has got abroad about *Mrs Leigh* and *Byron*!!!'

The streets were full of it. Even Mrs Clermont rattled through dark lists of Lord Byron's purported crimes in a chatty way to Annabella's mother: 'unnatural crime, incest, taking women into the house with his wife ...'

Lord Byron, at a dinner party at Holland House in 1812, leaned back in his chair and entertained everyone with a theory of incestuous love. It was in the Bible, and he could probably rattle from that into his stock statement that things that were immoral or even illegal in one culture might be perfectly acceptable in another, less than half a hemisphere away. He had talked about incest, and four years later, as his marriage fractured and his wife wanted to charge him with every evil and vice, someone remembered that night, that dinner, those words from Lord Byron's mouth.

And there was more.

In Byron's life, there was always the sense that the most important woman had just left the room as you came in. You felt the swish of her skirt. You smelt the edge of her perfume. But she had always just gone. Beautifully synchronous with his correspondence with Miss Annabella Milbanke, there was a ribbon of

experience and implication running through his letters
to Lady Melbourne, and to Thomas Moore. That great,
crashing disaster that he had waved careless under
Annabella's nose in February 1814 – his dangling on
the brink of something terrible 'which will probably
crush me at last' – he wrote to her aunt as 'that perverse
passion'. He was afraid, he confessed, that 'that perverse
passion was my deepest, after all.' Augusta's fourth child,
Elizabeth Medora, was born in April 1814. Not only
had 'Medora' been the name of a horse running at
Colonel Leigh's local racecourse on the day she was
born, it was also the name of Byron's heroine in *The
Corsair*. The theory was that this was Byron's child.

Byron remet his sister for the first time since he became
famous in the summer of 1813, as Annabella watched
the two of them on a sofa at Lady Glenbervie's. He had
thrown, too casual, a line about 'my sister, who is going
abroad with me', into a letter to Lady Melbourne
within the first month of their reacquaintance. And
then there was a report about the plague, and they
couldn't leave straightaway. Augusta wanted to take one
of her children with her and Byron said he couldn't see
why you didn't just get one where you were if you
wanted one, rather than having to cart one around with
you on the off-chance ... he spent a night with far too
many bottles of claret and Scrope Davies, 'feeling feverish', in September 1813 – and Augusta's overseas trip
was not mentioned again.

He took himself off to play platonism with the lady
with the poodle. Any affair, he said to Lady Melbourne,
'is better than the last – and I cannot exist without some
object of attachment'. Annabella became 'your A' in his

letters to Lady Melbourne, as opposed to 'my A', and, in April of 1814, as Annabella's father invited him to visit them in Seaham, when Medora was a month old, he wrote for Lady Melbourne's advice about the visit. 'I should be not only unwilling but unable to make the experiment without your acquiescence. Circumstances,' he reminded her, 'which I need not recapitulate may have changed *Aunt's* mind ... all this mystery. It is what no one else will think ...' But Lady Melbourne had not changed her mind about Byron's suitability for her niece: he could go to Seaham with her blessing.

Annabella now recalled her honeymoon, that trip she had made to Augusta's house twelve months before. She remembered how the first night there, after dinner, she sat waiting for Byron, who had finally appeared. He had been, she remembered, 'in a state of frenzy – black and enraged'. He stood, he watched her, and then he had said to his wife of a scant two months, 'now that I have *her* you will find I can do without *you* ... I told you you had better not come here, and you will find it is so.' Modest, in shorthand, she wrote now that his 'personal intercourse with me was less' while they were in Augusta's house – and that he said that he knew Augusta wore that daring new undergarment, *drawers*. 'It was his pleasure,' she wrote, 'to torture me as it were by an instrument so evanescent that I could not produce it to convince others, and I might even suspect it to be the phantom of my own Imagination, whilst I was writhing under its wounds.' She saw him lying on a sofa, demanding that Augusta and Annabella take turns at kissing him: 'I was sensible that he was more warm towards her than me.'

Byron sitting up late at night talking with his sister, laughing with her, while Annabella had been sent to bed on her own. He would come in, later, with ice in his voice: 'Don't touch me.' He had laughed, too, about the liaisons he had had while Annabella was writing to him through 1813 and 1814 – and all that time, he scoffed, you thought I was dying for you.

Annabella told Stephen Lushington her suspicions about her husband and his sister and the relationship they had had before Byron's marriage. But Lushington warned her that the malice of raising any implications about things that had happened *before* the marriage would, Annabella wrote, 'be altogether most injurious to *me* in a social view.' But she wrote herself a memo about it, so that she could see Augusta (against her lawyer's advice) and still be legally recognised as having considered the possibility of incest. There was a suspicion in her mind that 'an improper connection had at one time and might even still subsist between Lord Byron and Mrs Leigh', but there was no positive proof. With no positive proof, there could be no direct accusation. And Annabella wrote how kind Augusta had been, how she had done so much to 'mitigate the violence and cruelty of Lord Byron', and that it was 'possible that the crime, if committed, might not only be deeply repented of, but never have been perpetrated' again after Byron and Annabella were married.

'Oh, but it is worthwhile,' Byron had written to Lady Melbourne the week after Elizabeth Medora Leigh was born in 1814. 'I can't tell you why – and it is *not* an *Ape* and if it is – that must be my fault. However I will positively reform,' he promised, 'you must however allow that it is utterly impossible I can ever be half as well liked elsewhere – and I have been all my life trying to make some one love me – and never got the sort I preferred before.' It was another two months – that big gap up to June 1814, after Annabella had tentatively enquired if he really meant to visit – before he wrote to Annabella again. It was in June, too, that Lady Melbourne commented to Byron that the easy way two people 'accustom'd themselves to consider their situation [was] quite *terrible*'. The child born of an incestuous union would be an ape, according to folk-lore. Byron was never more specific than that.

Augusta, in February and March 1816, heard the sewage of rumours about her brother. She had tried to take care of him. She had tried to do the best thing by her sister-in-law – who now even refused to write to her, to see her. Friends confronted Augusta directly with the rumours of incest: 'if Lady Byron had ever heard such reports or if she had not treated them with the contempt they deserved, would she have invited me to come' into her home? she asked, plaintive. By the middle of March, Annabella had been gone for two months, and Augusta wondered whether, in duty to her husband and her children, she should leave London, leave Byron, and go home. As it was, she said to Hobhouse, she felt she had stayed 'long enough to *give the lie* to all rumours respecting herself'. But if she was to leave, Byron ('who is suspicious on these sorts of things') must believe that the suggestion had come from someone like Hobhouse. Otherwise he might think it was the wish of Augusta's husband ('[who] on the subject of reports has only been indignant and vexed, as it is but natural he should feel on the subject') or the persecution of her friends. Augusta was seven months pregnant, which no one seemed to take into account as they asked her to become her brother's keeper, run his household, run his errands, and provide full and detailed information to both him and to his wife. Augusta was exhausted.

When it seemed impossible for things to get worse, or more complex, or more defamatory, a series of letters arrived at Lady Byron's hotel from the one person she had not revisited as she rebuilt her image of Byron – Lady Caroline Lamb. Such a convenient character in the story: even the *same* biographer can swing from branding her that 'wicked and dishonourable madwoman' to endorsing her account of all Byron's indiscretions and misdemeanours by saying that, although 'the lady in question was not in all respects trustworthy … in this instance her information being confirmed by that from other sources, is of sufficient interest for inclusion'. Not that those other sources were named.

In the initial stages of the separation Lady Caroline had offered her allegiance to Byron – if Lady Byron threatened to leave him on account of something she had seen in a letter, she said, then she would tell Lady Byron that she had written it and it was a lie. Now Caroline bombarded Annabella with more than thirty pages – to which Annabella didn't reply – convincing her finally that they should meet (it was late March). She confirmed, in the course of that one conversation, every vile suspicion Annabella had had of Byron –

except her frequent sense that he was guilty of murder. Annabella wanted charges of sodomy and homosexual practices? Caroline assured her that Byron had buggered a number of his school-fellows at Harrow, and his page, and 'practised unrestrictedly' in the East. Annabella thought now of incest? Caroline *knew* that Augusta Leigh's fourth child, Elizabeth Medora, was fathered by Byron. He had boasted so much of the connection and it had taken her a while to work out who the woman was. But he had confessed it, she said, in the end. 'I am in love with a woman,' he had gushed, 'and she is with child, and if it is a daughter it will be called *Medora*.' There they sat, with Caroline's sister-in-law as a witness, the two extremities of Byron's involvements. As they were at the beginning of it all: Caroline, all wildfire and imprudence, and Annabella, still, calm, 'declaring no belief' in the litany of misdemeanours Caroline rattled through – although she feared that Caroline would read her reaction to the charge of sodomy as only confirming her suspicions.

'Lady Byron's fate,' said the Duchess of Devonshire, 'is the most miserable I have ever heard and he must be mad or a Caligula. Caro [Lamb] will have told you some of the stories. It is too shocking and her life seems to have been endangered whilst with him from his cruelty.'

Annabella went home. She picked up her pen and she wrote to Stephen Lushington that the interview had changed her 'strong impression relative to the 1st and 2nd reports [sodomy and incest] into *absolute* conviction'. She wrote a long memorandum of the interview for herself. The last pieces in place. This

Lord Byron, laid out for her in a hundred horrible, intimate and previously unconfirmed details, was a stranger to her. She need feel nothing for him.

But still it dragged on – disagreements over money, over arbitrators, over everything but the heinous evil of Lord Byron's character. Byron wrote verses that he didn't want published – the newspapers ran them. Byron wrote verses that he did want published – his publisher circulated them privately. And Byron wrote to his wife. But she didn't need to believe his sentences: she had believed his sentences, after all, when he wrote to her from all over England in 1813 and 1814. And now she found that she shouldn't have believed any of it. That he was sleeping with his sister and buggering boys and drunk half the week and who knew what else at the same time. He could write poetic letters. He could write pleading letters. He could write despondent letters. He could write resigned letters. None of them would touch her.

'If I did not believe,' he said, 'that you are sacrificing your own happiness as much – as I know – you are destroying mine: if I were not convinced that some rash determination – and it may be – promise – is the root of the bitter fruits we are now at the same time devouring and detesting, I would and could address you no more.'

'Were you then *never* happy with me?' he asked. 'Did you never at any time or times express yourself so? Have no marks of affection – of the warmest and most reciprocal attachment passed between us?' And he told Hobhouse that he and Annabella had 'lived on conjugal terms' up until the last, that people may have seen him often behave coolly towards his wife – but had they not been discovered just as often, Annabella sitting on Byron's knee, with her arms around his neck? 'I wish you would make it up,' he said simply to her. And, 'Oh Bell – to see you thus stifling and destroying all feeling all affections – all duties (for they are your first duties – those of a wife and mother).' She passed them all on to her legal adviser, with appropriate comments about his art – how deep, how cunning.

'There are reports which once circulated not even falsehood, or their most admitted and acknowledged falsehood, can neutralise, which no contradiction can obliterate, nor conduct cancel,' Byron wrote prophetic. 'Such have since your separation been busy with my name – you are understood to say, "that you are not responsible for these – that they existed previous to my marriage, and at most were only *revived* by our differences." Lady Byron, they did not exist – but even if they had, does their *revival* give you no feeling? – are you calm in the contemplation of (however undesignedly) raising up that which you never can allay? – and which but for you might never have arisen? – is it with perfect apathy you quietly look upon this resurrection of Infamy?'

She made no reply.

I, said Byron haughtily, I have raised no party – and I do not write my letters with a lawyer at my elbow. She requested an 'amicable arrangement'? He was, he said, 'open to the MOST amicable of arrangements. I am willing and desirous to become reconciled to Lady Byron and her friends.' But there were still weeks of it to come: lawyers from each side met each other in the street and discussed the case. Lady Byron signed a paper denying all the reports that raced on and on about her husband. Then an argument, the statement was burnt, and Lady Byron signed another paper saying only that she was not responsible for spreading the worst two reports. Which was quite a different thing. Byron wrote letters, and threw them in the fire. Hobhouse wrote letters, and threw them in the fire: Lady Byron, he wrote, 'may have been deceived in the expectations she formed in uniting herself with Lord Byron, but she was not deceived by Lord Byron, she was deceived by herself'. Duels were mooted. Lady Judith Milbanke bought a pair of pistols in case Byron rode to Kirkby to reclaim his daughter by force. Hobhouse wrote page after page of foolscap as the official record of Byron's camp. Lady Byron collected page after page of letters to shore up her side of the argument. She heard that London muttered that she didn't seem to care very much about her baby daughter, and she wrote some letters that her mother could pass around to prove her maternal affections.

She went back, again and again, over those fifty-four weeks of marriage to him, but she never went back another step. She never recalled her own words when she had refused his first offer of marriage: he is not the person best suited to my domestic happiness. She never saw herself as having contributed to the causes of separation. 'I was thought a devil because Lady Byron was allowed to be an angel,' Byron later deduced, 'and that formed a pretty antithesis.'

Finally, on Sunday, April 21, 1816, it was over. The arguments about financial arrangements and trustees. The altercations between lawyers and representatives. Byron signed the deed of separation. But the rumours, the questions, the riddles – the discussion of Lady Byron's secret: they went spinning on and on.

Lord Byron and his travelling possessions and companions were tucked into a replica of Napoleon's coach he had made for himself at the exorbitant cost of £500 while the bailiffs and duns camped at his door for money. He left Piccadilly on the morning of April 23 and the bailiffs were in there twenty minutes later, stripping the house of everything, even his squirrel and birds. He left in the care of trusty Hobhouse his official version of the disintegration of his marriage. London was full of rumours that Lady Byron intended to publish her side of the story: he had his ready for retaliation. 'I made no secret of hating marriage,' he attested, 'but was equally explicit in avowing my love for her ... The allegations at which she hints, my respect for her character, and confidence in her veracity, almost make me think they must have some foundation; and I am therefore inclined to believe that at some periods of my married life I might have been deprived of reason.

'I solemnly protest,' he vowed, sounding almost as legalistic as Annabella, 'that I am unconscious of the commission of any enormity which can have prompted Lady Byron to desert me, thus suddenly, thus cruelly.'

Byron sailed from Dover on April 25, 1816 and, much as Lushington assured Annabella that all London stood behind her and that 'there are not 20 persons who, tho ignorant of the particulars, are not satisfied that the separation has arisen from Lord Byron's gross misconduct,' he had to inform her that a number of fashionable ladies drove to Dover and disguised themselves as chambermaids 'for the purpose of obtaining

under that disguise a nearer inspection while he
remained at the Inn – and that on going to embark, he
walked through a lane of spectators'. Assembled to
snatch one last glimpse of that impossibly attractive,
limping poet.

X

THE DESERT

'Remember that I prefer the most
disagreeable certainties to hints and innuendoes –
the devil take everybody – I never can get any
person to be explicit about anything or any body,
and my whole life is past in conjectures of what
people mean – you all talk in the style of
Caroline Lamb's novels.'

Lord Byron

And then he was gone.

Annabella, who had never seen a desert, let alone felt the bare emptiness of one, said that she could see a desert stretching out before her. Alone in that great expanse of dry space. It was a dismal summer, cold, mean and grey. Annabella, having never before lost a night's sleep in her life, turned insomniac. She was 'positively reduced to a skeleton – pale as *ashes* – a deep hollow tone of voice and a *calm* in her manner quite supernatural'. There was no respite. There was no letting out of breath, no striking out on a new life – for Lady Byron or anyone else knotted up in the mess.

Lady Caroline Lamb, for one, was in no way ready to relinquish her part of the Byrons' saga. It didn't matter that she wasn't an intricate part of the story anymore – she simply wrote her own, published on May 9, 1816, in three duodecimo volumes, available from all the leading booksellers. *Glenarvon*, she called it, with a patently recognisable Byronic main character. Was it possible, the narrator wondered of this man, 'that a single woman existed who could resist cherishing every word he uttered'? She had been huddled over its final alterations as she wrote offering Byron her allegiance, her assistance, in winning Lady Byron back – rejected – and as she wrote the litanies of justification and vice that Lady Byron said turned her suspicions of incest and sodomy to certainty.

She used his body. She used his looks. She used his words, quoting directly the letter he had sent to her ending their relationship. And she augmented his behaviour and his personality. She made him a vampire. She made him a baby-killer. All this she was writing as she wrote to Annabella, and as she saw Annabella, and as she gossiped around London about the Byrons' marriage in the winter that opened 1816. 'And tell me,' she said even to Byron's trusted publisher who had with her – did Byron know? – an avuncular sort of relationship, 'tell me have you heard the reports, and have you breathed a word of what I told you?'

Through all her peskiness and persecutions in 1812, 1813, even 1814, Byron had forecast that he and Caroline would end like Paolo and Francesca, chained together in Dante's *Inferno* in perpetuity. But, I do think, he said at last of *Glenarvon*, that to kiss and tell, whatever it is, is slightly better than to fuck and publish.

'Caroline Lamb, and Lady Byron,' he said, 'my "Lucy" and my "Polly" have destroyed my moral existence amongst you – and I am rather sick of being the theme of their mutual inventions.'

The book, whatever it did for Byron's satanic reputation, destroyed what was left of Caroline's. By the time she finished two more novels, London had washed its hands of her to the extent that she had to write to her mother, wishing for her, because – she said – she was upset by some terrible new anonymous book she had read and wanted her mother to comfort her. That book was her own. After *Glenarvon*, she left Byron alone, later clearing him of 'the hideous calumnies concerning himself and Mrs Leigh (indeed of all calumnies involving the charge of crime)'. Her room was found to contain something of a shrine to him – portrait, candles, an altar cloth, crucifix – when she died, more than a decade later.

On the day *Glenarvon* was published, Augusta gave birth to the son she had lugged through the beginning of 1816. She had hardly heard from Annabella. Byron was gone. It must have seemed possible to begin to look ahead.

But this was just a brief hiatus: Annabella was about to launch a concerted campaign to extract an admission from Augusta about her relationship with her brother. She had marshalled her troops – seducing Augusta's best friend, Mrs Therese Villiers (practised in the arts of blackmail, emotional and financial, from a previous round with Queen Charlotte), to her cause. 'A very judicious letter of yours,' Mrs Villiers reported back to Lady Byron, 'which I have seen circulated respecting

Lord Byron's systematic cruelty has done much good, and even this extraordinary production *Glenarvon* tends to do you justice in the eyes of the world – for nobody doubts the correctness of *Glenarvon*'s character.'

'I do not know what letter of mine can have been shown as I never wrote any on the subject which I did not mean to be private,' Lady Byron assured her accomplice, all decorum, 'though I have no doubt it was circulated with the kindest intention.' And then, with much the same sort of kind intention, she began the letter that signalled her pursuit of Augusta Leigh. She would not for the world – she assured Augusta – have risked agitating her while she was still pregnant. But now –

She did not ask Augusta if she had ever slept with Byron. She did not ask who the father of Elizabeth Medora Leigh was. She did not use the word 'incest'.

She did write that 'circumstances in your conduct' compelled her not to see so much of her sister-in-law. And she levelled two charges: that she had heard that Augusta had not 'disguised your resentment against those who have befriended me'; and that Augusta had 'countenanced the arts which have been employed to injure me'. She wrote all this to the woman who had counselled and calmed her through the single year of her marriage, soothed her through Ada's birth (the 'Augusta' of the baby's name tacitly dropped almost as the ink dried on the separation), and taken her place running Byron's household. To the woman who had always written to her with affection, with understanding and compassion. To that 'dearest Augusta' whom she had been so afraid to lose as a sister should she ever leave Byron. 'I shall still not regret having loved and trusted you so entirely,' she offered, big. And she was nice enough to assure Augusta that, 'should your present unhappy dispositions be seriously changed' she would be happy to consider herself a faithful friend. Again. Annabella believed that her letter avoided 'all ambiguity of meaning' and 'precluded the occasion for further explanation'. But it was only the beginning.

How would you reply, if you were Augusta Leigh? Her latest child – her fifth – was less than a month old. She had had an inconceivably traumatic year: she had nursed her brother through an illness that resembled insanity, and she had stood by him as his marriage crumbled. She had stood by him through everything that London muttered about him – and her - worried that she stayed too long, worried that she could not stay long enough. She had tried, too, to be the best friend she could be to his wife. She had walked that tightrope between them: 'I have never *screened* him where I thought him wrong,' she had written to Annabella during the negotiations, 'but you will allow for my anxiety that he should not be accused *undeservedly*.' And then she had seen him – the one person who had ever spoiled her, taken her on holidays, helped her pay her ridiculously huge debts – leave the country, and she felt sure that she would never see him again. Her children were ill. Her husband had left it to her to find a buyer for their house. She was terrified that the reports about her and Byron would reach the Palace and she would lose her position with the Queen – which provided the family's only income. Now this.

She could not, she said, have replied by return of post 'under the influence of such [feelings] as your letter could not fail to produce'. Her letter managed,

much more successfully than Annabella's, to avoid all
ambiguity. To general accusations, Augusta said simply
(sounding quite like her brother), she could only give
general replies. But, even if she was on her deathbed,
she said, 'I could confirm as I *now* do that I have uni-
formly considered you and consulted your happiness
before and above everything in this world.'

The position she was in: the world despised her
brother, and the slightest appearance of coldness from
Annabella would look like an absolute confirmation of
the whole rumour of incest. Why else would someone
as honourable as Lady Byron turn away from her 'dearest Augusta'? And so, said Augusta, she was forced to
accept this 'limited intercourse' that Annabella offered,
even while Annabella said quite coolly that she no
longer considered Augusta as worthy of her 'esteem or
affection'. She had refused to shake the hand of one of
Annabella's friends at a dinner – that was the best she
could find to meet Annabella's first charge. As for the
second – that she had 'countenanced acts employed' to
injure her sister-in-law – Augusta was bewildered.
'Really you must have been cruelly misinformed and I
cruelly injured.' She didn't even want to know who said
these scurrilous things: she would not know how to
forgive them. 'My "present unhappy dispositions" – !'
she concluded, unwittingly waving a red flag at a bull.
'I have indeed in *outward* causes sufficient to make
anyone *wretched* but inward peace which none can take
away.'

Inward peace? Augusta Leigh? The woman marked
down by the good soul of Lady Byron as an egregious
sinner? Such a thing was not possible. Still, Lady Byron
conceded to Mrs Villiers, it was 'perhaps the best

letter she *could* have written'.

'Did you tell her,' asked Mrs Villiers from the sidelines, 'of his having betrayed her to others or do you think it possible to do this?'

Lady Byron was one of the first people to realise that it was possible to tell a story about Byron tilted slightly to suit any purpose or reinforce any impression. She had stated to her lawyer that *Lord Byron had never declared himself specifically guilty of any crime.* Insinuations – they were his stock in trade. But specific admissions: I did this, with this person, in this place. That he did not do. It created a vacuum that Annabella spent the rest of her life filling.

To Mrs Villiers she wrote that Augusta 'of course does not plead guilty, but her assertions are not exactly *to the point*, though it is evident she perfectly understands me.' She let Augusta dangle for three weeks before she replied that she didn't think Augusta owed her any 'obligations' – or, if she did, they would 'be only for the endurance of trials of which I endeavoured to keep you ignorant, though *you* were their cause. I was not the *less* anxious to spare your feelings – to hope and trust for the future even when I could not but have the strongest doubts of the past.'

Far from perfectly understanding Annabella, Augusta – who shot her reply back within a day or two of this – matter-of-factly pointed out that it was very hard for her to know how to answer Annabella when anything could have 'the appearance of *duplicity* which (with yr present opinions) you believe me guilty of'. She wished, she said simply, that Annabella could see every thought – past and present – that she had had. She was confident that there wasn't a single act she would choose to hide from her. 'You say, my dear A – *I have been the cause of your sufferings* – if I have it has been *innocently* ... Had I even entertained the *slightest* suspicions of any "*doubts*" of yours – I never could or would have entered your house – perhaps I did wrong as it is to do so – but I was,' Augusta allowed, 'under delusion certainly ...

'In respect to the *secret parts of my conduct openly unfavourable to you* – will you at a convenient opportunity explain *what* they were for I really cannot guess.'

Of this letter, Lady Byron reported to her cohort: 'Her eyes seem to be opened, and her feelings awakened in a manner that convinces me she was wholly ignorant of her having been the cause of so much suffering to me. She speaks from her heart I am sure – admits respecting what preceded my marriage as much as she could do on paper, maintains her innocence since, but seems to be suddenly made sensible of her extreme self-delusion.' Lady Byron added, charitable, that she 'had a confident hope of restoring the better part of her mind.'

I think I am justified in saying, said Mrs Villiers of her friend, 'that her eyes have been opened to the enormity she has been led into.' Which seemed to suggest that, had there been an incestuous relationship, it hadn't occurred to Augusta, before the descent of these two salving Christian ladies, that there may have been something inappropriate about sleeping with her half-brother.

'Perhaps with you,' Annabella suggested to that one person Byron had always claimed understood him better than anyone else in the whole world, 'he has not given way to the frantic agonies of Remorse.'

No, said Augusta, she had never seen those 'frantic agonies'. As for her own agonies, she had tried to say as little as possible about her brother 'fearing you might mistake the nature of my feelings – I am *certain*,' she said, 'they are and ever have been such as you could not disapprove.'

Well, said Annabella ignoring the opportunity to comment very explicitly on incest (as something of which she certainly would disapprove), she had seen Byron's agony – the only time she saw him 'on the very brink of suicide', she said, 'was on an occasion relating to his remorse about you.' And she collected statements from her own friends approving – endorsing – the unimpeachable attitude with which she had married Byron. Lord Byron, said the friend Annabella had stayed with during 1812, 'appeared so much to need a friend who could not only point out to him his errors, but also lead to a better mode of thinking ... Had I supposed for a moment that you had been bewildered by love of Talent, by that of notoriety, or by being what is called "in love", I should indeed have been most unhappy about you ... in marrying Lord B.,' she said, gratifyingly, 'you seemed clearly to sacrifice all self-gratification for the purpose of devoting yourself to him for his ultimate good ...' Pointing out his errors. A better mode of thinking. Surely some of the smallest things that could be said about reasons for marrying. His ultimate good.

But even to her most loyal advisers, Annabella's launch into the foray of confession and accusation was at odds her public stance of fair dealing. 'The step you have taken was attended with great risk,' one cautioned of her pursuit of Augusta, 'for tho the proofs and impressions [of Augusta's and Byron's liaison] were such as left no doubt on your mind, they were decidedly not such as could have been brought forward to establish a charge of that nature.' He concluded, though, that if Annabella could 'produce an acknowledgement of the fact, even previous to your marriage' he would be pleased that she had waded in. Still, he warned her, she may one day have to give 'a full explanation of the motives and grounds of your conduct'. He, himself, had advised against the persecution of Augusta Leigh. 'You must remember,' he waved at the crusading Lady Byron, 'that your position is very extraordinary.'

Mrs Villiers wrote to Augusta – who knew nothing of her collusion with Lady Byron – that she should think of Annabella as nothing less than her 'Guardian Angel'. The Guardian Angel assured Augusta, too, that she believed that 'Heaven is always open, and *this* hope for him is still dear to me.' In terms of writing letters to her beloved brother, the Guardian Angel recommended she '*rectify* instead of *soothing* or *indulging* his feelings – by avoiding therefore all phrases or *marks*, which may recall wrong ideas to his mind ... and let me also warn you against the levity and nonsense which he likes for the worst reason, because it prevents him from reflecting seriously.'

The tables were turned: where Annabella had received Augusta's guides to managing Byron before she married him, she now issued his sister with rules for further communication. They sounded suspiciously like the groundwork for lecturing – particularly the bit about avoiding 'levity and nonsense'. Augusta was the woman who had advised Lady Byron that her husband could be laughed out of anything ... and look where that had got everyone.

Was it not after all, Annabella suggested suavely, 'from seeing things in *one* point of view only' that Augusta could say that her feelings towards her sister-in-law and her brother had always been 'such as I could not disapprove?'

'I do not *quite* understand what you mean by *seeing things in one point of view*,' Augusta replied cautious, 'neither can I easily describe my own meaning and I am always so afraid of being too lenient to myself ... supposing he returns nothing could induce me' – and she broke off writing for two whole days – 'to see him again so frequently or in the way I have done.' Which seemed too casual a thing to say, somehow, to the wife of the brother you'd been sleeping with.

Annabella decided it was time to return to London. She had been staying on the coast at Lowestoft, with Ada (where the noise of a too-close nursery had disturbed her), indulging an interesting regimen whereby she would eat a plateful of mutton chops and then have a boat row her out to sea where she could 'unload her stomach'.

On the last day of August 1816, the first of several meetings took place between Byron's wife and his sister in Knightsbridge. In these meetings, said Annabella, Augusta made a full admission about having slept with Byron before his marriage. As for a confession about anything after that, Augusta denied it. Strangely, though, for someone so addicted to memoranda and deposition-making (she had her father attest to true copies of the letters she sent to Augusta, so she could keep them for her own records), Lady Byron did not make a single note about these interviews at the time.

And Augusta's letter to her sister-in-law immediately after their first conversation was to say how sorry she was to hear that Annabella had had a 'bad night' after the conversation, 'and for your *idea* of my *uncomfortableness*, which is however quite a *fancy of your own*. But I daresay I *looked* something or other which made you fancy.' With seemingly no reference to any affair or enormity, Augusta wrote to ask 'when I am likely to see you again, and tell me you are no longer sorry. I assure you I only feel and felt pleasure and comfort in seeing you.'

It wasn't the note of a woman who'd just been hauled up to face accusations of gross and incestuous misconduct. And, while Lady Byron had told people – including Augusta – that she wished to be *incognito* in London, enough people knew that she had visited her sister-in-law. Lady Byron, who would complain sometimes that it 'requires more than ordinary exertion to keep up the character of a saint', had already told her mother and Mrs Villiers that Augusta Leigh had placed herself completely in her power. For her part, Augusta, having seen her sister-in-law, and chatted about a manuscript that was expected from Byron at any time, may have been quite happy to leave the city and go home to her husband. Annabella and Augusta were friends again: that gossip about her affair with Byron simply *couldn't* be true.

In the face of this Annabella thought, first, that perhaps Mrs Villiers could now extract a confession from Augusta – but Mrs Villiers declined. And so she wrote to Augusta again, and told her that no less a person than Mrs Villiers – Augusta's closest friend – had heard from an unimpeachable source of Augusta's relationship with her brother: 'she had attached no credit to the report but after you left Town before, had received detailed information which *originated from Lord B, from an authority she could not doubt.*'

Your brother has betrayed you. Your brother has talked about you to the world. She did not tell Augusta that she herself was that source whose authority could not be doubted. This was her winning stroke. If Byron had told the world that he had slept with her, then the only protection she had against that slander was the protection of Lady Byron's friendship. And so Augusta agreed to betray him.

It was all about appearances. As Lady Byron had said, she had had Augusta Leigh's complicity in those first visits she made to doctors and solicitors. If she could bring Augusta into line by telling her that Byron had betrayed her and talked to people of his improper obsession with his sister, then she could also bring Augusta into line by threatening to tell Byron about Augusta's collusion in those first enquiries she made about leaving him. Augusta was the one person he held onto as loyal and faithful through the whole fiasco – he didn't know the reports on him she sent to his wife, her covert meetings, covert discussions, covert correspondence, covert diagnoses. Just as easily as Annabella could confirm allegations of incest to London by publicly ending her friendship with Augusta, she could destroy Byron's exalted opinion of his sister – the one person, he said, who had stood loyally by him. The sister who stood to inherit his estate. And needed to.

Augusta herself offered, flat, not to write to her brother again. That would be that. Annabella advised against that. Augusta must be persuaded to pass his letters on to his estranged wife. As she was. And, 'when I write to him,' she assured Annabella, 'it will be as you advise.' Mrs Villiers – who, Annabella assured Augusta, had 'acted the part she thought most friendly towards you, avoiding the duplicity of appearing to have any feeling towards him but horror, which was much encreased by his treachery' – even Mrs Villiers advised Augusta that 'not a letter, a note, a word should pass between' her and Byron 'without being submitted to' Annabella. And Augusta agreed.

The one person Byron cared about. The one intimate link he had with England, and she projected everything he said, everything she would reply, through the hostile prism of his estranged wife. Augusta's letters to Byron were never hoarded and saved with Lady Byron's filing-cabinet precision, but there was no evidence she ever told him this: she hinted at fears, at her contact with Annabella, at rumours that were said to have come from Caroline Lamb – and for the rest of his life, Byron filled up a good part of their correspondence trying to work out what she was talking about. As long as Annabella was seen to stand by her, Augusta Leigh's reputation was safe. As long as Byron continued to write loving and loyal and affectionate verses about his sister – which Annabella, considerate, could organise to be withheld from public readership – then Annabella's hold over Augusta's reputation was secure.

Augusta handed her a pile of the letters Byron had sent since leaving England. Annabella gasped to Mrs Villiers: 'they are *absolute love letters*.'

Lady Melbourne would have been proud of her niece.

'And so,' wrote Byron to his sister as she sat in her enforced confessional, 'so Lady B has been "kind to you" you tell me – "very kind" – umph – it is as well she should be kind to some of us, and I am glad she has the heart and discernment to be still *your* friend; you were ever so to her.' She hinted at the position she was in, but she never told him.

Byron puzzled over her letters: 'I think all these apprehensions very groundless,' he wrote a safe distance away from Annabella and Mrs Villiers. 'Really this is starting at shadows.' He tried, too, to soothe her concerns about the stories that circled London still attributed to Caroline Lamb: 'Who can care for such a wretch as Caroline?' he asked, 'or believe such a seventy times convicted liar? Whatever she may suppose or assert – I never "committed" anyone to her but *myself*. And as to her fancies – she fancies anything and everybody.'

Who believed Caroline? Lady Byron. The character of veracity. Who assured Augusta that she had never *corresponded* with Lady Caroline. And, technically, she hadn't. She had received all of Caroline's letters during the separation. But she had never replied, so there was not a correspondence.

After landing at Ostend and falling 'like a thunderbolt on the nearest chambermaid', Byron progressed across the Continent in his Napoleonic coach. Which frequently broke down. Arriving at Geneva, he wrote his age in the hotel registry as one hundred years.

He sat there through long, wet summer days with his new friends – Percy Bysshe Shelley, Shelley's mistress Mary Godwin – who spent her summer writing

Frankenstein – and Mary Godwin's step-sister Claire Clairmont. Claire Clairmont had known where he was going, had gone there to meet him. And during the dismal summer, Claire Clairmont slept with Lord Byron – as she had, briefly, in his last weeks in London: she was pregnant before he sailed from Dover. But he was as indifferent to her in the Swiss alps as he had been on Piccadilly: anything to sleep with. Claire's pregnancy was obvious by the end of summer, and Byron happily packed her back to Bath with Shelley and Mary. He never saw her again, although their daughter, Allegra, lived with him in Italy until she died when she was only five years old, in 1822.

Augusta heard tales of multiple mistresses, but Byron protested, 'Lord help me, I have had but one. Now don't scold; but what could I do?' He went on: 'I was not in love – but could hardly play the stoic with a woman who had scrambled eight hundred miles to unphilosophize me.' Augusta heard, too, that Byron had taken another page. No pages, he assured her. Then she heard that she herself had been spotted in Geneva dressed as a page, and had the devil of a job trying to convince the people who told this ridiculous confusion of a story that it wasn't true. She wrote this, as a kind of light entertainment, in a letter to Annabella. Who probably didn't get the joke.

Across the water, English tourists watched the notorious Lord and his radical friends (that Shelley – a vegetarian *and* an aetheist) through specially-focused telescopes. They travelled back to London and spread stories that the two poets were living in a 'league of incest' with Godwin's two daughters. There were even rumours that Godwin had sold the two girls to Byron and Shelley –

although no one could agree about the price paid.

The state Byron was in: to Augusta he said it felt like his heart had been trodden on 'by an elephant'. But Hobhouse — arriving to visit him in September — was pleased to be able to tell her that at least 'the scream' (which no one had mentioned before) that had filled Lord Byron's head had shut up. He was still such a dangerous and notorious person, that mothers warned their daughters it wasn't even safe to look at him.

The main thing, though, was that he was writing again. Annabella was always at him to 'give up the abominable trade of versifying', and after his prolific flurry of hit publications between 1812 and his marriage, the public had had only the *Hebrew Melodies* from him during 1815, and those two poems — *The Siege of Corinth* and *Parisina* — as the drama of the separation began. In Europe, there was plenty to write about. New instalments of *Childe Harold's Pilgrimage*: sales figures for the third canto in no way mirrored the insane success of the first two instalments — but there were 7,000 copies in circulation by the end of 1816. And it had lines aimed very pointedly at Annabella for a gossip-hungry readership: she didn't miss his dig that his daughter might be separated from him, but 'wilt love me; though to drain/*my* blood from out thy being were an aim'. When Sir Walter Scott reviewed the poem and commented uncharitably on her representation in it, she skitched a mutual friend onto him. Lady Byron, this friend assured Sir Walter, had 'borne treatment and wrongs exceeding anything I have ever heard of in married life' and would never have left Byron 'could she have continued to live with him without becoming herself worthless and debased'.

There were lines imputing Augusta, too, and separate whole verses for her, soft, loving:

> For thee, my own sweet sister, in thy heart
> I know myself secure, as thou in mine:
> We were and we are – I am, even as though art –
> Beings who ne'er each other can resign.

Most of which were not published until after his death. Verses that were, as London muttered, again about this familial *fondness*. But Annabella said she had arranged for Byron's publisher to cut several lines from *Childe Harold's Pilgrimage*, and whole verses were withheld from his next *Prisoner of Chillon* volume. Augusta herself requested the suppression of 'Epistle to Augusta' – which began, 'My sister, my sweet sister' – and the 'Lines on Hearing that Lady Byron was Ill', in which he referred to Annabella as his 'moral Clytemnestra' for the first of many times, were also withdrawn.

Byron left Switzerland and went down into Italy, arriving in Venice in early November. Where, noticing that Casanova's name had been almost worn away on one of the columns on St Mark's Square, Byron – in a civic mood – refreshed it, chipping its letters back into talismanic clarity. Venice was everything that life with Annabella had not been. Venice was swimming from party to party along the Grand Canal, one arm held high out of the water with a flaming torch to warn the boats and gondoliers that Lord Byron was nearby. Venice was a place where secrecy and assumed identities were a vital part of the cultural heritage – where a man could slip into a cloak and a mask, and be whoever he pleased for the evening, just as Byron had created identities in the crowded drawing rooms of London. By the end of the month, despite his resolve – as he assured Augusta – to give up 'gallivanting' on leaving England, he found himself at last at the end of the struggle of wretchedness he had endured, he said, since being parted from her, 'thank Heaven above – and woman beneath'. He took his first Venetian mistress, looked around for a palazzo to rent, and settled in.

This was not the sort of recovery Annabella had had in mind.

He began to put himself back together, to think about what he might do next. He thought, he said to Thomas Moore, that if he could manage to live another ten years (and he wasn't at all confident he would), 'you will see, however, that it is not over with me – I don't mean in literature, for that is nothing; and it may seem odd enough to say, I do not think it my vocation. But you will see that I will do something or other – the times and fortune permitting – that, "like the cosmogony, or the creation of the world, will puzzle the philosophers of all ages." But I doubt whether my constitution will hold out. I have, at intervals, exorcised it most devilishly.'

His daughter was at the top of his mind too – waiting for reports about her from Augusta, buying her trinkets and toys in the places he visited. He imagined meeting her again when she had grown up, lamenting the distance between them while she was small. She was to be, he decided, the comfort of his old age. And he made her the start and finish of his new *Childe Harold* canto:

Ada! Sole daughter of my house and heart?
When last I saw thy young blue eyes they smiled,
And then we parted, – not as now we part,
But with a hope. –

It was in October, 1816, through the watertight communication channel of Lady Melbourne via Hobhouse,
that he heard that Lady Byron considered travelling in
Europe and would take Ada with her. Knowing that
Augusta had some sort of contact with his wife (she did,
after all, pass Lady Byron's news of his daughter on to
him), he suggested that she would be 'the properest
channel of communication from me to her'. Not knowing – never knowing – that she already passed his letters
(those ones signed 'Love me the most, as I ever must
love you', and '*A thousand loves* to *you* from *me* – which
is very generous for I only ask *one* in return', and 'We
are the last persons in the world – who ought – or could
cease to love one another') on to Annabella. 'It is a very
deep privation to me to be withdrawn from the contemplation and company of my little girl,' he said simply.
And, 'my whole hope – and prospect of a quiet evening
(if I reach it) are wrapt up in that little creature Ada.'

For a man who posed about 'abominating children'
and 'admiring the character of Herod', he always
wanted to know how Ada was. It was concern. It was
curiosity – whatever liberty there was in getting about
Europe in a Napoleonic coach, he was also lonely for
the few people he cared about and had left behind:
Ada, Augusta, his friends. It was also the case that if Ada
left England, Byron himself would lose all his legal
rights as a father as long as she was beyond British
jurisdiction. He was, he said, firm: he had no intention,

either then or in the future, of taking Ada away from her mother – 'I think it would be harsh' – but he did not want her taken out of England to travel 'over the Continent at so early a time of life – and [be] subjected to many unavoidable risks of health and comfort; more especially,' he pointed out, 'in so unsettled a state as we know the greater part of Europe to be at this moment.' He would be happy for his child to be left with Lady Judith and Sir Ralph Milbanke '(who would be naturally fond of it) but my distress of mind would be very much augmented if my daughter quitted England – without my consent or approbation.' He had no wish to trouble his wife beyond this, he said: he just wanted the request made known to her. Lady Byron replied, through Augusta, that she had no intention of travelling at that time.

No, said Byron, that wasn't the question. The question asked for an assurance that Ada would not be taken from England. He decided to write directly to Annabella, but got distracted from the question of his daughter's travel arrangements: 'You will not relieve me – you will not believe me – but I loved and love you most entirely,' he wrote. 'Things which you know – and things which you did not know – made me what I was – or rather appeared to you – and amongst others – a want of confidence – had I trusted you – as I had almost resolved soon after our marriage – all would have been better – perhaps well.'

He finished by saying 'before God – that if there were a means of becoming reunited to you I would embrace it.' It was a backhanded way of suggesting it, defeated before the sentence was even finished. He may be in England in the spring, he went on, and then – so small — 'let me at least find my daughter there.'

A note came at Christmas, signed by Annabella and her father: 'There never has existed nor does there exist, the remotest intention of removing Miss Byron out of the kingdom.' But still no guarantee. Byron stormed to his dithering solicitor, Hanson, that he required 'an explicit answer ... I shall have no comfort till I know of this. It would be too late,' he said snidely of Hanson's usual way of addressing things, 'to wait for her being in readiness to set off — the infant might be over the Channel before you could prevent it.' To Augusta he said menacingly (on the day that should have celebrated his second wedding anniversary) that Lady Byron and her family had no idea 'what I can and will do if thoroughly roused and my reasonable requests treated with a heedless contempt'. 'They will end by driving me mad,' he said a fortnight later when he still had no clarification from his wife, 'if they have not already.'

What Lord Byron did not know — what he would not be told until March, almost twelve months after he left England — was that Ada was already beyond his reach and, on this at least, Annabella was, machinating, one step ahead of him. The solicitor Hanson, roused, had contacted Lady Byron's advocate Stephen Lushington and, through him, her father, Sir Ralph Milbanke. And he discovered — as he wrote to Byron — that a bill had been filed against Byron in Chancery. 'To deprive me,' Byron blustered, 'of my paternal right over my child.'

Lady Byron had claimed, during the negotiations for the separation, that it was Byron's intention to sue for custody of Ada — even though she knew he intended to leave the country in his Napoleonic coach, and would hardly be taking a months-old baby and a nursemaid along with him. Then she was sure, she said, that he would sue for custody and give Augusta guardianship of Ada. She was confident at the time that she could get Augusta to give her word that she would not agree to this. But that wasn't enough. Without Byron's knowledge, without paying any attention to his repeated statements – even before he left England – that a child should remain with its mother and that he would be happy for Ada to stay with hers because it would 'show the world I have no fight with her', Lady Byron had her daughter made a Ward of Chancery. This removed her family's rights to her – allowing her to live with her mother, but giving the Lord Chancellor authority to make the sorts of decisions that a parent – more specifically a father – would make. Like whether, at the age of ten months, a little girl should be packed off on her mother's inaugural European tour. Annabella had justified this to Augusta in terms of 'taking power out of his hands, as I should take from my child a knife which she would use to the hurt of herself and others. The complete exposure of his character to me,' she assured her sister-in-law, unconvincingly, 'has however produced no reverse of charitable regard.'

It was the last thing he expected. Had there not been a general understanding, he raged, that all threats and legal actions were put aside when the Deed of Separation was signed? Had he not already suffered enough 'if not by your design,' he wrote to his wife, 'at least by your means? ... Irritated I may have been – and may be – is it a wonder? – but upon such irritation beyond its momentary expression – I have not acted – from the hour you quitted me – to that in which I am made aware that our daughter is to be the entail of our dis-union – the inheritor of our bitterness.

'If you think to reconcile yourself to yourself,' he wrote, saying that he knew well her excuse for it all would be *duty and Justice*, 'you are again mistaken. You are not happy nor even tranquil – nor will you ever be so.' It was his piece of prophecy for her – along with this: 'no one was ever even the involuntary cause of great evils to others – without a requital – I have paid and am paying for mine – so will you.' He saw, he said, that the sickly fancy he had cherished of a reconcilia-tion was entirely useless. He stopped the letter with no wishes, no compliments, not even 'Yours'.

'I forgive everything up to this,' Byron railed to Augusta, 'but this I will never forgive; and no consid-eration on earth shall now prevail on me to look upon her as otherwise than my worst enemy. I curse her from the bottom of my heart, and in the bitterness of my soul; and I only hope she may one day feel what she has made me suffer. They will break my heart or drive me mad, one day or the other.'

He wrote to his solicitor, too: 'I request that you give me the best advice how to proceed in Chancery – because I am determined to *reclaim* the child to my-self – as the natural guardian ... I have done what I could to avoid extremities,' he said, 'but the die is cast, and I authorise – and desire you to take the proper steps and obtain for me the best advice – how and in what manner to assume the care and personal charge of my daughter. I will return directly if necessary.'

'Give me but a fair share of my daughter,' he wrote for his sister to tell Lady Byron, 'otherwise I come to

England and "law and claw before they get it" …
plaguing Bell herself – which,' he assured Augusta, 'I
really by the Great God wish to avoid.' And the next
day he asked again simply for that assurance that Ada
would not leave England without his consent: 'there is
a law and right for me also.' Failing all this, he said, he
would return and ask the Chancellor to deliver his
daughter to him as her natural guardian. Ada, he
thought now, would be his Orestes and his Elektra.
Both. She would wreak his revenge on that 'moral
Clytemnestra' of a wife. Which was a big role to cast
for someone who was only a year old.

Lady Byron's expectations of Ada were hardly any less
grandiose. She marked her daughter's first birthday
noting to herself that Ada had 'arrived at an age when
a watchful and judicious superintendence may form
the basis of good habits and prevent the rise of evil
ones.' Her definitions of 'watchful' and 'judicious' were
very strict. Her greatest interest in Ada was to ensure –
at just about any cost – that she did not grow into her
father. She piqued herself, too, on telling her friends
that she had never had to 'give Ada a negative impression' of him. Yet it seemed sometimes that she simply
never said anything to her daughter about him at all:
trying to sort out the way the world worked, and who
the people in it were supposed to be, Ada once had to
ask her mother whether the person everyone else had
whom they called 'father' was the same person as the
one she had and called 'grandfather'. More and more
often Lady Byron made trips, leaving Ada at home with
her grandmother: she even visited Newstead Abbey
anonymously in 1817, flinching as the housekeeper

talked about Lord Byron's wife who had never gone
with him there, and his sister, whom he loved very
well, very well indeed, and finding herself (if only she'd
meant to be funny) 'rooted in his bedroom'. Byron's
snide remark during the separation proceedings that his
daughter showed a great acquaintance with her grandmother but didn't really know her *nearer* relations
still seemed apt. If Ada missed her, Annabella suggested
easily, 'my portrait may afford her some consolation.
I beg,' she wrote to her mother, 'it may be shown to her
with these words, "Pretty, pretty mama, give her a
kiss".'

Ada figured, in Annabella's thinking, as some*thing* to
be trained and controlled, rather than as some*one* to be
loved and nurtured. Nurses were sacked the minute
they showed any sort of attachment to 'the child', and
Annabella said flatly that she objected 'to her being
with anybody except those whom I mention to you as
approving of.' Governesses, similarly, Annabella determined were a force of evil: they either lacked the
qualities of mind to teach someone as brilliant as Ada,
or, like the nurses, they formed an inappropriate fondness for her. They were also, dangerous, potential
spreaders of stories: in the first year without Byron – as
through the rest of her life – much of Lady Byron's
social energy was devoted to seeking out people who
took his part or questioned her story, and setting them
straight. Her recollections of her own prodigy determined that Ada would be as brilliant as she had been,
as young. Although, as Ada sat learning her alphabet
when she was only two, Annabella emphasised that it
was 'not so much for the sake of early acquirement, as
to fix her attention, which from the activity of her

imagination is rather difficult.' There would be nothing more dangerous than the unfettered imagination of a child – especially Byron's child.

It seemed something of an understatement for Annabella to admit that there was not a lot of innate maternal affection lurking in her. Infancy, she noted, cannot soothe acute grief – although, she conceded, 'it may sometimes rouse from stupor.' Still, she wanted Ada to at least like her. It was a horrible thing when, suddenly, Ada was screaming 'war whoops worse than the Americans' if she was left alone in a room with her mother. She made no connection between this behaviour and the fact that, as her daughter's teeth began to come through, she herself had just lanced Ada's gums 'with so little compunction as to make the nurse flinch', as she cheerfully described it to her own mother. But the 'war whoops', Annabella deduced, were more the result of Ada's nanny at the time teaching 'the child to play the hypocrite': telling the 18-month-old Ada sweet things about Annabella while her mother was in the room – teaching her to hate Annabella when she wasn't there.

She noted that Ada was 'seldom voluntarily affectionate, except after she has felt an impulse to be naughty'. If her daughter fidgeted and scratched, Annabella had her hands tied in small black bags, turning them into ineffectual paws. If this didn't stop her squirming, she would be locked in a cupboard for at least half an hour. It was no wonder that other nannies could record that Ada poured so much concentration into doing her maths to please her mother. 'Ada loves me as well as I wish,' she said, 'and better than I expected, for I had a strange prepossession that she would never be fond of me.'

To ensure that no one else taught her either not to love her mother or – worse – to love some other missing parent, Annabella determined to keep Ada away from her aunt, for fear that Augusta's 'delusion might tempt her to put ideas into Ada's mind that might take root there – something of "poor Papa", &c'. 'Ada's intellect is so far advanced beyond her age that she is already capable of receiving impressions that might influence her – to what extent I can't say,' Annabella explained. 'My apprehensions may be exaggerated, but I have an insurmountable repugnance to Ada's being in her company.'

To another friend she wrote, quite earnestly: 'I am sick, quite sick, of taking my own part. I never did it but as an act of duty towards Ada, and the pains on which that principle I have taken … have been the most laborious and vexatious of my life.'

In Venice, without his wife, Byron was fulfilling the one sort of duty he set any store by and having a lovely time – writing through the night and sleeping until two in the afternoon. He had a mistress and a box at the theatre; he had *conversazione* to attend, Italians to challenge to swimming races along the Grand Canal ('I left him in the bubbles'), and friends from England to visit. Letters came from Augusta, still full of hints and insinuations and circumlocutions: Byron told her flatly that half the time he couldn't work out if she had a broken heart or an earache. 'I have received all your letters,' he assured her, 'which are full of woes – as usual – megrims and mysteries.' Two weeks later, he wrote again, 'I repeat to you again and again – that it would be much better at once to explain your mysteries – than to go on with this obscure hinting mode of writing. What do you mean? What is there known? or can be known? which *you and I* do not know much better?' It was, he wrote of signing the separation, 'on your account principally that I gave way at all – for I thought they would endeavour to drag you into it – although they had no business with anything previous to my marriage with that infernal fiend.' Time and Nemesis, he vowed, would requite him in the end.

In the summer of 1817, he still sat drinking with friends, turning his wife's treachery over and over, the odious behaviour of her advisers, the fact that he had never squarely been told what Lady Byron's charges were against him. It became bigger and bigger with every sentence, every glass of hock, until Byron finally drew up a statement offering to tear up the Deed of Separation – that supposedly amicable document, nothing more than an agreement between two people, and with no real legal force – and take the whole matter to the courts. It became a better idea as nights and flagons wore on.

'It has been intimated to me,' he wrote, 'that the persons understood to be the legal advisers of Lady Byron, have declared "their lips to be sealed up" on the cause of the separation between her and myself. If their lips are sealed up, they are not sealed up by me, and the greatest favour *they* can confer upon me will be to open them ... I have been, and am now utterly ignorant of what description her allegations, charges, or whatever name they may have assumed are; and am as little aware for what purpose they have been kept back – unless it was to sanction the most infamous calumnies.'

Let them take me to court. If they take me to court, they will have to name these terrible crimes I have committed, and I will stand proved or acquitted once and for all. That the world may know. That I may know. 'I call upon her and hers to say their worst, pledging myself to meet their allegations – whatever they may be – and only too happy to be informed at last of their real nature.' Mr Hobhouse, he said, had made this same suggestion the very day before the Deed was signed – throw it out the window and take it all into a tribunal. Make them state their reasons.

But Mr Hobhouse, in 1817, was appalled by such a suggestion – 'it will gratify Lady Byron's friends to think that Byron is annoyed,' he blustered, 'and I should think no one can suppose that Lady Byron's counsellors meant that their lips were sealed on Lord Byron's account or at his desire – but merely because they were her counsellors in a private and delicate affair.'

Even his friends, even drinking, thought it would be best to let it lie. It would pass – it virtually had passed. No one, they assured him, had these terrible thoughts of him anymore. In fact they still couldn't see why he had thought it was imperative to leave England in the first place – it was part of political banter to charge someone with incest, with homosexuality: the Prince of Wales' own brother had been accused of incest by his political opponents. It hadn't affected him at all. Incest was almost the *frisson* of the century. Hobhouse – who could be as staid and proper as Annabella – always maintained that there hadn't been the slightest necessity for Byron to leave the country. Rumours came, rumours went: what was a season without them? Everyone else got on with life, things, living: Byron –

and Annabella – hung on, clung on, fast and tight and always.

The friend entrusted to take the ultimatum back to London passed it on to Lord Byron's legal nemesis, Stephen Lushington. Who took no action and filed it away, until it was dragged out and published in a newspaper fifty years after Byron wrote it – years after they were all dead – when it shouldn't have mattered to anyone anymore. Lushington did show it to Annabella, who wrote succinctly in her journal: 'a blight in the evening. Received from Dr Lushington the copy of a paper written by Lord B Date Venice Aug 9 1817. It is probably the effect of advice. Could not read. Heart heavy.' It had to be the effect of advice. Everything Annabella did was the effect of advice.

XI

THAT LIFE

... Now I'll put out my taper
(I've finished my paper
For these stanzas you see on the *brink* stand)
There's a whore on my right
For I rhyme best at Night
When a Cunt is tied close to *my Inkstand*.

Lord Byron

While Annabella convinced herself and the world that the end of her marriage was nothing more than her doing her duty, her reaction to her husband's appalling behaviour – rather than an action she had chosen to take – Byron did not see himself as anything other than abandoned by her. Byron, model husband, had been a disaster of a role – best then to become again reckless, seductive Byron. The centre of a new city's attention, the dashingly prolific poet. To revel in being, as Venice matter-of-factly labelled him, 'the great English peer and poet'.

Between the end of 1816 and the first months of

1818, he rattled through *The Prisoner of Chillon, Manfred* (Lord Byron has given us such a picture of himself, commented one critic on the poem, which implied an incestuous relationship between two of the characters, colouring '*Manfred* into his own personal features' – 'he practically gives you away,' Annabella wrote to Augusta, 'and implies that you were guilty *after* marriage'), and *Beppo*. By the middle of 1818, he was writing his infamous satire, *Don Juan*, and his memoirs.

Sometimes it seemed that England was further away than Byron could imagine, that he was almost dead to it. If he stayed away long enough, he thought, he might even manage to forget the language altogether. Other times it was so sharp, so clear, in front of his eyes that he could write the most scathing descriptions of its people and everything they carried on with, even though he hadn't been there for years. He poured them into *Don Juan* – particularly, it seemed, his recollections of Lady Byron, so similar to the shape of the poem's Donna Inez, a misguided wife who sends in a troop of doctors to try to prove her husband is mad.

'If the bitch Inez resembles any other bitch that's fair,' Byron commented. 'Nature is for the poet and the painter.' He went on: 'Hobhouse talks to me about the woman – and of the thing being forgotten – is it so? *I* have *not* forgotten – nor *forgiven*. – And Ellice talks of my standing "*well and high*" – who cares how I stand – if my standing is to be shaken by the breath of a bitch – or her infamous Setters on? – If she was Scylla with all her dogs – I care not – I have swum through Charybdis already.'

His wife's mother had written to the Prince Regent to beg 'His Royal Highness's consideration of the relief

it would afford Sir Ralph and Lady Noel to be enabled
to call their insulted and injured daughter by another
title than that of Byron, viz. by the title of Wentworth,
Lady Noel waiving her claim.' Nothing ever came of
the request – maybe it was never sent, just filed with all
Annabella's other papers. In any case, Lady Byron
didn't seem to mind being Lady Byron at all: she
received invitations on the strength of it – all the way
through to the end of her life – and she used it for
favours.

He was her commodity. She traded.

She was, if anything, still the thing he reacted against.
In all the extremity of his Venetian life, there was the
sense that it was a little bit wilder in reaction to
the charge of 'dereliction' England had flung at him.
The city was the smorgasbord where even Byron could
satisfy his 'passion for women which is expensive in
its variety every where but less so in Venice ... more
than half [of £5000] was laid out on the Sex – to
be sure I have had plenty for the money – that's
certain – I think at least two hundred of one sort or
another – perhaps more, for I have not lately kept
count.' Shelley reported that he allowed 'fathers and
mothers to bargain with him for their daughters', and
'associates with wretches who seem almost to have
lost the gait and physiognomy of man, and who do
not scruple to avow practices which are not only not
named, but I believe seldom conceived in England'.
And Annabella's trusty invalid friend, still not dead,
carried from Venice the gratifying report that Byron
was 'enormously fat, his face bloated and complection
pasty. Nothing remains of that fine antique outline so

peculiar to his head.' He had no association with the *ladies* of Venice, and had to *pay* the shopkeeper's wife he kept 'for the loss of her affection'. His beauty, she told Lady Byron, 'is gone, quite gone'. His solicitor's son commented, chilling, that Byron's knuckles were sunk into mounds of fat.

Byron, even by Byron's standards, was well and truly debauching, and this reckless abandon drove more and more distance between him and England. It reinforced his sense, as he explained to Scrope Davies, of the 'circumstances under which I quit England [and] the rumours of which I was subject – if they were *true* I was unfit for England, if false, England is unfit for me.' And, so far from that English disapproval and even with whatever obesity he went up to and starved himself down from, Byron had found himself in a glamorous city where he, again, was the very lion at its centre. The best beloved, as though he walked always lit up by one of those gig-lamps. Men almost competed for his friendship, reaching hysterical states when he suggested that he might move to another town, depriving them of his sparkling company. Women fought catfights over him on the edge of the Grand Canal, and occasionally pushed each other into it arguing over him. Single young women pined over the fact that Lady Byron would not be so kind as to divorce her husband, so that one of them might have the chance of marrying him. And through all this, he dispensed charity, attended the two leading salons, and rode his horses at full pelt along the Lido. This was what it was to be Lord Byron.

In the spring of 1819, he met and fell for Teresa Guiccioli – a young Italian countess, only a year married and a little longer out of a convent education. And gasped, in his usual understated way, that he was certainly in love, never coming back, 'tired of promiscuous concubinage, and with an opportunity now of settling for life.' All within a minute and a half of meeting her. At about the same time, a parcel came from London with a copy of a Parisian magazine that claimed to be publishing a new short story by Lord Byron, called, *The Vampyre*. Based on a fragment of a story he had played with for Shelley, Mary, Claire Clairmont and his doctor in the dismal Genevan summer of 1816, it was written up by that same doctor and presented with this implied noble authorship. To make the allusion unmistakable, the doctor gave his Byronic character the same name as Caroline Lamb had named her character in *Glenarvon*. Goethe thought it was the best thing Byron had ever written. There were bound to be a few dead bodies in His Lordship's past, he suggested. Byron snarled: 'Damn *The Vampyre* – what do I know of vampires? It must be some book-selling imposture – contradict it with a solemn paragraph.' The excitement of the whole thing was raised by a rumour doing the laps of Paris that it was His Lordship himself who was the vampire – it was said that he drank the blood of a murdered mistress from a cup made out of a skull. I have a personal dislike of vampires, Byron assured the magazine's editor, 'and the little acquaintance I have with them would by no means induce me to reveal their secrets.'

On top of which, he had a little dalliance – despite the prospect of everlasting union with Teresa – with a girl called Angelina who thought that Byron might marry her. Her family sent round a priest and a family friend to reason with him, and he treated them both to coffee. Assuring everyone that the liaison had ended, he went to her house at midnight one night in mid-May, 1819, for another assignation: 'I tumbled into the Grand Canal,' he wrote spiritedly to his publisher, 'and not choosing to miss my appointment by the delays of changing – I have been perched on a balcony with my wet clothes on ever since … my foot slipped in getting into my Gondola to set out (owing to the cursed slippery steps of their palaces) and in I flounced like a Carp – and went dripping like a Triton to my Sea-Nymph – and had to scramble up to a grated window.'

But before he set off for this tryst Byron wrote another letter – the letter most often credited with proving his desperately incestuous passion for Augusta. Written as he waited to go out through the canals for a midnight rendezvous with some woman whose surname is lost.

He wrote to his 'dearest love', that he had never ceased to feel 'for a moment that perfect & boundless attachment which bound & binds me to you – which renders me utterly incapable of *real* love for any other human being – what could they be to me after *you*? My own' – there was a short word crossed out – 'we may have been very wrong – but I repent of nothing except that cursed marriage – & you refusing to continue to love me as you had loved me – I can neither forget nor quite *forgive you* for that precious piece of reformation …

'Circumstances may have ruffled my manner – & hardened my spirit – you may have seen me harsh & exasperated with all things around me; grieved and tortured with your new resolution, – & the soon after persecution of that infamous fiend who drove me from my Country ... but remember that even then *you* were the sole object that cost me a tear – and *what tears*! do you remember *our* parting?' It was written on May 17, 1819. Which was, coincidentally, Annabella's twenty-seventh birthday.

It is partly detective work and hypothesis that make it known (or assumed) that this letter was addressed to Augusta: the name and the address of the person it was sent to have been long crossed out. The letter has been used – through more than a hundred years – to prove one woman or another (perhaps that Mary Chaworth who he had had a crush on when he was a teenager, who had seen Lady Byron in the first months of her marriage, or perhaps someone else altogether) the single, abiding, soul-mated love of Byron's life. The consensus – stacked up by the secondary evidence of other letters, other comments – is that it was sent to Augusta Leigh. His dearest love. As opposed to Annabella: that infamous fiend.

Augusta passed a letter on to Lady Byron in June, commenting 'he is surely to be considered a *maniac*.' They met, the two women, in Tunbridge Wells, and Annabella noted that Augusta looked 'repressed and oppressed'. Augusta handed over the paper, and asked for Annabella's advice on how to reply. You have two options, said Annabella, as she always did – either break off all correspondence with him, or take no notice of it when you write back. Annabella could at least comfort her sister-in-law that, as Byron's words opened 'nothing new to me in regard to the writer's mind, it gives me no other pain than what arises from feeling for *your* grief in receiving a fresh proof of the continuance of that passion which you most wish to be extinguished'.

Augusta suggested that the letter was merely raving, but Annabella dismissed that out of hand. It was, she said, 'a well known fact in the nature of man that, unless a purifying repentance has taken place, there can be no medium between aversion and love.' Byron, she said, had shown himself 'incapable of the true attachment which is devoted to the welfare of its object.' The attachment of which she considered herself a past master. She would not burn the paper as Augusta had asked: she suggested that Augusta keep it as evidence of her perpetual claim that nothing had happened between her and her brother after his marriage. She made a copy of it for her own file. 'No one can be more fully aware of the *Precipice* on which I stand than I am,' Augusta wrote. And she opted again for the 'gentler expedient' of writing him a dull, flat letter of ordinary events that paid no attention to his passionate words.

'I am at too great a distance to scold you,' Byron wrote to Augusta in July, 'but I *will* ask whether *your* letter of the *1st* July is *an answer* to the letter I wrote you before I quitted Venice? What? Is it come to *this*? Have you no memory? or no heart? You *had* both – and I *have* both – at least for *you*.

'I write,' he said, 'presuming that you received *that* letter. Is it that you fear? Do not be afraid of the past; the world has its own affairs without thinking about *ours*.' Which could not have been further from the truth had it tried.

In the time around May 17, 1819, there was the sense in Byron's life – in Byron – that everything was starting to run slightly out of control. England so far away that his sister sent domestic monotonies in exchange for his greatest fondness, his greatest love. While he juggled liaisons with Venetian women, and avoided Teresa Guiccioli's husband's suspicions (and stiletto: the Count was not known as a reasonable man, nor was he averse to a little murder to get his own way). Paris thought that he drank the blood of his mistress from a skull; Rome believed he kept the abandoned Lady Byron locked in a castle. And against all of this extremity, everyone in England, from his publisher through every supposed friend he had in Christendom, was working themselves into a lather about the publication of his latest poem, *Don Juan* – Byron's version of that archetypal character, more an innocent than a Casanova, and his lusty adventures, bawdy humour, and innate inversion of vice and virtue. It was, they all said, depraved and corrupting. Byron knew, on the other hand, that it was the best thing he'd ever written, yet it seemed the rest of the world wanted it put under the bed, in a box and forgotten. People seemed convinced that he'd only written it to be difficult, to give them all more infamy to attach to (or try to scrub from) the name of Lord Byron. They made it the eleventh commandment not to read it, Byron scowled, even though a book had never been known to lift a petticoat.

'Confess it,' he wrote to his banker, 'confess it you dog – and be candid – that it is the sublime of *that there* sort of writing – it may be bawdy – but is it not good English? – it may be profligate – but is it not *life*, is it not *the thing*? – Could any man have written it – who has not lived in the world – and tooled in a post-chaise? in a hackney coach? in a vis-à-vis? – on a table? – and under it? ... I had such plans for the Don – but the *Cant* is much stronger than *Cunt* – nowadays, that the benefit of experience in a man who had well weighed the worth of both monosyllables must be lost to despairing posterity.'

The world tightened further around Byron: he considered eloping to America with Teresa. He considered moving to Venezuela without her. She fell ill – he was sure it was 'consumption' and prepared himself for a tragic death-bed scene. Then Byron himself caught a fever and came out of a delirium to see his valet weeping on one side of the bed and Teresa on the other.

He finished, besides all this, the memoirs he had begun in the languor of the previous Venetian summer – trying them out as a piece of writing the way he tried out comedies and novels every so often. He included them in reports of his works-in-progress for his publisher. They were the length of several sheets of letter paper; or they ran to forty pages and he anticipated another twenty. He handed them over to Thomas Moore, who had gone with him to Lady Caroline Lamb's party all those years ago in 1812, when Byron had tripped on the step and seen Annabella for the first time, and who had, as many years before, joked with Byron about being his 'editor and historiographer'. Show them to whomever you like, Byron said, but don't publish them until I am dead. They ran up to 1816. He wrote later to Lady Byron, asking if she would read them – 'and mark what you please. I wish you to know what I think and say of you and yours. You will find nothing to flatter you – nothing to lead you to the most remote supposition that we could ever have been – or be happy together. But I do not choose to give to another generation statements which we cannot arise from the dust to prove or disprove without letting you see fairly and fully what I look upon you to have been – and what I depict you as being. If seeing this – you can detect what is false – or answer what is charged – do so, your mark shall not be erased … The truth I have always stated – but there are two ways of looking at it – and your way may not be mine.'

She drafted answers – outraged on behalf of Ada: of course the memoirs should not even have been written, let alone the inappropriateness that *she* was expected to involve herself with them. 'If, as I have every reason to expect, your representation is partial, falsely coloured, and affectedly candid, the mode of refutation which you suggest would be very inadequate.' In the end, her lawyers dictated an impersonal note of terse brevity, declining his offer to show them to her. Let it lie.

Even three and a half years out from their signatures slashed across the Deed of Separation, the world still concerned itself with this estranged couple. Madame de Staël sent on to Byron a petition from a group of people in Denmark. They wanted the poet and his wife to know that they prayed for their reconciliation. Hot on the heels of that love letter that Augusta had passed on to Annabella. 'You will smile – as I have done – at the importance which they attach to such things,' Byron wrote to his wife, 'and the effect which they conceive capable of being produced by composition … perhaps it may not offend you – however it may surprise – that the good people on the portions of Denmark have taken an interest in your domestic affairs which have now – I think – nearly made the tour of Europe – been discussed in most of its languages – to as little purpose as in our own.' (And you might mention to my wife, he scrawled on the piece of paper wrapped around a letter to Augusta the next month, that I want to remarry: isn't there any way this can be done without compromising her blessed virtue and purity?)

In the middle of all this mess in Italy – an imminent revolution, women, fever, and being half a continent away from his publisher who wanted to slice *Don Juan* down to inoffensive ribbons – Byron decided it was time to go back to England. He sent packets of letters off announcing his coming, one of which duly reached Augusta, who duly informed Annabella. 'Luckily,' Augusta added, '(or *unluckily* perhaps) I do not die easily – or I think this stroke would about finish me.' What, she wanted to know, did Annabella advise? She was almost seven months pregnant. When he had suggested coming home two years before, she had written – at Annabella's instruction – the suggestion that she might not be able to see him when he got to England. Which he had dismissed as ridiculous.

It was very simple, said Annabella as 1819's summer ended. Augusta should write to her brother in Calais, where he would find the letter waiting for him on his way through. And she should simply tell him that she would not see him. 'It can scarcely be doubted,' Annabella pointed out, 'from the whole series of his correspondence, that you are his principal interest in England.' Perhaps Annabella anticipated hearing

Byron's howl of outrage as he arrived within sight of British soil to find that Augusta was still all full of her mysteries and alarms and – outrageous – refusing to even see him after all the distance he had travelled to see her.

But in Italy, Teresa Guiccioli began to exert her own emotional blackmail. As Byron came closer and closer to leaving Venice, she found herself suddenly struck down by a terrible and mysterious malaise, and managed to convince both her father and her husband that the only recuperative measure that would work was for Byron to be called to her bedside.

Augusta. Teresa. Augusta. Teresa. England. Italy. He could stay, easy, in this romantic liaison, undemanding, devoted. He could go back to England, to whatever moral army Lady Byron might raise. To the quagmire of insinuations he didn't understand in Augusta's letters – her fears and worries. To a public that wanted to lynch him rather than laud him, that said his *Don Juan* was destroying the morality of its readers. But he had been away for three and a half years. To see Augusta. To see Hobhouse. Perhaps he would even see Lady Byron – and Ada. To drink brandy again with his banker – an easier thing to imagine.

To kiss Teresa.

Everything in his Venetian palace was packed and bundled into boxes. He wrote to Teresa that he must leave Italy as he could not bear to be in it and not entirely with her. He wrote to John Murray, his publisher in London, that he would probably return on business. Everything he owned, packed up and ready to go – everything except his guns.

But he was Lord Byron. He was that man with such big and diabolic plans dished out to him by Fate and Destiny that it would be futile for him to try and stand against them. And so he stood in the stripped and dismantled rooms of his house.

He was dressed for the journey, in that limbo when everything is almost ready and you wish yourself two miles on the way and gone. He had his gloves on. He had his hat on. He had his walking cane in his hand. All he had to do was to go downstairs, get into his gondola, go across to the mainland, and begin the westerly journey towards the English channel. His boxes were packed into the boat. His goodbyes were made. There was nothing for it but to leave. And he paused. He stopped. He waited.

London was a different place now: there had been little post for him from England recently – he wondered blank if it was that people there didn't really want to see him. It was the middle of the day: he wondered idly about the time. Thought about the journey ahead of him. Thought about Teresa Guiccioli, south of him now, while England loomed west.

There was a small bustle behind him: his guns being packed up – the last thing to be loaded onto the gondola. The sun was high in the sky: he looked into its brightness. England. Italy. He drew a breath and, 'by way of a pretext,' wrote one of Teresa's companions, still with him in Venice, 'declares that if it would strike one o'clock before everything was quite in order (his arms being the only thing not yet quite ready) he would not go that day.

'The hour strikes and he remains. Evidently he had not the heart to go.'

The clock struck. His guns were not in the boat. He would not go home. He made excuses to England. You tell my sister, he asked his publisher: I can't bring myself to tell her. He wrote − pathetic − to Teresa not that a clock struck at a random moment. No, he assured her, love had won. He was on his way to her in Ravenna. He would stay in Italy. The clock struck one. His guns were not in the boat.

He never returned to England. He never saw his beloved sister or his daughter again. Or his wife.

XII

THE DICTIONARY OF NATIONAL BIOGRAPHY

'It is a fact, I assure you: I should have
positively destroyed myself, but I guessed that _____
or _____ would write my life, and with this fear
before my eyes, I have lived on. I know so well the
sort of things they would write of me – the excuses,
lame as myself, that they would offer for my
delinquencies, while they were unnecessarily
exposing them, and all this done with the avowed
intention of justifying, God help me! what cannot
be justified, my unpoetical reputation, with which
the world can have nothing to do! One of my friends
would dip his pen in clarified honey, and the
other in vinegar, to describe my manifold
transgressions, and as I do not wish my poor fame
to be either preserved or pickled ...
I have written my memoirs to save the necessity
of their being written by a friend or friends, and
have only to hope they will not add notes.'

Lord Byron

The Secret

When Byron, hoping for creative prowess, swam in the Kastalian Spring at Delphi he took it on trust that his spring was the one that would bring him the blessings of the muses. It was the end of 1809, thirty years or more before the site would be positively identified as Delphi and excavations began to uncover and reconstruct what can be seen today.

At Cape Sounion, in the ruins of the Temple of Poseidon perched on the Athenian peninsula, he scratched his name into a column and wrote about wanting to sit, and sing, and die, swan-like, on its marble step. But when Byron went to Sounion, only two of the temple's columns were standing. With seventeen or so pillars, the ruins now stand more complete than when Byron rode up to it almost two centuries ago. The rock he carved his name into was the inner surface of one of the column's blocks. It is now enclosed, part of its core, while the temple's shape is visible again: you can know that Byron was there, and that he has left something essential in the reconstructed shapes, but you cannot see him directly.

There is a weight to everything it is possible to discover about this man, this marriage – there were more than 5,000 books, chapters, theses, articles, scripts, tributes and dissertations relating to Byron between 1973 and 1994 alone. Someone's shard of suspicion about him could be combined with all the pieces other people had collected. Fragments, like those fragments of stone monuments in Greece, are patched together and rounded up into a life. It is partial, reconstructed, but it is closer to a whole.

Byron's affinity with Greece was strong and fatalistic. He may have returned home from his first travels in 1811 announcing that, if the call was to be in favour of any population for their way of living and their humanity, then he thought it was probably the Turks (which was about as contrary to raising yourself up as a sympathetic Greek as you could get), but it was Greece that he carried deep at the centre of himself. He was fated to return there; he was fated to die there; he'd been trying to get back ever since that inconvenient wave of the plague swept through in 1813. Lady Byron had used these alarming notions in part of her original statement about his insanity: if he believed that he would die on going back to Greece, she argued, wasn't it her *duty* to prevent him from going? And wasn't it *madness* to want to go somewhere where you were sure you would die? And then she left him anyway and he had no reason not to work his way back across Europe.

He arrived, finally, on the Grecian mainland, at the marshy dank town of Missolonghi, on January 5, 1824. He had left Italy, left Teresa, and sailed across the Adriatic to lend his reputation and his finances to the Greek war of independence against the Turks. You have only to come, people told him, we have only to mention your name, and the Greeks will rally – the factions will be united: 'you will be received as a saviour,' they wrote. 'Be assured, My Lord, that it depends only on yourself to secure the destiny of Greece.' He had written, you see, a sweet verse on the field of Marathon wondering aloud when Greece might again be free, and a group of idealistic Englishmen sent him back with a boatload of money and goodwill and the promise of military assistance, to fulfil his own suspicion (pencilled in at the return end of a discarded *Childe Harold* stanza) that it would be him himself who led Greece to her freedom. And then, at least, if he did die there, he would die a glorious battlefield death. And it would all have been worth something.

Byron, it was observed, was received like a delivering angel at Missolonghi. Even Hobhouse was overcome with a deifying pen when he wrote from London of the whole world and glory and success spilling out from his friend: 'you will have, indeed you have, a very handsome fortune – and if you have your health, I do not see what earthly advantage you can wish for that you have not got. Your present endeavour is certainly the most glorious ever undertaken by man.' This was Byron's time. This was Byron's place. That 'thing beyond poetry' that he had assured Tom Moore he would be capable of, if he could just live another ten years: this had to be it.

By the time Hobhouse's letter reached Missolonghi, Byron was dead. He went riding in the rain, and died of a cold and a muddle of doctoring at Easter, 1824. His physicians, without even a common language between them, attached leeches to him against his wishes and then couldn't stop the bleeding. 'Too close to my temporal artery,' he quipped, 'for my temporal safety.' He was only thirty-six years old.

The woman who embalmed him said he had soft white flesh, like a chicken's. The Greeks, who had touted the idea of crowning Byron king if they won their freedom, suggested that he should be buried on the Athenian Acropolis. In the end, though, his lungs were left in a canister as a keepsake for the people of the

Missolonghi, and the rest of him was put back together after a brutal autopsy (it took two men to tear his skull away from his brain), barrelled up in alcohol and sent back to England.

Hobhouse met the ship as it came up the Thames: he needed three days to work himself up to look at the corpse of his friend. Which he didn't recognise – the hair long and straggly, with unheard-of whiskers and Byron's teeth, of whose whiteness he had always been inordinately proud, stained brown and garish by the preserving fluid. Augusta too, distraught, could hardly find the shape of her brother under the heap of flesh and moustaches. People swam out to the boat to try and see the body (Hobhouse presented the most persistent with snatches of the fabric that had wrapped the corpse), and queued to pay their last respects as Byron lay in state in Great George-street. Tickets were sold to control numbers.

Lady Byron didn't go.

It had fallen to the new, seventh Lord Byron – Byron's cousin, whose alliance with Annabella during the separation he had never forgiven – to tell her that her husband was dead. It was May 14 when the news reached England. She had no right, she said, to be considered in these things, but she did have her feelings, and she would like to hear any reports that came about his last hours. She was happy for Hobhouse to arrange the funeral – and she was happy for Lord Byron's friends to publicise her happiness about this. The coldness of the woman, spat Hobhouse, thinking how her gestures would be perceived by a public, at a time like this. The sixth Lord Byron was buried in the church at Hucknall Torkard, down the road from Newstead

Abbey, on July 16, 1824. His coffin was lowered down into the vault, next to his mother, the church upstairs teeming with so many people that it took five hours to get the quarter-mile-long funeral procession along the road. The vault was not closed until the next morning.

They sent Byron's valet, Fletcher, down to see Lady Byron as soon as he arrived back in the country. He had been with Byron when he died. He had been entrusted with Byron's last words. He brought them to Lady Byron, and 'found her in a fit of passionate grief, but perfectly implacable'.

Lord Byron's deathbed scene. If ever there was a man with confessions to make, propped up on his pillow with the end nigh. If ever there was a man in need of a final religious revelation – although there was a Bible from Augusta next to his bed. (His friends suppressed this piece of information: the world mustn't think that Byron lost his nerve at the last minute.) If ever there was a man with secrets to blast into daylight – Byron had even censored his own diary. 'If I could explain at length the *real* causes which have contributed to this perhaps *natural* temperament of mine, this Melancholy which hath made me its bye-word, nobody would wonder; but this is impossible without doing much mischief. I do not know what other men's lives have been, but I cannot conceive anything more strange than some of the earlier parts of mine. I have written my memoirs, but omitted *all* the really *consequential* and *important* parts, from deference to the dead, to the living, and to those who must be both ...' And then at the critical moment: 'I must not go on with these reflections,' he broke off, 'or I shall be letting out some secret or other to paralyse posterity.' The tantalisingly unsaid thing: but at least he had written his memoirs.

On his deathbed, Byron had called to his valet, Fletcher. There were things, he said, that need to be passed on – messages, important. No time, he snapped, for Fletcher to fetch paper or a pen. He named his wife, his daughter, his sister – said that Fletcher should go to Lady Byron: 'you know all – you must say all – you know my wishes,' and 'tell her everything – you are friends with her.' His voice dropped, and he muttered inaudibly, raising his head to ask Fletcher to be sure and follow his commands faithfully.

My Lord, said Fletcher, I haven't been able to hear a word you've said.

Byron cried: 'Oh my God! Then all is lost, for it is now too late! Can it be possible you have not understood me?'

'No my Lord, but I pray you to try and inform me once more.'

'How can I? It is too late now. It is all over.'

And Annabella heard this story, striding around and around the room, begging Fletcher to try and remember, to try and hear the lost words that her husband had said.

'Go to Lady Byron and tell her –'

She 'walked the room in convulsive struggles to repress her tears and sobs … the gates of eternity were shut in her face, and not a word had passed to tell her if he had repented.'

This is how it is. Always something unsaid, something unclarified, some message that doesn't quite get through. Everyone striving for completion in a muddle of unfinished sentences, unresolved arguments, unclarified moments. They fade. Or they are forgotten completely. Or they are raised up and turned over, combed and combed, spiralling out, growing huge, never closed.

In any case, they had already burnt his memoirs – fast, rash – almost as soon as the news of his death reached London. A group of men in dark suits who had never been a quarter of the distance Byron had surged in his life. His publisher, John Murray. John Cam Hobhouse, his closest friend. Thomas Moore, the fellow poet – the man entrusted with those unrevised slabs of Byron's life laid across sheet after sheet of foolscap. (Show it to anyone, just don't publish it till I'm dead.) His banker. Someone to stand as a representative for his sister as the beneficiary of his will (who had worked, unknown to Augusta, for Annabella's part during the separation). Someone to observe for Annabella. These men stood in judgement over him more definitively than any jury of society hostesses. These men who were supposed to be on his side.

Moore objected: surely this league of honourable gentlemen could just agree to lodge the pages safe with a bank – not this. Not destroy them. Not burn them to nothing but supposition. Hobhouse stood firm: he hadn't read the memoirs but he had it on authority that their erotic episodes made them 'fit only for a brothel' and would 'doom Lord Byron to everlasting infamy if published'. Augusta's representative asserted that Mrs Leigh was adamant that they be burnt for Lady Byron's sake. Lady Byron's representative was certain they were being burnt for Augusta's.

Byron's telling of his own life turned to a little pile

of dusty ashes in the dregs of an unseasonal early summer fire. Kindled up for the purpose. Leaving it open for the rest of the world, for the rest of time, to say what it would of him without his own contradiction or confirmation. The pages of his memoirs – the one copy of his telling of that story that London had wound into the centre of itself – fed into the flames of John Murray's fire on May 17, 1824. Perpetuating all those secrets.

And that should have been the end of it.

You could be forgiven for thinking that this would all have been a weight lifted from Lady Annabella Byron's shoulders – that she would finally let out the retributive breath she had been holding for eight years, step light back into the world, and begin a new life. New gig-lamped moments. New happiness. New vivacity, as she had had in 1812, and in those short months in 1814 when she was certain that marrying Byron was the Right Thing to Do. Instead, she ordered herself a set of widow's weeds, covered herself with their heavy blackness, and was still wearing her widow's cap at the other end of her life. Her long, long life: she had another thirty-six years to live – her husband's lifetime over again. Another thirty-six years assembling and augmenting and fine-tuning the story of that one sliver of time: the fifty-four weeks she spent under the same roof as Lord Byron.

She never got out of the habit taken up in those first months of stamping herself as right to have left him, of bringing people around to her side. She justified it by saying she was concerned about the pernicious influence her husband could have – even dead – on the morality of new generations of readers. As biographies of Byron were published, she would go to great lengths to contradict this statement or that insinuation. Thomas Moore's biography, stating that the memoirs 'afforded no light whatsoever' on the cause of the separation, announced that Annabella's parents turned her against her husband and kept her from returning to him. She wrote her own pamphlet in reply, had it run off by more than one printer so that no one ever knew exactly how many copies there were, and sent it to everyone she could think of. Including the King. Lady Byron, that pillar of veracity, had never sprung to Augusta's defence in print – in fact, through every successive year, she blamed Augusta more and more.

It was Augusta: it always came back to Augusta. Precisely what Lady Byron thought she was guilty of may have changed through the years, but that she was the cause of everything was a given. Towards the end of her life, Lady Byron wrote, melodramatic: 'I look back on the past as a calm spectator, and *at last* can speak of it. I see what was, what *might* have been, had there been one less person among the living when I married.'

In 1816, she remembered much later, she had been told unequivocally by Byron that he was the father of Augusta's fourth child, Medora. But in 1820, she had gazed fondly at that child, 'felt the most tender affection' for her and, wondering why, had gone back to her old home on Piccadilly, gazing into the room 'where I have sat with him'. In 1842, when she had taken Medora into her care and introduced her to Ada and her friends, there was no question that Medora was Byron's daughter. Lady Byron, said Medora, 'informed me of the cause of the deep interest she felt, and must

ever feel, for me. Her husband had been my father ...
I was made to feel that I was to be Ada's sister in all
things,' she continued, 'as I was really.'

'I would save you if it be not too late,' Annabella
wrote to Augusta about Medora's wellbeing, 'from
adding the guilt of her death to that of her birth.'

Augusta replied, somehow naïve, 'I sent Certificates
of her own Baptism ... to disprove [the] assertions.' As
if this one tiny common-sense document would undo
years of Annabella's suspicions – her certainties.
Annabella, with that particular kind of Christian charity,
sent this letter back to Augusta unopened. Their correspondence, she wrote on the outside of the envelope,
she considered closed.

Another long silence. Augusta herself had vowed to
say nothing at all of Annabella, of the whole debacle of
her brother's marriage, for as long as possible. When
Byron was already dead five or more years, she allowed
herself the observation that 'nothing in the whole
world but the welfare of one's children should induce
one, or justify one, in abandoning one's husband.' Lady
Byron, she said, 'may have considered this point, but
she ought to have behaved differently.'

And then their last meeting: Augusta, almost seventy years old, travelling down from London to
Reigate on a train (at Annabella's command: Augusta
had only been on a train once before and was terrified)
for an anonymous interview in an anonymous hotel. It
was April 8, 1851: thirty-five years after Byron had left
England. Thirty-five years after the Deed of Separation
had been signed. Lady Byron wanted Augusta to confess that she had deliberately and maliciously kept up
Byron's hatred of Annabella, and convinced him to stay

away from England rather than encouraging him finally to realise that Annabella had been his best friend, and that he must come to London and to her. She believed, she recited, that 'he *must* have come, had he lived, to the belief that *from first to last*, I had been his only truly devoted friend.' It had come to this.

Annabella sat, waiting for Augusta to admit – again – to ruining her life. Augusta. Whom she had called her truest friend. Whom she had even once feared might be wrongly blamed by an ignorant public for the end of the Byrons' marriage. Whom she had called treacherous within weeks for asking why she would not see Byron, give him another chance. Whom she remembered, ultimate and extreme, as the woman into whose heart she would happily have plunged a dagger. Whom she then blamed for promoting the marriage in the first place – drawing her in, Annabella said in the first years of her separation, with all her encouraging and endorsing letters about her brother. Now, a new charge. By 1851, Annabella believed this infallible: he would have come back to me if his sister hadn't kept in front of his eyes the image of me that he must hate.

Augusta, disoriented, said as much as she had come to say. It knocked Lady Byron back into her chair, and into such a welter of surprise that she had to leave the room. 'Is that all?' she asked, as she left. Is that all?

All Augusta had said was that John Cam Hobhouse had said that she, Augusta, had gone out of her way to support Annabella during the mess of the separation, that she had risked (Hobhouse noted) losing not just Byron's affection, which was most dear to her, but – more vital – being named in his will. She had nothing more to get off her chest. This was unpardonable. Lady Byron refused to come back into the room. Refused to see her again. Refused again to open or read any of the letters Augusta sent.

That triangle of emotions: Byron, his sister, his wife. He had written to Annabella about Augusta from Italy: 'whatever she is or may have been, *you* have never had reason to complain of her − on the contrary − you are not aware of the obligations under which you have been to her. − Her life and mine − and yours and mine were two things perfectly distinct from each other − when one ceased the other began − and now both are closed ... she and two others were the only things I ever really loved,' Lord Byron had told his wife. 'I may say it now,' he wrote at the supremely advanced age of thirty-two, 'for we are young no longer.'

He had asked her to take care of his sister, who would not benefit from his will until after Lady Byron's own death. And Annabella had promised. Annabella had given her word. And ignored it for the most part of her very long life. While Augusta lived on in debt and poverty, finally having to sell even the poems Byron had written to her when he left his wife and England in 1816: *my sister! my sweet sister.* 'Only hard necessity,' she wrote, 'could have induced me to part with them, or indeed any − but these last of all.'

Worse than anything from Byron, Augusta had once presumed − outrageous − to *forgive* Annabella. Forgive her for 'all and everything that has agonised, and I may say all but destroyed me. I can believe,' Augusta had written, 'that you have been actuated throughout by a principle which you thought the right one.' That Augusta Leigh, the most unsaved and sullied soul in the world, should presume to say she *forgave* the righteous Lady Byron. But when Augusta was dying, Annabella asked that 'two words of affection, long-unused', be whispered to her. *Dearest Guss*, whispered Augusta's daughter on Annabella's instruction. Which was said to move Augusta to tears.

Augusta Leigh died in October, 1851 – she had lived thirty-seven years in a world of Lady Byron's neuroses, her obsessions, her bugbears, thirty-seven years in a world where Annabella could denounce her at any moment. It was no wonder she cried.

Annabella adopted black-edged notepaper to mark Augusta's death.

'Did anyone really mourn Mrs Leigh's passing?' asked Byron's daughter, Ada. Surely it was just 'a sad end to a bad life'?

Yes, replied Annabella, 'there *is* one who "personally laments" – Perhaps because "a Byron" cannot be unmourned by me – The World knew not how to deal with them, and if I did not believe in a prolonged being, I should be guilty of the blasphemy of saying God was unjust – why were they not placed under other conditions?'

Ada's own Byronic traits: the drinking, the flirtations, the gambling, the grandiose ideas of her own purpose and destiny. Annabella could and had overlooked these, had side-tracked them with religious questions. Ada was never mad – as Byron had been – and Ada was never publicly humiliated. It must have been one of Annabella's greatest achievements to launch Ada into a world of London society who found her to be 'entirely lacking in paternal sparkle'. The famous portrait of Byron as a suave, swashbuckling hero in his Albanian turban had been bought by Judith Milbanke in the year of her daughter's marriage, and kept hung behind a heavy green velvet curtain. It was a condition of her will that Ada not be allowed to look at it until she was either married or had come of age – and even then, only with Lady Byron's permission. Ada didn't even see the shape of her father's handwriting until she was in her twenties and married herself. This mysterious man.

In 1851, she went to Newstead Abbey herself – stood, melancholy, hearing stories from its new owner, one of Byron's friends from Harrow. She paused for a long time in the bedroom. She felt so strongly, she wrote to her mother, that he might walk in at any moment. 'I do love the venerable old place, and all my *wicked forefathers.*' Lady Byron was apocalyptic: this melancholy, this *empathy* with the Byrons. This was an unforgivable desertion. She unleashed a diatribe on her treacherous daughter. Ada had been among the 'partizans of Byron', who believed – so wrongly, so ignorantly – that his wife had 'taken a hostile position towards him'. Lady Byron drew herself up: 'you must be convinced,' she said, justifying left, right and centre, 'of my repugnance to anything like self-justification.' It was her beatific silence, for which she had paid with her own 'social disadvantage', that allowed the memory of Byron to be exalted to the 'Mythic idea, generally entertained'. She had saved him from 'involving himself in what would have injured his private character and reputation still further. The proofs and witnesses are in existence.' That was what her vendetta came down to – the proofs and witnesses. The black and white definitions of people as for Lady Byron, or against her.

When Ada died, in November 1852, she asked – treachery again – to be buried next to her father. She was, as her father had been, only thirty-six years old.

Lady Byron would have the last word over them all – over Byron, over Medora, over Augusta, over Ada. The spirit of Byron, frequently contacted in those popular Victoria seances, may have lamented what a 'damned hard thing' it was to hear so much being said of your life, unable to contradict it: Annabella took the precaution of assembling reserve troops to carry on her fight. Towards the end of her life, she met Mrs Harriet Beecher Stowe, who came to lunch one day. Beecher Stowe would write – in the future – not only *Uncle Tom's Cabin*, but also *Lady Byron Vindicated*. Publishing incest unmistakable in black and white. 'I will tell you everything,' Lady Byron had said during their pleasant afternoon together in 1856, implying that she had never told anyone else everything – or possibly anything – before. 'She said,' wrote Mrs Stowe, agog with her scoop, 'that he had slept with his sister' and 'that there was a daughter'.

An incendiary device published ten years after Annabella's death, and – coincidentally – just after John Cam Hobhouse's. Which was a shame: it would have been interesting to have seen his response to it all. He was the man who had recorded gossip that 'Lady Byron had said Byron had boasted to her of going to bed with his sister. I implied,' he wrote, 'that if he had, she was more villainous in mentioning it than he in doing it.'

The fragile morality of the times: as someone else said, you had the choice of Lady Byron's word over her husband's – 'why should she be believed rather than Lord Byron? On account of his general "immorality" in the ordinary sense of the term? If so, the word of the average woman must be much more trustworthy than that of the average man. Yet is it? Everybody knows that it is not.'

She left her youngest grandson, Ralph, obliged by her will to take the name Milbanke, to continue the battle. His life was consumed by Lady Byron's story – fighting an elderly Dr Stephen Lushington for access to her papers, and then using them to publish (but only privately, tastefully) books that set out Lady Byron's truth about her own life – the most comprehensive edition appearing as recently as 1921, edited by his own widow. He proved the usefulness of his existence when Virginia Woolf's father, Sir Leslie Stephen, in the hulkingly respectable *Dictionary of National Biography*, slandered his grandmother by suggesting that she'd left Byron for no more reason than offence at his not eating with her, and offence that Augusta inspired sweeter, softer poetry than she did. Ralph bombarded Sir Leslie with protests until, he said, Sir Leslie gave his word as both a scholar and a gentleman to amend the entry. When Sir Leslie, ill, resigned as *DNB* editor – the information uncorrected – Ralph said it was this slander on Lady Byron's good name that had driven him to nervous breakdown. The enormity of mistakenly defaming Lady Byron would, of course, drive one to such a collapse.

Their story ran, as most stories do, on a sine wave. Whenever another book was published, whenever

anyone involved died, it would suddenly be promised
that now – finally – under the terms of this person's
will, or among that person's most personal documents,
the secret at the base of the Byrons' marriage would be
revealed. There was the wonderfully-titled and mostly-
imagined *Only Authentic Edition: The Private Life of
Lord Byron, Comprising his Voluptuous Amours, Secret
Intrigues, and Close Connection with Various Ladies of Rank
and Fame in Scotland and London, at Eton, Harrow,
Cambridge, Paris, Rome, Venice, &c, &c, with Particular
Account of the Countess Guiacolli* [sic]*, and, Never Before
Published, Details of the Murder at Ravenna which Caused
his Lordship to Leave Italy; Various Singular Anecdotes of
Persons and Families of the Highest Circles of Haut Ton;
Compiled from Authentic Sources, with Extracts from
Unburnt Documents and Familiar Letters from his Lordship
to his Friends, being an Amusing and Interesting Expose of
Fashionable Frailties, Follies, Debaucheries, with Numerous
Engravings* – a fabulous invention by an Anglican vicar
in 1836. Its author claimed to have found 'a hand-written note in the gutter' which revealed the secret: 'Lady
Byron told Dr Lushington that Byron committed an
unnatural crime on her.' This in a fantastic book that
also had Byron leaping out of sideboards and rowing
eloping women around the Bay of Naples (where he'd
never been).

The authoress of a *jeu d'esprit* published with the
libretto of that rousing operetta, *Zameo, White Warrior*,
suggested that the answer to the secret was Byron's
'other wife living', and another daughter, Medora
Gordon Byron, who lived off the Strand while Byron
and Annabella lived on Piccadilly. Whom Byron would
visit regularly. And naturally, Lady Byron was upset to

find that her husband preferred sitting next to a smoky fire in a tiny room under the shadow of St Paul's to sitting in the barren opulence of 13 Piccadilly Terrace. Not to mention the whole other wife, other child situation. Another answer. When Annabella's assiduous lawyer, Dr Stephen Lushington, died, newspapers announced breathily that her secret had not died with him, and that an announcement about the evil root of the Byron marriage would be published shortly. But he himself had said once that Lady Byron's 'noble husband … has given cause for a separation which can never be revealed' – and no more revelations came. When John Cam Hobhouse died, leaving private papers which were not to be opened until the 20th century, it was decided categorically that these would contain a copy of Byron's infamous memoirs, and that this would settle the secret question once and for all. But nothing.

One sheet of paper was found among Lady Byron's papers – a draft bill written to compel Byron to sign the Deed of Separation but never filed. The cause: 'unhappy differences'.

And when a box of papers collected by Byron's flamboyant friend Scrope Davies was discovered in one of Lloyd's bank vaults in London only twenty or thirty years ago, then certainly they were going to reveal everything … but the most exciting thing was a disintegrating newspaper clipping from a hundred years before, announcing that Byron wound papers into his hair to create those trademark rich brown curls as he slept: don't let the cat out of the bag, he begged Davies – I'm as vain as a girl of sixteen of my curls.

In the insanity of it all, to establish the one thing that *could* be established, Byron's body was exhumed during a survey of the vault in 1938. There had always been rumours that the Greeks had sent home someone else's body. Not to mention the rumours that Byron was one of the living dead, and probably off sucking blood from the necks of virgins rather than rotting decently where he was supposed to be. All this macabre exercise proved was, in the first case, that the most ridiculous activities were still possible in the name of Lord Byron 114 years after his death and, in the second, that his 'sexual organ showed quite abnormal development'. Which somehow doesn't seem surprising. Strangely, none of the surveying party were perturbed by the fact that his right foot was disconnected from his leg in the bottom of his coffin, or that only his arms and shins were decomposing. The rest of him, the superintending vicar was happy to inform the world, looked very like the portraits painted of him – and most particularly like the memorial plaque erected upstairs in the church itself. You'll see it on the way out.

There's a wonderful trick to secrets. They will always be the worst thing that you can imagine them to be. You will go into the deepest part of yourself, find the most unspeakable darkness there, and assume that this is the hidden thing in somebody else's life, somebody else's marriage. If the worst thing in your world would be to discover that your lover had another wife, it will be that. If the worst thing in your world would be – as it was for Lady Holland discussing the Byrons – finding that Lord Byron had not paid a whole year's rent, it could be that. If the worst thing in your world would be – as it came to be in Byron's story at the end of the 20th century – discovering that he was a paedophile, it would be that. Of course, somebody else's 'worst thing' will also be the last thing another person could conceive of. Virginia Woolf's observation that you can only imagine for someone a life you could have lived yourself bled into the dilemma of horrified biographers in the 1950s and 1960s, who certainly could not entertain a previous theory that Byron had *sodomised* Annabella, that she had enjoyed it and *then* found out the mortal sin it was and left him for fear of her particularly upright and religious friends finding out.

Biography stutters along with this inconceivable, unbearable fact: that there is something we don't know. And the rudeness that the shadowy moments which fall between those gig-lamped highlights, the day-to-day existence, might actually have been more important – have held more answers – than anything that was trumpeted, fanfared or written down by someone somewhere. But what does it matter that someone notices? What does that guarantee? We embroider, not for any malicious or sinister reason, the stories we tell. Just for the sake of a good story. And then we tell it again, harder to step down from the elevated version. Over and again, until the *truth* is the version that we keep repeating and the embellishments are solidified. The partial is rounded up into the whole. Facts, moments, which used to be speculation are presented as absolute. In 1830, one of Byron's letters was published with an omission. By 1974, it was suggested that Byron *might* have written something about an affair with Augusta in the missing words. By 1999, that space had become a solid statement that he left an explicit revelation of incest. And as someone constructs one version, other moments will be found to support it. Byron mentioned, casual, in a conversation in Italy that three women had been visiting with his wife during the first months of their marriage, and that he knew them all to be 'birds of the same nest' – his former amours. Which sent everyone back to search for evidence of such a meeting to prove he had slept with this woman, or not with that one. But was it the morning when Lady Caroline Lamb and her mother-in-law came to call on Annabella and Augusta? Or was it the morning that Annabella met Mary Chaworth-Musters, one of her husband's first loves, in a room with Caroline Lamb and Lady Melbourne? Perhaps it had been a different visit altogether – one that no one had thought worth commenting on at the time.

The secret will morph with each generation, so the story can be told over and over again. By the 1850s, two Victorian women debated whether Byron had tried to kick or to stab his wife – it had to be one of these two things that had driven her away. With a bout of medico-note-taking that Annabella would have approved of, doctors – at the far end of the 20th century – found a new explanation. Byron, manic depressive: look at his mood swings, his lavish spending sprees when he was already up to his neck in debt. Look at the way he decorated his study with skulls, his periods of frenzied promiscuity (those two hundred-plus women he boasted of in eighteen Venetian months alone) which are clearly the result of the heightened sex drive manic depressives experience.

And the *British Medical Journal* – at the same time – announced Byron as anorexic: Professor Arthur Crisp, emeritus professor of psychological medicine at St George's Hospital Medical School, London, believed that Byron not only feared obesity but any weight gain. Byron's letters about his dietary regime are presented: he never gave up his habit of dosing himself with vinegar and laxatives.

Overall, the evidence is now conclusive: 'Lord Byron was a fat child treated badly by his obese mother, and psychiatrists now believe he suffered from eating disorders through his short adult life.' Labels now exist to explain everything all at once, whereas before bad moods and strange eating habits were simply facets of who Byron was.

The generous luxury of his story, though, is that it will adapt to whatever your particular area of interest is. Byron's diet. Byron's sleeping patterns. Byron's poetry. Byron's liaisons with men. Byron's spending habits. Byron's brush with a hippopotamus – serious academic time was devoted, during 1855, to the vexed question of whether the hippopotamus he claimed to see at the Exeter Exchange in 1813 *was* a hippopotamus or – it was hypothesised – a tapir. Byron may have *said* that he saw a hippopotamus, but it was open to debate. And if Byron was not even to be allowed this statement, unquestioned, there was hardly a hope that his statements about his women, his fears, his poetry, his secrets could be taken on trust. The world, like Lady Byron, was never going to be finished with it.

'And what do you make of the Byron-Leigh controversy?' Virginia Woolf had one character ask another in 1921.

'That he had a child by his grandmother,' replied the other – 'very inaccurately,' said Woolf, 'but rather to the point.'

Lady Byron always maintained, of course, that she was motivated by concern about his effect on those new generations of readers, but if she'd put him behind her, then new generations of readers may not have been half so interested in it all. She talked about it to her friends and she talked about it to people she thought were more partial to Byron. She wrote and wrote and wrote. As one of her friends commented, 'her narratives and memoranda were given away right and left. The confidantes who knew her best, her peculiarities, her troubles with her daughter ... thought her mind was touched. Suspicions had become delusions.'

'I am sure,' said another, 'that Lady Byron was a woman of the most honourable and conscientious intentions, but she was subject to a constitutional idiosyncrasy of a most peculiar kind, which rendered her, when under its influence, absolutely and persistently unjust ... in such moments she seemed to take sudden and deep impressions against person and things, which, though the worst might pass away, left a permanent effect.'

While her gallant Dr Lushington gushed, 'if there was a wonderful person in the world, it is Lady Byron: her energy of mind, her bodily exertions, the strength of her affection, the cool decision of her judgement ... I am in boundless admiration of her heart, intellect and governed mind.' She was one of his longest-term and highest-paying clients.

All that time Annabella poured into Byron. The epiphany she had at forty – 'not to see things as they are, then, is my greatest intellectual defect' – she put aside again. The malignancy of her fights with her daughter, her son-in-law, a stream of maids and governesses and tutors. Her immutable standards. The day she told someone that it was a better thing for their daughter to die than to live and be Catholic. And contradictory, against this bitterness, this awfulness, she stood as a philanthropist and mentor for a whole generation of younger women, to whom she wrote inspirational letters and signed herself '*Eve*'. This was Lady Byron proto-feminist, that Annabella who did good big things, all altruism and disinterested motivation. She was interested in mesmerism, in phrenology, in regular bleeding by leeches to keep her constitution healthy. The cycle of over-indulgent feeding that she and her single lady friends kept up was marked down as a sign of sexual frustration: it seems that Annabella never even danced again, let alone kissed another man. Ever.

'Oh! How could you love him?' someone once asked her.

'My dear,' she replied, 'there was an angel in him.'

She always meant to write her autobiography. She began it again and again – myriad versions of her honeymoon, the first weeks of her marriage. It would peter off after that – she always went back to the beginning. Started over. Wondering sometimes if she would ever be able to 'perform the duty of making such a statement without afterwards experiencing all the pangs of conscience'. It was a pleasant thing sometimes – sometimes in the middle distance she saw Byron on the beach at Seaham, scrabbling over the rocks and calling for her to follow him. Or standing, gazing out to the horizon for hours. By the time he had been dead thirty years, these were pleasant things to remember.

Among all the versions that she worked up of that sliver of her life, she would glance in at the truth and then sheer away. That terrible scene when he finally came to see her in November, 1814 – all the farce of two people in a room, completely unsure if they even recognised each other, clumsy, rushing, retreating, falling over furniture. 'Again I lost the Ideal in the Real,' she conceded forty years later: 'the face was less refined, something more complex in the expression – it responded with a kind of reservation. *He* was not as happy as his *letters* ...' And then she could skip ahead to her life after he left: where she went, what she did, how her mother felt: 'it was impossible to make her look upon me but as –'

And another version broke off, unfinished.

She went over and over the marriage – but never back one step further to the decision she had made in August, 1814, a month before she accepted Byron's proposal: 'you do not appear to be the person whom *I* ought to select as my guide, my support, my example on earth with a view still to Immortality.' Or to her original sketch of him from 1812 where she proved to herself that he was unsuitable.

There was, though, one scrap of paper torn off from a larger sheet. On it, in her handwriting, a line from one of her husband's poems: '*I've lived not in vain.*' It had been important enough to register it as she read it, to write it down, and to file it to be catalogued with everything else she had written and thought and wondered and copied and bought and taken back and *saved*.

This sliver had, somehow, to be taken into account with the screeds of paper she kept: *I've lived not in vain.*

The night swung from May 15 to May 16, 1860. Lady Annabella Byron was a day shy of her sixty-eighth birthday, in that quiet part of night where time always seems to run differently. That last night, maybe she thought about all this. All that her life had been. All that she had thought once it might be. That God, that soul, that Duty, that had directed everything. Or perhaps she remembered that Byron had told her, in bed the night before she met Augusta, that she made him happy. Or that she had done things, after him, that were nothing to do with his life or his legacy. Opened schools. Campaigned for the end of slavery. Called for prison reform. Sponsored preachers and missionaries. Or that she still saw that empty desert of time and space running away from her feet. Without him. Always without him.

Lady Byron's life — letters, papers, journals, notes, memoirs, essays and depositions: it sits now in a series of boxes and folders and envelopes deposited at the Bodleian Library at the University of Oxford. Sorted into 460 buff-coloured boxes, strong, durable cardboard but shaped low, flat and rectangular. They should hold lingerie — a piece of silk scarf, or a camisole. But instead there are diaries, crumbling spines tied together with grubby white archive tape. Newspaper clippings that feel like chalk. Byron's handwriting — fast — and Lady Byron's more precise, and so much more plentiful with all the copies she made of her own letters and other people's. Augusta Leigh's letters, even more flourishes than Byron's. Letters from Annabella's parents, friends, confidantes, acquaintances, advisers.

From Lady Caroline Lamb, running on into fourteen, sixteen pages each.

A mess of moments: shake them through the sieve of the story you want to tell. Sift out the shape of Annabella Milbanke, the young woman who loved Lord Byron's soul, who married him, who realised – for whatever reason – that this was an insupportable thing to do. Who left him. And who hardened into someone obsessed, someone consumed, with that one decision, that one action. All the rest of her life. Through years and years, she never managed to shake herself free from the moment of marrying him. She was Lady Byron. It defined her.

The way a letter was folded into a sheet of foolscap before the modernity of envelopes: a restrained sort of origami. Refold the letters back into their unopened rectangles, recreate the form of Byron, of Lady Byron, of everyone who was involved in their marriage. Give them a chance to undo, or avoid, the mess.

Filed carefully: a note about the contents of the first drawer of her davenport. 'Consists of packets of letters to be sent according to directions,' she jotted down, 'or burnt at my death.' Who knew how much truth was lost – or how much there had been in the first place.

It came, then, at that still part of the morning, before dawn, when it is possible to imagine anything in the world. Her grand-daughter, also called Annabella, and one of her trusty harem of attendant women-friends, were with her: a sculptor would come and take a cast of her hand the day after she died, to add to the memento mori she left. She had had trouble breathing for some days – despite leeches and cupping and bleed-ing. Prosaic, she succumbed to bronchitis and pleurisy.

At four in the morning of May 16, 1860, Lady Annabella Byron died.

No one bothered to record her last words.

'When shall we three meet again?'
      'In heaven, I trust.'

References

page 1
'The least word BLJ, 13.11.1814.
'In heaven LP 131, fol. 144.
page 2
an agony Brent (1974), p. 112.

The Beginning page 3
'The sun may Paston and Quennel (1939), p. 79.
page 5
'I can truly say LP 29, 9.2.1812.
The London 'season' Pool (1993), p. 53.
page 6
There was hardly Byron (1809), p. 48.
young ladies had Pool (1993), p. 51.
'Your Annabella Ogilvy (1921), p. 136.
page 7
Went to a ball Elwin (1962), p. 116.
'twenty guineas LP 29, 8.3.1812.
page 8
'I am quite LP 29, fol. 86, 9-10.4.1812.
page 9
Annabella, taken LP 117–118, Journal 29.3.1812.
'too kind-hearted Elwin (1962), p. 105.
baa-ing and bleating Strickland (1974), p. 69.
'when she was silly Elwin (1962), p. 104.
page 10
'no one will LP 29, 15.3.1812.
her cousins could LP 29, 15.4.1812.
'the turns taken Hobhouse (1909–1911), vol. i, p. 100.
Oh! Many a time Childe Harold's Pilgrimage, I: 82, 92.
page 11
Caroline begged him Manchester (1992), p. 64.
he had presented Eisler (1999), p. 342.
'mad, bad and Cecil (1954), p. 126.
'many passages in LP 117–118, 24.3.1812.
page 12
a morning party Jenkins (1972), p. 59.
club-footed climb Eisler (1999), p. 341.

page 13
eyes whose gaze Lovelace (1921), p. 16.
his valet couldn't Low (1977), p. 98.
their fabric so Eisler (1999), p. 314.
could not dance ibid, p. 343.
page 14
'violence of his LP 117–118 and LP 29, 25.3.1812.
page 15
the knowledeagble age Basham (1992), p. 4.
leave a party LP 29, 26.3.1812.
page 16
'What is to become Elwin (1962), p. 86.
'would rather not LP 29, 16.7.1810.
... Reforming Byron Soderholm (1996), pp. 74–75.
'I cannot worship Elwin (1962), p. 106.

page 19 This Life
'[Byron] says himself Page (ed.) (1985), p. 13.
page 20
When he was announced Grosskurth (1997), p. 19.
Chubby, he sparred Moore (1878), p. 417.
page 21
souvenired so many Paston and Quennell (1939), p. xi.
'an ague and Eisenberg (1987), p. 16.
1st At twenty -three Grosskurth (1997), pp. 126–127.
page 22
style of life Murray (1998), p. 22.
He arrived in Manchester (1992), p. 60.
page 23
It was estimated Grosskurth (1997), p. 151.
The street in Cecil (1954), p. 124.
page 24
'In short, Duchess of Devonshire in Christiansen (1994), p. 192.
'the fact is Byroniana, pp. 83–84.
it was fashionable Murray (1998), p. 20.
'men about town Trelawny (1973), pp. 78, 87.
'I could not Ogilvy (1921), p. 131.
page 25
while she would LP 29, 26.3.1812.

page 27 The Season
'Indeed I rather BLJ, 1.12.1822.
'met with much Elwin (1962), p. 109.
page 28
'without exception of ibid.
'angelic – or demon-like Foot (1998), p. 74.
page 29
'wants the calm LP 29, 15.4.1812.

References

Love comes on   Wilson (1929), p. 592.
page 30
he nominated Caleb   Elwin (1962), p. 110.
Lord Byron making   Duchess of Devonshire, 4.5.1812,
   in Elwin (1962), p. 115.
page 31
'I consider it   LP 29, 26.4.1812.
The truth, she held   Jenkins (1972), p. 22.
she thought most   Cecil (1954), p. 87.
carried into dinner   Bruce (1953), p. 296.
not her admirers   Blyth (1972), p. 236.
page 32
As the Prince Regent   Ogilvy (1921), p. 131.
'once you told   Eisler (1999), p. 351.
page 33
'nothing criminal   Cecil (1954), p. 128.
she had been assured   LP 131, fol. 131.
page 34
a little practice   Elwin (1962), p. 112.
'exert my eloquence   LP 29, 29.4.1812.

The 1812 Overture   page 35
'I have no   BLJ, 25.9.1812.
'undeceived her by   LP 117–118, 2.5.1812.
page 36
Annabella's over-arching   Elwin (1962), p. 114.
page 37
'propensity towards coquetry   LP 117–118, 16.6.1812.
page 38
'When I returned   Elwin (1962), p. 216.
she saw him flinch   ibid, p. 116.
'You know how   LP 29, 13.4.1812.
page 39
If she had stayed   LP 359, [June 1814].
to be clipped   Manchester (1992), p. 80.
page 40
'It is true   BLJ, 10.9.1812.
page 41
'There was and is   ibid, 13.9.1812.
'but you are   ibid, 18.9.1812.
'she deserves a   ibid, Sept. 1812.
'At this moment   ibid, 28.9.1812.
page 42
life isn't a   Woolf (1984), p. 35.
page 43
music – he could not   Elwin (1962), p. 105.
She had no love   ibid, p. 88.

page 44
As Annabella herself ibid, p. 189.
one gentleman was ibid, p. 103.
'an oration on LP 29, 9.4.1812.
a point of inviting ibid, 13.4.1812.
page 45
Passions, she wrote Elwin (1962), p. 119.
page 46
She excused herself ibid, p. 153.
fine lady's companion Medwin (1824), p. 36.
with 'consistent principles Elwin (1962), p. 156.
page 47
'a man possessed ibid, p. 157.
They appear to me ibid, p. 152.
And that, said BLJ, 24.10.1812.

Absence and the Heart page 49
'I congratulate BLJ, 14.11.1812.
one of her beaux Elwin (1962), p. 488.
page 50
the most 'probable LP 29, 1.5.1813.
page 51
who burnt him Soderholm (1996), p. 52.
bit through glasses Cecil (1954), p. 130.
page 52
'very happy to BLJ, 12.2.1813.
She did, one Elwin (1962), pp. 161–162.
he was accused of ibid, p. 164.
page 53
petty-sounding evasion Murray (1998), pp. 255–256.
page 54
'unreserved friendship Elwin (1962), pp. 166–167.
page 55
ended up stored in Paston and Quennell (1939), p. ix.
surprising amount of emotion BLJ, 1.5.1812.
'You will not reject Elwin (1962), p. 167.
'I must be candid BLJ, 25.8.1813.
page 56
impulse of ill-judged Elwin (1962), p. 168.
'I perceive that BLJ, 31.8.1813.
'act then towards Elwin (1962), p. 169.
page 58
'She seems to have BLJ, 5.9.1813.
yes, he would ibid, 22.8.1813.
he was passing Eisler (1999), p. 418.
'the great object BLJ, 6.9.1813.
page 59
'"As your friend Elwin (1962), p. 170.

References

'*My dear friend* BLJ, 26.9.1813.
page 60
'*If you are fatigued* Elwin (1962), p. 173.
It ran through six Page (1988), p. 31.
page 61
Byron's descriptions Elwin (1962), p. 174.
So she is melancholy BLJ, 8.10.1813.
'*ceased on both sides* ibid, 23.10.1813.
page 62
'*I am not exacting* Elwin (1962), p. 175.
he even declared BLJ, 10.11.1813.
She wondered whether Elwin (1962), p. 176.
page 63
'*You wrong yourself* BLJ, 29.11.1813.
page 64
She is a very ibid, 30.11.1813.
And he confessed ibid, 6.2.1814.
he originally thought Gunn (1968), p. 98.
Five editions Page (1988), p. 33.
It sold, unprecedented Smiles (1911), p. 91.
'*I was more pleased* Franklin (1992), p. 15.
page 65
'*You have thought* Elwin (1962), p. 186.
'*There is one sentence* BLJ, 12.2.1814.
page 66
'*pray take care* ibid, 15.2.1814.
'*I will comment* Elwin (1962), p. 188.
That interest, he assured BLJ, 19.2.1814.
page 67
it was hardly fair Elwin (1962), p. 189.
she could not seek ibid.
Byron was back to BLJ, 3.3.1814.
page 68
there was 'something ibid, 27.2.1814.
'*I still hope the best* Elwin (1962), p. 190.
'*A letter from* Bella BLJ, 15.3.1814.
'*You do not know* ibid, 15.3.1814.
page 69
I have been prevented Elwin (1962), p. 191.
This, said Byron, laying BLJ, 20.4.1814.
page 70
I wish to see you Elwin (1962), p. 193.
You tell me what BLJ, 29.4.1814.
'*My heart* ibid, 30.4.1814.
page 71
'*Pray write* Elwin (1962), p. 197.
He signed himself BLJ, 21.6.1814.
Last year, she thought Elwin (1962), p. 198.

before they met ibid, p. 200.
page 72
(published with Page (1988), p. 36.
'Write to me BLJ, 1.8.1814.
she still only wanted Elwin (1962), p. 202.
page 73
'I did – do BLJ, 10.8.1814.
because 'a comparative view Elwin (1962), p. 203.
page 74
He bounced BLJ, 16.8.1814.
Lord Byron, clearly ibid, 9.9.1814.
page 75
'a very pretty Gunn (1968), p. 111.
page 76
She wrote one Elwin (1962), p. 208.
He looked up Gunn (1968), p. 112.
page 77
'Your letter,' BLJ, 18.9.1814.
To Lady Melbourne ibid, 18.9.1814.
And then on Monday ibid, 19.9.1814.
'my third letter ibid, 20.9.1814.

November 2, 1814   page 79
'There could not Moore (1878), p. 412.
So wonderful Lady Granville, in Basham (1992), p. 11.
page 80
I always thought Elwin (1962), p. 216.
'all our relatives to Countess of Jersey, 5.10.1814, in Jeaffreson (1883), p. 282.
confidence 'built on Selina Doyle, 24.9.1814, in Elwin (1962), p. 218.
'I know you Emily Milner, 2.10.1814, in Elwin (1962), p. 219.
Lady Caroline Lamb wrote Low (1977), p. 103.
page 81
Augusta confessed Elwin (1962), p. 221.
'I received a letter ibid.
'It gives me much BLJ, 7.10.1814.
page 82
Annabella began, overwhelming Elwin (1962), p. 212.
who later commented, Hobhouse's journal, 26.4.1816, in LP 251.
page 83
the first time he had BLJ, 26.9.1814.
'my good and evil ibid.
page 84
'If you were here Elwin (1962), p. 224.
'I never like ibid, p. 225.
'calm,' she felt LP 390, Narrative Q.
'the character of BLJ, 17.10.1814.
page 85
'coarser, more sullied Elwin (1962), p. 228.

'hardly articulate   ibid, pp. 227–228.
She waited 'till   ibid, p. 228.
page 86
'Seriously, if she imagines   BLJ, 29.4.1814.
Like Byron telling   ibid, 4.11.1814.
Like Annabella declaring   Elwin (1962), p. 178.
page 87
his discovery that   BLJ, 13.11.1814.
Her passions,   ibid, 6.11.1814.
'Do you know   ibid, 13.11.1814.
page 88
He fell back   LP 131, fol. 132.
She thought: I am sure   Stowe (1870), p. 157.
To be together   BLJ, 23.12.1814.
page 89
Annabella was, she wrote   Elwin (1962), p. 233.
'to yourself   BLJ, 20.11.1814.
'I wish for you   Elwin (1962), p. 237.
page 90
'try to be ready   BLJ, 5.12.1814.
they might 'love   ibid.
'I have learned   Elwin (1962), p. 237.
'With regard to   BLJ, 23.12.1814.
Lord Byron stood   Marchand (1957), vol. ii, p. 497.
to write, famously   Grosskurth (1997), p. 219.
Hobhouse admired her   Hobhouse (1909), vol i, p. 192.
page 91
Hobhouse, usually prosaic   ibid, p. 193.
Nor in his mistakenly   Lovell (1966), p. 34.
if she was not happy   Marchand (1957), vol. ii, pp. 505–506.

Marriage   page 93
'Good breeding demanded   Murray (1998), p. 231.
page 94
stick is not thicker   Laudermilk and Hamlin (1989), p. 89.
sold by him   Kalyanavaca (ed.) (1997), p. 113.
page 95
He turned to her   Medwin (1966), p. 37.
she arrived at Halnaby   Elwin (1962), p. 250.
In one version   Austin (1869), p. 6.
And another maid   Elwin (1962), p. 251.
Lord Byron had Lady   Moore (1961), p. 28.
page 96
Or Lord Byron   The Life, Writings, Opinions and Times... (1825), p. 278.
'Good God   Grosskurth (1997), p. 221; Moore (1961), p. 55.
page 97
as much a fiend   LP 131, fol. 58.
he had two natural   ibid, fol. 5.

page 98
I am a fallen   LP 129, fol. 2, 2.1.1816.
'Nobody understands me   Gunn (1968), p. 124.
page 99
guilty of murder   LP 131, fol. 53.
Byron wrote happily   BLJ, 10.1.1815.
'I think you now   LP 331, fol. L.
page 100
'I have quite enough   BLJ, 2.2.1815.
Annabella to play   Soderholm (1996), p. 96.
page 101
in bed, Lord Byron   LP 390, Narrative R.
page 103
'made yourself   Elwin (1962), p. 266.
Annabella caught   ibid, p. 292.
this Lady Byron   Gunn (1968), pp. 130–131.
page 104
As long as you   Elwin (1962), p. 264.
page 105
'I have never mixed   Mayne (1929), p. 143.
a complete blank   Page (1988), p. 41.
'and he was kind   LP 390, Narrative S.
fool to invite   Elwin (1962), p. 302.
page 106
'Dearest, now that   BLJ, 15.4.1815.
'Lord and Lady Byron   Gunn (1968), p. 137.
Lady Byron walked   Mayne (1929), p. 185.
page 107
an American visitor   Elwin (1962), p. 305.
page 108
'She walks in beauty   Coote (1988), p. 67; Nathan (1829), p. 2.
page 109
Augusta who defended   Gunn (1968), p. 139.
She thought, one night   Elwin (1962), p. 303.
Yet 'as soon as   Prothero (1899–1901), vol. i, p. 210.
page 110
'very flat indeed   LP 29, 31.8.1815.
'perfectly ferocious   Elwin (1962), p. 317.
page 111
'yrs always most   BLJ, 1.9.1815.
Annabella sat reading   Pierson (1992), p. 85.
sure he heard   Mayne (1929), p. 190.
page 112
Byron shouted   LP 129, fol. 9.
page 113
'the idea of Bailiffs   Elwin (1962), p. 320.
page 114
'great anxiety   ibid, p. 319.

References

Things, Hobhouse wrote Hobhouse's journal, 25.11.1815, in LP 251.
page 115
'Lord Byron wished LP 129, fol. 55.
'ennui of a monotonous Gunn (1968), p. 139.
his sense of religion Elwin (1962), pp. 322–323.
page 116
'all inexorable pride Gunn (1968), p. 140.
wanted a wife who Elwin (1962), p. 332.
page 117
'will you still Gunn (1968), p. 159.
On December 9, Elwin (1962), p. 336.
Mrs Clermont told LP 251.
Of course he would Grosskurth (1997), p. 240.
page 118
publisher had no idea Burton and Murdoch (1974), p. 67.
Annabella didn't know BLJ, 2.1.1816.
page 119
Lady Byron chattered Elwin (1962), p. 345.
an enquiry was Scull, MacKenzie and Hervey (1996), pp. 30, 33.
page 120
bottle of laudanum Coote (1988), p. 71.
her husband's own Hobhouse (1870), p. 71.
No, no ibid, p. 71.
his 'principal insane LP 129, Statement for Dr Baillie, fol. 3, 8.1.1816.
page 121
Lord Byron's agitated Eisler (1999), pp. 478–479.
he sent a note BLJ, 6.1.1816.
page 122
Coming down Mayne (1929), p. 202.
page 123
sweeping out past LP 129, fol. 30.

Constructing Separation page 125
'There is no reason BLJ, 26.2.1816.
page 127
'Dearest Duck Hobhouse (1870), p. 55.
'it would be most Elwin (1962), p. 355.
page 128
The same woman who Hobhouse (1870), p. 72.
Byron, she recalled Prothero (1899–1901), vol. iii, pp. 295–296.
Annabella wrote pages LP 129, Statement given to my mother,
    fols. 7–12 incl., 18–19.1.1816.
page 129
My husband said Elwin (1962), p. 341.
insanity hidden skeletal ibid, p. 252.
page 130
Annabella is a good to John Murray, in Gunn (1968), p. 151.

page 131
Leaving London,   Elwin (1962), p. 350.
page 132
divorces would still   Thompson (ed.) (1990), vol. ii, p. 30, and vol. iii, p. 267.
A full divorce   Pool (1993), p. 185.
page 133
'she will break   Elwin (1962), p. 364.
Hobhouse, Annabella now   to Lushington, 11.2.1816, in LP 88, fol. 14.
page 134
sit for a portrait   Augusta to Annabella, 19.1.1816, in Gunn (1968), p. 155.
'I must never   Elwin (1962), p. 362.
'loves me distractedly   ibid, p. 365.
'that unremitting principle   ibid, p. 366.
'I would willingly   LP 30, fol. 1.
her mother counselled   Elwin (1962), p. 373.
page 135
'By the bye   ibid, p. 369.
'Poor thing!   ibid, p. 370.
for him is best   LP 30, 22.1.1816.
'the truest of friends   ibid, 27.1.1816.
page 136
'I being in a   ibid, 24.1.1816.
page 137
people already said   Elwin (1962), pp. 373, 404.
page 138
Under the circumstances   ibid, p. 379.
page 139
'For once in my   Gunn (1968), pp. 160–161.
page 140
'cruel and wicked   Elwin (1962), pp. 385–386.
page 141
'under the persuasion   ibid, pp. 408–409.

The Secret   page 143
'I have often   Gardiner (1969), p. 160.
'Happiness,' she wrote   Marchand (1957), vol. ii, p. 578.
page 144
He had, for all   Mayne (1924), p. 221.
'brought before a   Ogilvy (1921), p. 166.
an affair with   Elwin (1962), p. 387.
page 145
He confessed, finally   Hobhouse's journal, 12.2.1816, in LP 251.
'There are reports   Gunn (1968), pp. 170–171.
page 147
Hobhouse amazedly heard   Hobhouse's journal, 29.2.1816, in LP 251.
'unnatural crime, incest   Elwin (1962), p. 433.
dinner party at Holland   Mrs Villiers to Lady Byron, 18.5.1816,
    in Lovelace (1921), p. 34.

References

page 148
'which will probably   BLJ, 19.2.1814.
'that perverse passion   ibid, 25.11.1813.
'my sister, who   ibid, 5.8.1813.
Any affair,   ibid, 11.10.1813.
'your A   ibid, 30.4.1814.
page 149
'I should be not   ibid, 18.4.1814.
'in a state   Elwin (1962), p. 293.
Modest, in shorthand   LP 390, Narrative R.
'It was his pleasure   Elwin (1962), p. 295.
'I was sensible   ibid.
page 150
Byron sitting up   Gunn (1968), p. 129.
'be altogether most   LP 30, 28.2.1816.
'mitigate the violence   Elwin (1962), p. 441.
'Oh but it is   BLJ, 25.4.1814.
page 151
'accustom'd themselves   Grosskurth (1997), p. 196.
Friends confronted   Elwin (1962), p. 330.
stayed 'long   ibid, p. 438.
Otherwise he might   Marchand (1957), vol. ii, p. 590.
page 152
'wicked and dishonourable   in first unpublished draft of Lovelace,
    cited by Elwin (1962), p. 419.
'the lady in   Lovelace (1921), p. 36, note.
every vile suspicion   Elwin (1962), p. 456.
page 153
'Lady Byron's fate   Fleming (1998), p. 11.
'strong impression   LP 88, fol. 54, 27.3.1816.
page 154
'If I did not   BLJ, 4.3.1816.
'lived on conjugal   LP 251, fol. 29.
page 155
but had they not   Hobhouse (1870), p. 98.
'I wish you would   BLJ, 4.3.1816.
She passed them all   Elwin (1962), p. 400.
'There are reports   BLJ, 25.3.1816.
page 156
Lady Byron, he wrote   Hobhouse (1870), p. 10.
'I was thought   Gardiner (1969), p. 161.
page 157
'I made no secret   Lord Byron in Hobhouse (1870), pp. 97–98.
'There are not 20   LP 88, fol. 105, 13.4.1816.
'for the purpose   ibid, fol. 114, 6.5.1816.

The Desert page 159
'Remember that I   BLJ, 21.8.1817.

could see a desert   LP 131, fol. 169.
It was a dismal   Rudolf (1984), vol. incl.
'positively reduced   Lovelace (1921), p. 57.
page 160
Was it possible   Mayne (1937), p. 209.
'And tell me   Paston and Quennell (1939), p. 70.
But, I do think   Hodge (1996), p. 62.
page 161
'Caroline Lamb   BLJ, 20.1.1817.
'the hideous calumnies   Lytton (1913), p. 121.
Her room was found   Blyth (1972), p. 230.
(practised in the   Hedley (1975), pp. 265–266.
'A very judicious   LP 80, fol. 38, 18.5.1816.
page 162
'I do not know   ibid, fol. 42, 23.5.1816.
'circumstances in your   ibid, fol. 79, 3.6.1816.
page 163
'all ambiguity of   Gunn (1968), p. 188.
'I have never   LP 80, fol. 50, 27.3.1816.
page 164
'Really you must   Gunn (1968), p. 189.
page 165
'Did you tell her   ibid, p. 190.
'of course does not   LP 114, fol. 47, 15.6.1816.
'obligations' –   LP 80, fol. 87, 30.6.1816.
'the appearance of   Gunn (1968), p. 191.
page 166
'Her eyes seem   Elwin (1975), p. 60.
I think I am justified   Lovelace (1921), pp. 227–228.
'Perhaps with you   LP 80, fol. 101, 17.7.1816.
page 167
she had never seen   ibid, 24.7.1816.
'on the very brink   Elwin (1975), p. 117.
'The step you   Col. Doyle, 9.7.1817, ibid, p. 61.
page 168
'Guardian Angel   ibid, p. 67.
'rectify instead   LP 80, fol. 115, 30.7.1816.
'levity and nonsense   Elwin (1975), p. 76.
page 169
'from seeing things   LP 80, fol. 114, 30.7.1816.
'I do not quite   ibid, fol. 122, 7.8.1816.
'unload her stomach   Moore (1977), p. 15.
In these meetings   Gunn (1968), p. 192.
page 170
And Augusta's letter   Elwin (1975), p. 83.
'requires more than   ibid, p. 93.
Augusta Leigh had placed   ibid, p. 87.
an unimpeachable source   ibid.

References

page 172
'when I write   ibid, p. 90.
'acted the part   LP 80, 12.9.1816.
'not a letter   Elwin (1975), p. 89.
'they are absolute   LP 114, fol. 121.
page 173
'And so,'   BLJ, 8.9.1816.
'I think all these   ibid, 27.8.1816.
never corresponded *with*   Elwin (1975), p. 104.
landing at Ostend   Polidori (1911), p. 32.
page 174
'Lord help me   BLJ, 8.9.1816.
Then she heard that   Elwin (1975), p. 90.
'league of incest   BLJ, 15.5.1819. Price quoted as £700 and £800
   for Claire and Mary respectively by Hodge (1996), p. 156.
page 175
at least 'the scream   MacDonald (1991), p. 100.
a dangerous and   Coote (1988), p. 105.
gossip-hungry   Christiansen (1994), p. 196.
'borne treatment   Joanna Baillie in Elwin (1975), p. 136.
page 176
For thee, my   Epistle to Augusta, XV1, i–iv.
this familial fondness   Elwin (1975), p. 123.
Augusta herself requested   ibid, p. 84.
page 177
'thank Heaven above   BLJ, 18.12.1816.
'you will see   ibid, 28.2.1817.
page 178
Ada! Sole   Childe Harold's Pilgrimage, III, i.
those ones signed   BLJ, 28.10.1816; 15.10.1816; 27.8.1816.
'It is a very   Normington (1995), p. 97.
'my whole hope   BLJ, 1.10.1816.
page 179
'I think it would be   ibid.
'before God   ibid, 1.11.1816.
page 180
'an explicit answer   ibid, 26.12.1816.
'what I can and   ibid, 2.1.1817.
'They will end   ibid, 13.1.1817.
'To deprive me   ibid, 5.3.1817.
page 181
'taking power   Elwin (1975), p. 132.
'if not by your   BLJ, 5.3.1817.
page 182
'I forgive everything   ibid, 25.3.1817.
'I request that   ibid, 25.3.1817.
'Give me but   ibid, 10.5.1817.

page 183
'arrived at an age   Stein (1985), p. 18.
page 184
'my portrait may   Elwin (1975), p. 133.
flatly that she objected   ibid, p. 168.
'not so much for   Stein (1985), p. 22.
page 185
Infancy, she noted   Mayne (1929), p. 291.
'war whoops worse   Moore (1977), p. 8.
'seldom voluntarily   Elwin (1975), p. 218.
'Ada loves me   Strickland (1974), p. 86.
page 186
'delusion might tempt   Gunn (1968), p. 206.
'Ada's intellect is   Elwin (1975), p. 180.
'I am sick   Mayne (1929), p. 281.
'I have received   BLJ, 3-4.6.1817.
'I repeat to you   BLJ, 19.6.1817.
page 187
'It has been intimated   ibid, 9.8.1817.
page 188
'I call upon   ibid.
'it will gratify   Grosskurth (1997), p. 316.
part of political   Chapman (1975), p. 213.
Incest was almost   Murray (1998), p. 6.
Hobhouse – who could   Nicolson (1948), p. 21.
page 189
'a blight in the   LP 250, fol. 30, 27.10.1817.

That Life   page 191
... Now I'll put out   BLJ, 8.1.1818.
page 192
Lord Byron has given   The Day and New Times, 23.6.1818,
   in Gunn (1968), p. 205.
Sometimes it seemed   McDayter, in Cardwell (ed.) (1997), from p. 127.
If he stayed away   BLJ, 20.1.1817.
'If the bitch   ibid, 26.1.1819.
'His Royal Highness's   Mayne (1929), pp. 279–280.
page 193
she received invitations   Elwin (1975), pp. 3, 177;
   Moore (1961), pp. 149–150.
'passion for women   BLJ, 8.8.1818.
'fathers and mothers   Page (1988), p. 59.
'enormously fat   Elwin (1975), pp. 176–177.
page 194
'circumstances under   Burnett (1981), p. 103.
page 195
'tired of promiscuous   BLJ, 6.4.1819.
Goethe thought   Frayling (1991), p. 6.

References

'*Damn* The Vampyre   BLJ, 24.4.1819.
drank the blood   Frayling (1991), p. 6.
I have a personal   *The Life, Writings, Opinions and Times...* (1825), p. 221.
page 196
'*I tumbled into*   BLJ, 18.5.1819.
'*dearest love*   ibid, 17.5.1819.
page 197
(perhaps that   Gribble (1910); Moore (1905), vol. incl.
'*he is surely*   Elwin (1975), pp. 183–184.
'*repressed and oppressed*   Gunn (1968), p. 207.
page 198
'*a well known*   Elwin (1975), p. 184.
She made a copy   ibid.
'*I am at too*   BLJ, 26.7.1819.
page 199
Rome believed he   Origo (1962), p. 99.
Byron's version   Eisler (1999), p. 612.
made it the eleventh   BLJ, 29.10.1819.
'*Confess it*   ibid, 26.10.1819.
page 200
'*and mark what*   ibid, 31.12.1819.
page 201
'*If, as I have*   LP 40, fol. 122.
'*You will smile*   ibid, fol. 88, 20.7.1819.
page 202
dismissed as ridiculous   BLJ, 28.10.1816.
'*It can scarcely*   Gunn (1968), p. 209.
page 204
post for him   Origo (1962), pp. 165–167.
'*by way of*   ibid, p. 165.

The Dictionary of National Biography   page 207
'*It is a fact*   Lovelace (1921), p. 119.
page 208
there were more   Goode (1997) vol. incl.
page 209
'*you will be received*   Nicolson (1948), p. 170; Grosskurth (1997), p. 443.
a sweet verse   Don Juan, III.
(pencilled in at   Eisler (1999), p. 228.
page 210
received like a delivering   Pietro da Gamba to
    Countess Teresa Guiccioli, 8.1.1824, in Origo (1962), p. 437.
'*you will have*   Grosskurth (1997), p. 468.
'*Too close to*   Murray (1824), p. 11.
The woman who embalmed   Marchand (1957), vol. iii, p. 1232.
crowning Byron   Blackstone (1975), p. ix.
page 211
(it took two men   Medwin (1824), p. 519.

Augusta too, distraught   Hodgson (1878), pp. 147–148.
The coldness   Hobhouse (1909–1911), vol. iii, p. 53.
page 212
'found her in   Grosskurth (1997), p. 474.
the world mustn't   Hobhouse (1909-1911), vol. iii, p. 38.
'If I could explain   Detached Thoughts, 74, 76,
     from Quennell (ed.) (1990), p. 637.
page 213
On his deathbed   Maurois (1963), p. 423.
His voice dropped   Normington (1995), p. 133.
'walked the room   Stowe (1870), p. 299.
page 214
'fit only for   Gay (1993), vol. iii, p. 95.
Augusta's representative   Lovelace (1921), p. 11.
page 215
still wearing her   Pierson (1992), p. 294.
page 216
'afforded no light   Moore, in *Daily News*, 28.9.1869, in *Miscellaneous
     Collection of Newspaper Cuttings Relating to Lord Byron*, vol. ii.
She wrote her own   Moore (1961), p. 312.
Towards the end of   Lovelace (1921), p. 140.
in 1820, she   Mayne (1929), p. 303.
'informed me of   Mackay (1870), p. 33.
page 217
'I would save   LP 84, fols. 135–136, 20.1.1841.
'I sent Certificates   ibid, fol. 144.
'nothing in the whole   Hodgson (1878), p. 202.
page 218
'he must have   Elwin (1975), p. 7.
plunged a dagger   LP 131, fol. 97.
By 1851, Annabella   Normington (1995), p. 175.
'Is that all?   Gunn (1968), p. 262.
page 219
'whatever she is   BLJ, 28.10.1820.
'Only hard necessity   Briscoe (1924), p. 227.
'all and everything   Gunn (1968), p. 234.
page 220
'Did anyone really   LP 43, fol. 240, 15.10.1851.
Yes, replied Annabella   LP 58 fol. 217, 16.10.1851.
page 221
'entirely lacking in   Normington (1995), p. 143.
The famous portrait   Medwin's *Conversations*, in Gardiner (1969), p. 218.
'I do love the   LP 43, fol. 125, 15.9.1850.
'partizans of Byron   LP 58, fol. 23, 17.9.1850.
page 222
The spirit of Byron   Quevedo Redivivus, *A Spiritual Interview
     with Lord Byron*, in Moore (1961), epigraph.
'I will tell you everything   Stowe (1870), p. 162.

References

'Lady Byron had said Normington (1995), p. 95.

page 223

'why should she Austin (1869), p. 4.

obliged by her will Stein (1985), p. 207.

slander on Lady Pierson (1992), p. 325.

page 224

'a hand-written Mitford (1836), p. 103.

Zameo, White Warrior Byron (1834), pp. v–x.

page 225

When Annabella's assiduous Standard, 20.3.1873, in *Miscellaneous Collection of Newspaper Cuttings relating to Lord Byron, vol. ii.*

'noble husband Moore (1974), p. 454; Vogelsberger (1987), p. 28.

no more revelations Blyth (1972), p. 187.

One sheet of paper Elwin (1975), p. 7.

a disintegrating Gronow, 19.9.1869, in Page (1985), p. 41.

page 226

'sexual organ Churchwarden Arnold Houldsworth, in Manchester (1992), p. 154.

right foot was Manchester (1992), p. 154, and Barber (1939), p. 137.

Lady Holland discussing Lushington to Annabella, 30.4.1816, LP 88, fol. 113.

page 227

he was a paedophile Eisler (1999), pp. 384–385.

horrified biographers Moore (1974), Appendix 2.

In 1830 one of Byron's letter to Moore, 22.8.1813, in Moore (1833), vol. i, p. 520; Marchand note in BLJ, 22.8.1813 ['Byron hinted to Moore of his liaison with Augusta Leigh. ("I am, at this moment, in a far more serious, and entirely new, scrape than any of the last twelve months, - and that is saying a good deal. ★★★★ It is unlucky we can neither live with nor without these women.") That he told him more is suggested by the asterisks] and Marchand (1957), vol. i. p. 404 ['All that can be said is that the circumstantial evidence in Byron's letters cannot be ignored, and that certain aspects of his life and correspondence cannot be explained sensibly in any other terms (than by a relationship with Augusta)']; and Eisler (1999), p. 398 ['To gossipy Tom Moore he confided: "I am, at this moment, in a far more serious, and entirely new scrape than any of the last twelve months – and that is saying a good deal." He followed this schoolboy boast with a full confession of his affair with his sister'].

page 228

'birds of the same Medwin (1824), p. 74 and annotation by Lady Byron, Lady Caroline Lamb and John Galt, in Medwin (1966), pp. 69-70.

But was it Jenkins (1972), p. 92.

Annabella met Mary Prothero (1899–1901), vol. iii, p. 210.

By the 1850s Taylor (1958), p. 294.

(those two hundred-plus BLJ, 8.9.1818.

heightened sex drive One Foot in the Past, BBC2, June 23, 1998.

Byron as anorexic 'Mad, bad and now anorexic', in *Sydney Morning Herald*, 10.10.1998.

page 229

a hippopotamus N&Q (1855), in Santucho (1977), p. 247.

'And what do you make Woolf (1988), p. 484.

page 230

'her narratives and John Robertson in Austin (1869), p. 67.

'I am sure William Howitt in Austin (1869), pp. 56–57.

'if there was Lovelace (1921), p. 195.

'not to see Praz (1970), p. 76.

page 231

The day she told Kosky (1989), p. 123.

a philanthropist and mentor Basham (1992), p. 15.

Lady Byron proto-feminist ibid, p. 12.

The cycle of Elwin (1975), p. 208.

'Oh! How could Stowe (1870), p. 299.

'perform the duty Mayne (1929), p. 281.

page 232

'Again I lost LP 131, fol. 132.

'it was impossible ibid.

'you do not appear Elwin (1962), p. 203.

she proved to herself ibid, p. 153.

'I've lived not Childe Harold's Pilgrimage, IV, 137, in LP 118, fol. 139.

page 234

'Consists of packets LP 118, fols. 130, 131.

a sculptor would come Pierson (1992), p. 310.

page 235

bronchitis and pleurisy ibid, p. 14.

BIBLIOGRAPHY

This book began life focusing on all of the women – wives, daughters, mistresses – associated with Lord Byron and narrowed down later on to concern itself with Annabella Milbanke and everything she and Byron did to each other. This bibliography, however, relates to the larger focus.

Miscellaneous Collection of Newspaper Cuttings Relating to Lord Byron. vol. i, 1812–1833, vol. ii, 1834–1880. London: The British Library.

The Monthly Review or Literary Journal, England, May–August MDCCCXV (vol. LXXVII). London: 1815.

Zambelli Papers, vol. iii, British Library, Add. MS. 46,873; vol. iv, British Library, Add. MS. 46,874.

The Life, Writings, Opinions and Times of the Right Hon. George Gordon Noel Byron, Lord Byron ... in the course of the biography is also separately given copious recollections of the lately destroyed MS, originally intended for posthumous publication and entitled, 'Memoirs of my Own Life and Times', by the Right Hon. Lord Byron, by an English gentleman, in the Greek military service and comrade of his Lordship. London: Matthew Iley, 1825.

Byroniana: The Opinions of Lord Byron on Men, Manners and Things, with the Parish Clerk's Album Kept at His Burial Place, Hucknall Torkard. London: Hamilton Adams and Co., 1834.

In Chancery Hobhouse v. Bland, 1853. British Library, Add. Ch. 72,103.

Police News Edition: Life of Lady Byron – Compiled from the Best Authorities Together with a Summary of the 'True Story' told by Mrs Harriet Beecher Stowe with Descriptive Matter – Private Letters – and Full Particulars of the Great Scandal to which is Appended a Vindication of Lord Byron with Correct Portraits of Lord and Lady Byron, Their Daughter and Mrs Stowe. G. Purkess, 286 Strand, and all newsagents.

The True Story of Lord and Lady Byron as Told by Lord Macaulay, Thomas Moore, Leigh Hunt, Thomas Campbell, the Countess of Blessington, Lord Lindsay, the Countess Guiccioli, by Lady Byron and by the Poet Himself, in answer to Mrs Beecher Stowe. London: John Camden Hotten, 1869.

Byron Painted by His Compeers, or, All About Lord Byron from His Marriage to His Death, as Given by Various Newspapers of His Day, Shewing Wherein the American Novelist Gives a Truthful Account and Wherein She Draws on Her Own Morbid Imagination. London: Samuel Palmer, 1869.

Adams, Joseph, M. D., *An Illustration of Mr Hunter's Doctrine, Particularly Concerning the Life of the Blood, in Answer to the Edinburgh Review of Mr Abernethy's Lectures.* London: W. Thorne, 1814.

Airlie, Mabell, Countess of, *Lady Palmerston and her Times*. London: Hodder and Stoughton, 1922.

Amos, William, *The Originals: Who's Really Who in Fiction*. London: Johnathan Cape, 1985.

Angelo, Henry, *The Reminiscences of Henry Angelo*. London: Henry Colburn and Richard Bentley, 1830.

Arnheim, Rudolf, *Art and Visual Perception: A Psychology of the Creative Eye*. Berkeley: University of California Press, 1974.

Arnold, Matthew, 'The Function of Criticism at the Present Time', in Con Davis and Finke (eds), *Literary Criticism and Theory: The Greeks to the Present*.

Ashton, John, *Gossip in the First Decade of Queen Victoria's Reign*. London: Hurst and Blackett, 1903.

Austen, Jane, *Pride and Prejudice*. London and Glasgow: Collins Clear, 1954.

Austin, Alfred, *A Vindication of Lord Byron*. London: Chapman and Hall, 1869.

Babbage, Charles, *Passages from the Life of a Philosopher*. London: Longman, Green, Longman, Roberts and Green, 1864.

Barber, Thomas Gerard, *Byron, and Where he is Buried*. Hucknall: Henry Morley and Sons, 1939.

Basham, Diana, *The Trial of Women: Feminism and the Occult Sciences in Victorian Literature and Society*. Basingstoke: Macmillan, 1992.

Baum, Joan, *The Calculating Passion of Ada Byron*. Hamden, CT: Archon, 1986.

Bedford, John Harmer, *Wanderings of Childe Harold: A Romance of Real Life, interspersed with Memoirs of the English wife, the foreign mistress, and various other celebrated characters*. London: Sherwood Jones and Co., 1825.

Beecher Stowe, Harriet, *Lady Byron Vindicated*. London: Sampson, Low, Son and Marlton, 1870.

Bellamy, R. L., *Byron the Man*. London: Kegan Paul, Trench, Trubner and Co., 1924.

Bennett, Alan, *The Madness of King George*. London: Faber and Faber, 1995.

Berlin, Isaiah, *The Proper Study of Mankind*. London: Pimlico, 1998.

Bettany, W. A. Lewis (ed.), *The Confessions of Lord Byron: A Collection of His Private Opinions of Men and Matters, Taken from the New and Enlarged Edition of His Letters and Journals*. London: John Murray, 1905.

Blackstone, Bernard, *Byron: A Survey*. London: Longman, 1975.

Blain, Virginia, Patricia Clements and Isobel Grundy, *The Feminist Companion to Literature in English: Women Writers from the Middle Ages to the Present*. London: B. T. Batsford, 1990.

Blakey, Dorothy, *The Minerva Press*. London: Bibliographical Society, 1939.

Block, Andrew, *The English Novel 1740–1850*. London: Dawsons, 1963.

Blunden, Edmund, *Leigh Hunt's Examiner Examined*. London: Cobden-Sanderson, 1928.

Blyth, Henry, *Caro: The Fatal Passion*. London: Rupert Hart Davis, 1972.

Bold, Alan (ed.), *Byron: Wrath and Rhyme*, London and Totowa, NJ: Vision, and Barnes and Noble, 1983.

Borch-Jacobsen, Mikkel, 'What Made Albert Run?', *London Review of Books*, May 27, 1999.

Bibliography

Boyes, Megan, *Love without Wings*. Derby: J. M. Tatler and Son, 1988.

Brecknock, Alfred, *Byron: A Study of the Poet in Light of New Discoveries*. London: Cecil Palmer, 1926.

Brent, Peter, *Lord Byron*. London: Weidenfeld and Nicolson, 1974.

Brewster, Sir David, *A Treatise on the New Philosophical Instruments*. London: John Murray, 1813.

Briscoe, Walter A. (ed.), *Byron, the Poet: A Collection of Addresses and Essays*. London: George Routledge and Sons, 1924.

British Council, *Byron 1788–1824*. London: British Council, 1988.

Brown, David Blayney, *Turner and Byron*. London: Tate Gallery, 1992.

Bruce, Ian, *Lavallette Bruce: His Adventures and Intrigues Before and After Waterloo*. London: Hamish Hamilton, 1953.

Bryant, Arthur, *The Age of Elegance 1812–1822*. London: Collins, 1975.

Brydges, Sir Egerton, *An Impartial Portrait of Lord Byron, as a Poet and a Man, compared with all the Evidences and Writings regarding him, up to 1825*. Paris, Galignani, 1825.

Burnett, T. A. J., *The Rise and Fall of a Regency Dandy: The Life and Times of Scrope Berdmore Davies*. London: John Murray, 1981.

Bushell, Peter, *London's Secret History*. London: Constable, 1983.

Bustacchini, Gianfranco, *Ravenna: Capital of Mosaics*. Ravenna: Cartolibreria Salbaroli, 1988.

Butler, E. M., *Goethe and Byron*. Nottingham: University of Nottingham–Byron Foundation Lecture, 1949–50.

Byron, A. I. Noel (Lady), *Remarks Occasioned by Mr Moore's Notices of Lord Byron's Life*. London: Richard Taylor, 1830.

Byron, George Gordon (Lord), *Byron's Letters and Journals*, vols. 1–12 + one supplemental, edited by Leslie A. Marchand. London: John Murray, 1974–1994 (listed in references as 'BLJ').

Byron, George Gordon (Lord), *Selected Letters and Journals*, edited by Leslie A. Marchand. London: Picador, 1984.

Byron, George Gordon (Lord), *Complete Poetical Works*. Oxford and New York: Oxford University Press, 1970.

Byron, George Gordon (Lord), *Hours of Idleness*. London: S. and J. Ridge, 1807.

Byron, George Gordon Noel [sic] (Lord), *A Narrative of the Circumstances which Attended the Separation of Lord and Lady Byron; Remarks on his Domestic Conduct, and a Complete Refutation of the Calumnies Circulated by Public Writers*. London: R. E. Edwards, 1816.

Byron, George Gordon (Lord), *Selected Poems*. (Edited with a preface by Susan J. Wolfson and Peter J. Manning.) London: Penguin, 1996.

Byron, Medora Gordon, *Celia in Search of a Husband*. London: Minerva Press, 1809.

Byron, Medora Gordon, *The Spinster's Journal*. London: Minerva Press, 1816.

Byron, Medora Gordon, *Zameo: or the White Warrior: An operatic romance … by Medora Gordon Byron, a minor … to which is prefixed a memoir of Miss Byron … [a jeu d'esprit, representing the author as a natural daughter of Lord Byron] written by Mrs Jane Briancourt*. London: John Duncombe and Co., 1834.

The Secret

Burton, Anthony, and John Murdoch, *Byron: An Exhibition to Commemorate the 150th Anniversary of his Death in the Greek War of Liberation, 19 April, 1824.* London: Victoria and Albert Museum, 1974.

Calder, Jenni, 'The Hero as Lover: Byron and Women', in Alan Bold (ed.), *Byron: Wrath and Rhyme.*

Calvino, Italo, *Six Memos for the Next Millennium.* New York: Vintage, 1993.

Cardwell, Richard (ed.), *Lord Byron the European: Essays from the International Byron Society.* Lewiston, Queenstown, and Lampeter: Edwin Mellen, 1997.

Cecil, David, *The Young Melbourne and the Story of his Marriage with Caroline Lamb.* London: Constable and Co., 1954.

Chapman, John S., *Byron and the Honourable Augusta Leigh.* New Haven and London: Yale University Press, 1975.

Chew, Samuel C., *Byron in England: His Fame and After-Fame.* London: John Murray, 1924.

Christensen, Jerome, 'Setting Byron Straight: Class, Sexuality and the Poet', in Elaine Scarry (ed.), *Literature and the Body: Essays on Persons and Populations.*

Christiansen, Rupert, *Romantic Affinities: Portraits from an Age 1780–1830.* London: Vintage, 1994.

Cockle, Mrs, *Reply to Lord Byron's 'Fare Thee Well'.* Newcastle: Hodgson, 1817.

Cockshut, A. O. J., *Truth to Life: The Art of Biography in the Nineteenth Century.* London: Collins, 1974.

Con Davis, Robert, and Laurie Finke, (eds), *Literary Criticism and Theory: The Greeks to the Present.* New York and London: Longman, 1989.

Coote, Stephen, *Byron: The Making of a Myth.* London: Bodley Head, 1988.

Courtney, William Prideaux, *The Secrets of our National Literature.* London: Archibald Constable and Co., 1908.

Crompton, Louis, *Byron and Greek Love: Homophobia in 19th-century England.* London: Faber and Faber, 1985.

Crook, Nora, and Derek Guiton, *Shelley's Venomed Melody.* Cambridge: Cambridge University Press, 1986.

Curreli, Mario, e Antony L. Johnson (a cura), *Paradiso degli Esuli Shelley e Byron a Pisa.* Pisa: ETS Editrice, 1988.

Dallas, Robert Charles, *Recollections of the Life of Lord Byron, from the Year 1808 to the End of 1814.* London: Charles Knight, 1824.

Dangerfield, Elma, *Byron and the Romantics in Switzerland, 1816.* London: Ascent, 1978.

Eagleton, Terry, *Literary Theory: An Introduction.* Minneapolis: University of Minnesota Press, 1983.

Ehrsam, Theodore G., *Major Byron: The Incredible Career of a Literary Forger.* London: John Murray, 1951.

Eisenberg, Elizabeth, *Lord Byron: Mad, Bad and Dangerous to Know.* The Nottinghamshire Heritage Series, Derby: John Hall and Sons, 1987.

Eisler, Benita, *Byron: Child of Passion, Fool of Fame.* New York: Alfred Knopf, 1999.

Elfenbein, Andrew, *Byron and the Victorians.* Cambridge: Cambridge University Press, 1995.

Bibliography

Eliot, T. S., *On Poetry and Poets*. London: Faber and Faber, 1957.

Elwin, Malcolm, *Lord Byron's Wife*. London: Macdonald, 1962.

Elwin, Malcolm, *Lord Byron's Family: Annabella, Ada and Augusta 1816–1824*. (Edited from the author's typescript by Peter Thomson.) London: John Murray, 1975.

Evans, Ivor H., *Brewer's Dictionary of Phrase and Fable* (14th edition). London: Cassell, 1992.

Fleming, Anne, *In Search of Byron in England and Scotland*. Sussex: Old Forge Press, 1988.

Fleming, Anne, *The Myth of Bad Lord Byron*. Cuckfield: Old Forge Press, 1998.

Foot, Michael, *The Politics of Paradise: A Vindication of Lord Byron*. London: Collins, 1988.

Fox, Caroline, *Memories of Old Friends: Being Extracts from the Journals and Letters of Caroline Fox Of Penjerrick, Cornwall, from 1835 to 1871*, (Horace N. Pym, ed.) London: Smith, Elder and Co., 1882.

Franklin, Caroline, *Byron's Heroines*. Oxford: Clarendon, 1992.

Frayling, Christopher, *Vampyres: Lord Byron to Count Dracula*. London: Faber, 1991.

Gamba, Count Peter, *A Narrative of Byron's Last Journey to Greece, Extracted from the Journal of Count Peter Gamba who Attended His Lordship on that Expedition*. Paris: Galignani, 1825.

Garber, Frederick, *Self, Text and Romantic Irony: The Example of Byron*. Princeton, NJ: Princeton University Press, 1988.

Gardiner, Marguerite (Countess of Blessington), *Lady Blessington's Conversations of Lord Byron*, (Ernest J. Lovell, ed.), Princeton, Princeton University Press, 1969.

Gatton, John Spalding, *Dictionary of Literary Biography*, vol. 96, British Romantic Poets, 1789–1832, 2nd series.

Gay, Peter, *The Bourgeois Experience: Victoria to Freud*. vol. i, 'Education of the Senses', New York: Oxford University Press, 1984; vol. ii, 'The Tender Passion', New York: Oxford University Press, 1986; vol. iii, 'The Cultivation of Hatred', New York: W. W. Norton, 1993; vol. iv, 'The Naked Heart', New York: HarperCollins, 1996.

Gillen, Mollie, *Assassination of the Prime Minister: The Shocking Death of Spencer Perceval*. London: Sidgwick and Jackson, 1972.

Gittings, Robert, and Jo Manton, *Claire Clairmont and the Shelleys*. Oxford and New York: Oxford University Press, 1992.

Godwin, William, *Caleb Williams*. London: New English Library, 1975.

Goode, Clement Tyson, Jr, *George Gordon, Lord Byron: A Comprehensive Annotated Research Bibliography of Secondary Materials in English 1973–1994*. Maryland and Folkeston: Scarecrow, 1997.

Gould, Stephen Jay, Umberto Eco, Jean-Claude Carriere and Jean Delumeau, *Conversations about the End of Time*. London: Penguin, 1999.

Gould, Stephen Jay, *Questioning the Millennium: A Rationalist's Guide to a Precisely Arbitrary Countdown*. London: Random House, 1997.

Graham, Peter W. (ed.), *Byron's Bulldog: The Letters of John Cam Hobhouse to Lord Byron*. Columbus: Ohio State University, 1984.

Graham, Peter W., *Don Juan in Regency England*. Charlottesville and London: University Press of Virginia, 1990.

Graham, William, *Last Links with Byron, Shelley and Keats*. London: Leonard Smithers and Co., 1898.

Grebanier, Bernard, *The Uninhibited Byron: An Account of His Sexual Confusion*. London: Peter Owen, 1970.

Gribble, Francis, *The Love Affairs of Lord Byron*. London: Eveleigh Nash, 1910.

Grosskurth, Phyllis, *Leslie Stephen: Writers and their Work*. No. 207, Essex: Longmans Green and Co., 1968.

Grosskurth, Phyllis, *Byron: The Flawed Angel*. London: Hodder and Stoughton, 1997.

Grun, Bernard, *Timetables of History: A Chronology of World Events*. London: Thames and Hudson, 1975.

Grylls, R. Glynn, *Claire Clairmont: Mother of Byron's Allegra*. London: John Murray, 1939.

Guiccioli, Teresa, *My Recollections of Lord Byron and Those of Eye-witnesses of his Life*. London: Richard Bentley, 1869.

Gunn, Peter, *My Dearest Augusta: A Biography of the Honourable Augusta Leigh, Lord Byron's Half-Sister*. London: The Bodley Head, 1968.

Halevy, Elie (trans. by E. I. Watkin and D. A. Barker), *England in 1815: A History of the English People in the 19th Century*. London: Ernst Benn, 1949.

Hamilton, Ian, *Keepers of the Flame: Literary Estates and the Rise of Biography*. London: Pimlico, 1992.

Hart, Chris (ed.), *Lives of the Great Romantics by their Contemporaries*, vol. 2, London: William Pickering, 1996.

Hedley, Olwen, *Queen Charlotte*. London: John Murray, 1975.

Henley, William Ernest, *Essays*, vol. iv. London: David Nutt, 1908.

Hibbert, Christopher, *George IV: Regent and King 1811–1830*. London: Allen Lane, 1973.

Hobhouse, John Cam, *General Correspondence*. vol. I of the Broughton correspondence, 1774–1817: British Library Add. MS. 36,456 vol. IV of the Broughton correspondence, 1825–February 1826: British Library Add. MS. 36,461.

Hobhouse, John Cam, *Exposure of the Mis-Statements contained in Captain Medwin's Pretended 'Conversations of Lord Byron'*. London: John Murray, 1824.

Hobhouse, John Cam (Lord Broughton), *Remarks on the Exclusion of Lord Byron's Monument from Westminster Abbey*. Not published, 1844.

Hobhouse, John Cam (Lord Broughton), *A Contemporary Account of the Separation of Lord and Lady Byron; also of the Destruction of Lord Byron's Memoirs*. Privately printed: London, 1870.

Hobhouse, John Cam (Baron Broughton), *Recollections of a Long Life – With Additional Extracts from His Private Diaries Edited by His Daughter, Lady Dorchester*. London: John Murray, 1909–1911.

Hodge, Jane Aiken, *Passion and Principle: The Loves and Lives of Regency Women*. London: John Murray, 1996.

Bibliography

Hodgson, Rev. James T., *A Memoir of the Reverend Francis Hodgson, Scholar, Poet and Divine*. London: Macmillan, 1878.

Holland, Tom, *The Vampyre: Being the True Pilgrimage of George Gordon, Sixth Lord Byron*. London: Little, Brown, 1995.

Holmes, Richard, *Shelley: The Pursuit*. London: Weidenfeld and Nicolson, 1974.

Horwood, Richard, *An A–Z of Regency London*. London, 1985.

Hough, Graham, *Two Exiles: Byron and D. H. Lawrence*. Nottingham: University of Nottingham–Byron Foundation Lecture, 1956.

Howard-Hill, T. H., *Bibliography of British Literary Bibliographies* (2nd edition). Oxford: Clarendon, 1987.

Huber, Werner, 'Dead Poets' Society: Byron, Post-Modernism and the Biographical Mode', in Richard Cardwell (ed.), *Lord Byron: The European*.

Hudson, Glenda A., *Sibling Love and Incest in Jane Austen's Fiction*. New York: St Martin's Press, 1992.

Hunt, Leigh, *Lord Byron and Some of His Contemporaries with Recollections of the Author's Life and of His Visit to Italy*. Paris: A. and W. Galignani, 1828.

James, Henry (edited with introductions and notes by Leon Edel and Lyall H. Powers), *The Complete Notebooks of Henry James*. New York and Oxford: Oxford University Press, 1987.

James, Henry, *The Aspern Papers*. Stockholm: The Continental Book Company, 1947.

Jameson, Mrs K., *The Romance of Biography: or, Memoirs of Women Loved and Celebrated by the Poets from the Days of the Troubadours to the Present Age*. London: Saunders and Oatley, 1837.

Jeaffreson, John Cordy, *The Real Lord Byron: New Views on the Poet's Life*. London: Hurst and Blackett, 1883.

Jenkins, Elizabeth, *Lady Caroline Lamb*. London: Sphere, 1972.

Johnson, Paul, *The Birth of the Modern: World Society 1815–1830*. London: Phoenix, 1992.

Jones, F. L. (ed.), *Maria Gisborne and Edward E. Williams: Shelley's Friends: Their Letters and Journals*. Norman: University of Oklahoma Press, 1951.

Kalyanavaca (ed.), *Moon and Flowers*. Birmingham: Windhorse, 1997.

Kitchin, Laurence, *Three on Trial: An Experiment in Biography*. London: Pall Mall Press, 1959.

Kosky, Jules, *Mutual Friends: Charles Dickens and the Great Ormond Street Children's Hospital*. London: Weidenfeld and Nicolson, 1989.

Lamb, Lady Caroline, *Glenarvon* (1816): a facsimile reproduction with an introduction by James L. Ruff. New York: Scholar's Facsimiles and Reprints, 1972.

Laudermilk, Sharon H., and Teresa L. Hamlin, *The Regency Companion*. New York and London: Garland, 1989.

Lessenich, Rolf P., *Lord Byron and the Nature of Man*. Köln: Böhlan Verlag GmbH, 1978.

Lewis, Matthew, *The Monk*. Oxford: Oxford University Press, 1980.

Longford, Elizabeth, *Byron's Greece*. London: Weidenfeld and Nicolson, 1975.

Lovelace, Mary, Countess of, *Ralph, Earl of Lovelace: A Memoir*. London: Christophers, 1920.

Lovelace, Mary, Countess of, *Astarte*. New edition, edited by Mary, Countess of Lovelace. London: Christophers, 1921. ['Of this edition 125 copies only have been printed for sale in the British Empire and 66 copies only for sale in the United States of America.']

Lovric, Michelle (ed.), *Deadlier Than the Male*. Sydney: Allen and Unwin, 1997.

Low, Donald A., *That Sunny Dome: A Portrait of Regency Britain*. London: Dent, 1977.

Lytton, Victor, 2nd Earl of Lytton, *The Life of Edward Bulwer, 1st Lord Lytton*. London: Macmillan, 1913.

MacDonald, D. L., *Poor Polidori: A Critical Biography of the Author of 'The Vampyre'*. Toronto, Buffalo and London: University of Toronto Press, 1991.

Mackay, Charles, *Medora Leigh: A History and Autobiography*. New York: Harper and Bros, 1870.

Mackay, William, *The True Story of Lady Byron's Life: Christmas Comic Version*. London: Mackay and Co., 1869.

Maggs, Norman, *Educating Ealing: How Lady Byron Did It*. Ealing: Monographs for Megalopolis, 1996.

Maitland, Frederic William, *The Life and Letters of Leslie Stephen*. London: Duckworth, 1906.

Manchester, Sean, *Mad, Bad and Dangerous to Know: The Life of Lady Caroline Lamb*. Cornwall: Gothic Press, 1992.

Manning, Peter J., *Byron and His Fictions*. Detroit: Wayne State University Press, 1978.

Marchand, Leslie A., *Byron: A Biography*. New York: Alfred A. Knopf, 1957.

Marlowe, Derek, *A Single Summer with Lord Byron: The Summer of 1816*. Middlesex: Penguin, 1973.

Martin, Philip W., *Byron: A Poet Before his Public*. Cambridge: Cambridge University Press, 1982.

Masson, Madeleine, *Lady Anne Barnard: The Court and Colonial Service under George III and the Regency*. London: George Allen and Unwin, 1949.

Mayne, Ethel Colburn, *Byron*. London: Methuen, 1924.

Mayne, Ethel Colburn, *The Life and Letters of Anne Isabella, Lady Noel Byron, from Unpublished Papers in the Possession of the Late Ralph, Earl of Lovelace*, (2nd edition). London: Constable and Co., 1929.

Mayne, Ethel Colburn, *Enchanters of Men*. London: Mellifont, 1937.

Maurois, Andre, *Byron*. (A new edition translated by Hamish Miles.) London: The Bodley Head, 1963.

McCormick, Donald, *Love in Code: Or, How to Keep Your Secrets*. London: Eyre Methuen, 1980.

McCormick, Donald, *Erotic Literature: A Connoisseur's Guide*. New York: Continuum, 1992.

McDayter, Ghislaine, 'What Do I Know of Vampires?', in Richard Cardwell (ed.), *Lord Byron: The European*.

Medwin, Thomas, *Conversations of Lord Byron: Noted During a Residence with His Lordship at Pisa, in the Years 1821 and 1822.* London: Henry Colburn, 1824.

Medwin, Thomas, *Conversations of Lord Byron: Revised with a New Preface by the Author for a New Edition, and Annotated by Lady Byron, John Cam Hobhouse, Sir Walter Scott, Sir Charles Napier, John Murray, John Galt, William Harness, Roberth Southey, Lady Caroline Lamb, Leigh Hunt, Mary Shelley, E. J. Trelawny, William Fletcher, Countess Teresa Guiccioli, and others who knew the poet personally.* (Ed. Ernest J Lovell, Jr) Princeton: Princeton University Press, 1966.

Mellanby, Helen, *Animal Life in Fresh Water.* London: Chapman and Hall, 1963 (sixth edition).

Milbanke, Ralph, Earl of Lovelace, *Astarte: A Fragment of Truth Concerning George Gordon Byron, Sixth Lord Byron. Recorded by his grandson, Ralph Milbanke, Earl of Lovelace.* London: The Chiswick Press, 1905.

Millingen, Julius, *Memoirs of the Affairs in Greece: containing an account of the military and political events, which occurred in 1823 and following years. With various anecdotes relating to Lord Byron and an account of his last illness and death.* London: John Rodwell, 1831.

Mitford, J., *Extract of a Letter Containing an Account of Lord Byron's Residence on the Island of Mitylene,* printed with *The Vampyre.* London: Sherwood, Neely and Jones, 1819.

Mitford, J. Esq., *Only Authentic Edition: The Private Life of Lord Byron, Comprising His Voluptuous Amours, Secret Intrigues, and Close Connection with Various Ladies of Rank and Fame in Scotland and London, at Eton, Harrow, Cambridge, Paris, Rome Venice, &c, &c, with Particular Account of the Countess Guiacolli [sic], and, Never Before Published, Details of the Murder at Ravenna which Caused His Lordship to Leave Italy; Various Singular Anecdotes of Persons and Families of the Highest Circles of Haut Ton; Compiled from Authentic Sources, with Extracts from Unburnt Documents and Familiar Letters from His Lordship to His Friends, being an Amusing and Interesting Expose of Fashionable Frailties, Follies and Debaucheries, with Numerous Engravings.* London: H. Smith, 1836.

Moers, Ellen, *Literary Women.* New York: Doubleday, 1976.

Moore, Doris Langley, *The Late Lord Byron.* London: John Murray, 1961.

Moore, Doris Langley, *Byron: Accounts Rendered.* London: John Murray, 1974.

Moore, Doris Langley, *Ada, Countess of Lovelace: Lord Byron's Legitimate Daughter.* London: John Murray, 1977.

Moore, Frank Frankfort, *He Loved But One: The True Story of Lord Byron and Mary Chaworth.* London: Eveleigh Nash, 1905.

Moore, J. Sheridan, *Byron: His Biographers and Critics,* delivered to the Australian Patriotic Society, November 15, 1869. Sydney: John Ferguson, 1869.

Moore, Thomas, *Notices of the Life of Lord Byron.* Paris: A. W. Galignani, 1831.

Moore, Thomas, *The Letters and Journals of Lord Byron, with Notices of His Life* (new and revised version). London: Chatto and Windus, 1875.

Moore, Thomas, *Prose and Verse, Humorous and Satirical, with Suppressed Passages from the Memoirs of Lord Byron*, with notes and introduction by Richard Herne Shepherd. London: Chatto and Windus, 1878.

Murray, John, *Notes on Captain Medwin's Conversations with Lord Byron ('Conversations of Lord Byron, as related by Thomas Medwin, Esq., compared with a portion of his Lordship's correspondence')*. London: John Murray, 1824.

Murray, John, *Lord Byron and his Detractors*. London: Ballantyne, 1906.

Murray, Venetia, *High Society: A Social History of the Regency Period, 1788–1830*. London: Viking, 1998.

Nadel, Ira Bruce, *Biography: Fiction, Fact and Form*. London: Macmillan, 1984.

Nathan, Isaac, *Fugitive Pieces and Reminiscences of Lord Byron*. London: Whittaker, Treacher and Co., 1829.

Nicolson, Harold, *Byron: The Last Journey April 1823–April 1824*, new edition with new preface. London: Constable, 1948.

Noel, The Hon. Roden, *Life of Lord Byron*. London: Walter Scott, 1890.

Normington, Susan, *Byron and His Children*. Stroud: Sutton, 1995.

Nye, Robert, *The Memoirs of Lord Byron: A Novel*. London: Hamish Hamilton, 1989.

Ogilvy, Mabell Frances Elizabeth, Countess of Airlie, *In Whig Society 1775–1818: Compiled from Hitherto Unpublished Correspondence of Elizabeth, Viscountess Melbourne, and Emily Lamb, Countess Cowper, later Viscountess Palmerston*. London: Hodder and Stoughton, 1921.

Origo, Iris, *A Measure of Love*. London: Jonathon Cape, 1957.

Origo, Iris, *The Last Attachment: The Story of Byron and Teresa Guiccioli*. London: Fontana, 1962.

Ormond, Richard, and Rogers, Malcolm (eds.), *Dictionary of British Portraits*, vol. ii. London: Batsford with the National Portrait Gallery, 1979.

Ovington, John, *Conversations on Matrimony Intended as an Accompaniment to the Letters Lately Published on the Duties, Advantages, Pleasures and Sorrows of the Marriage State*. London, 1815.

Page, Norman (ed.), *Byron: Interviews and Recollections*. Basingstoke: Macmillan, 1985.

Page, Norman (ed.), *A Byron Chronology*. Boston: G. K. Hall, 1988.

Paglia, Camille, *Sexual Personae: Art and Decadence from Nefertiti to Emily Dickinson*. London and New Haven: Yale University Press, 1990.

Parker, Derek, *Byron and his World*. London: Thames and Hudson, 1968.

Paston, George, and Peter Quennell, *'To Lord Byron': Feminine Profiles Based on Unpublished Letters 1807–1824*. London: John Murray, 1939.

Pierson, Joan, *The Real Lady Byron*. London: Robert Hale, 1992.

Pool, Daniel, *What Jane Austen Ate and Charles Dickens Knew*. New York: Simon and Schuster, 1993.

Porter, Roy, *A Social History of Madness: Stories of the Insane*. London: Phoenix, 1996.

Prantera, Amanda, *Conversations with Lord Byron on Perversion, 163 Years After His Lordship's Death*. London: Abacus, 1988.

Praz, Mario, *The Romantic Agony* (translated by Angus Davidson). London and New York: Oxford University Press, 1970.

Bibliography

Prince, Rosa, 'Tragedy of man who invented computer 150 years too soon,' *The Independent on Sunday*, March 1, 1998, p. 3.

Prothero, Rowland (ed.), *The Works of Lord Byron – Letters and Journals*, vols. iii, iv, and v. London and New York: John Murray and Scribner's, 1899–1901.

Prothero, Rowland, *Lord Byron and his Detractors*. London: Ballantyne (printed for private circulation), 1906.

Quennell, Peter (ed.), *Byronic Thoughts: Maxims, Reflections, Portraits from the Prose and Verse of Lord Byron*. London: John Murray, 1960.

Quennell, Peter, 'Review of Doris Langley Moore's *The Late Lord Byron*', *The Observer*, July 9, 1961.

Quennell, Peter, *Byron: The Years of Fame*. London: Collins, 1967.

Quennell, Peter, *Byron: A Self Portrait in his Own Words*. Oxford: Oxford University Press, 1990.

Raeper, William, *George MacDonald*. Tring: Lion Books, 1987.

Raphael, Frederic, *Byron*. London: Thames and Hudson, 1982.

Read, Herbert, *Byron*. London: Longmans, Green and Co., 1966.

Reiman, Donald H. (ed.), *The Romantics Reviewed: Contemporary Reviews of British Romantic Writers, Part B – Byron and Regency Society Poets (in five volumes)*. New York and London: Garland, 1972.

Richardson, Joanna, *The Regency*. London: Collins, 1973.

Ricks, Christopher, *Keats and Embarrassment*. Oxford: Clarendon, 1974.

Rolls, Mrs Henry, *A Poetical Address to Lord Byron*. London: W. Hone, 1816.

Rossetti, William (ed.), *The Diary of Dr John William Polidori, 1816: Relating to Byron, Shelley, Etc*. London: Elkin Matthews, 1911.

Rowse, A. L., *Homosexuals in History: A Study of Ambivalence in Society, Literature and the Arts*. London: Weidenfeld and Nicolson, 1977.

Rowse, A. L., *The Byrons and the Trevanions*. London: Weidenfeld and Nicolson, 1978.

Rudolf, Anthony, *Byron's Darkness: Lost Summer and Nuclear Winter*. London: The Menard Press, 1984.

Santucho, Oscar José, *George Gordon, Lord Byron: A Comprehensive Bibliography of Secondary Materials in English, 1807–1974*. Metuchen, NJ: Scarecrow, 1977.

Scarry, Elaine (ed.), *Literature and the Body: Essays on Populations and Persons*. Baltimore and London: The Johns Hopkins University Press, 1988.

Scull, Andrew, MacKenzie, Charlotte, and Hervey, Nicholas, *Masters of Bedlam: The Transformation of the Mad-Doctoring Trade*. Princeton: Princeton University Press, 1996.

Shattok, Joanne, *The Oxford Guide to British Women Writers*. Oxford: Oxford University Press, 1993.

Shilstone, Frederick W., *Byron and the Myth of Tradition*. Lincoln and London: University of Nebraska Press, 1988.

Simmons, J. W., *An Inquiry into the Moral Character of Lord Byron*. London: John Cochran, 1826.

Smiles, Samuel, *A Publisher and his Friends*. London: John Murray, 1911.

Soderholm, James, *Fantasy, Forgery and the Byron Legend*. Lexington: University of Kentucky Press, 1996.

Spence, Lewis, *Introduction to Mythology*. London: Senate, 1994.

Spufford, Francis and Uglow, Jenny (eds), *Cultural Babbage: Technology, Time and Invention*. London: Faber and Faber, 1996.

Stein, Dorothy, *Ada: A Life and Legacy*. Cambridge, MA: MIT, 1985.

Stephen, Leslie, *Dictionary of National Biography*, vol. VIII, London: Smith, Elder and Co., 1885.

Stephen, Leslie, *Studies of a Biographer*. London: Elder Smith and Co; Duckworth and Co., 1907.

Stocking, Marion Kingston (ed.), *The Journals of Claire Clairmont*. Harvard: Harvard University Press, 1968.

Stone, Lawrence, *The Family, Sex and Marriage in England 1500–1800*. London: Weidenfeld and Nicolson, 1977.

Stone, Lawrence, *Broken Lives: Separation and Divorce in England 1660–1875*. Oxford: Oxford University Press, 1993.

Storch, Robert D. (ed.), *Popular Culture and Custom in Nineteenth Century England*. London and Canberra: Croom and Helm, 1982.

Storey, Mark, *Byron and the Eye of Appetite*. London: Macmillan, 1986.

Strachey, Lytton, *Literary Essays*. London: Chatto and Windus, 1948.

Strickland, Margot, *The Byron Women*. London: Peter Owen, 1974.

Stürzl, Erwin A., *A Love's Eye View: Teresa Guiccioli's La Vie de Lord Byron en Italie*. Salzburg: Institut für Anglistik und Amerikanistik, 1988.

Summers, Montague, *A Gothic Bibliography*. London: The Fortune Press, 1949.

Taylor, Gordon Rattray, *The Angel-Makers: A Study in the Psychological Origins of Historical Change, 1750–1850*. London: Heinemann, 1958.

Thompson, F. M. L. (ed.), *The Cambridge Social History of Britain 1750–1950, vol. II: People and their Environment; vol. III: Social Agencies and Institutions*. Cambridge: Cambridge University Press, 1990.

Thomson, David, *Europe Since Napoleon*. London: Longman, Green and Co., 1958.

Thorslev, Peter L., *The Byronic Hero: Types and Prototypes*. Minneapolis: University of Minnesota Press, 1962.

Train, John (ed.), *Love*. London: HarperCollins, 1993.

Trelawny, Edward John, *The Relations of Percy Bysshe Shelley and his two wives, Harriet and Mary, and a Comment on the Character of Lady Byron*. London: Printed for private circulation only by Richard Clay and Sons, 1920. Printed for Thomas J. Wise, Hampstead, NW London. Edition limited to thirty copies.

Trelawny, Edward John, *The Relations of Lord Byron and Augusta Leigh with a Comparison of the Characters of Byron and Shelley and a Rebuke to Jane Clermont [sic] on Her Hatred of the Former*. London: Printed for private circulation only by Richard Clay and Sons, 1920.

Trelawny, Edward John, *Records of Shelley, Byron and the Author* (edited by David Wright). London: Penguin, 1982.

Trueblood, Paul Graham (ed.), *Byron's Political and Cultural Influence in 19th Century Europe: A Symposium*. London: Macmillan, 1981.

Turney, Catherine, *Byron's Daughter: A Biography of Elizabeth Medora Leigh*. Newton Abbot: Readers Union, 1975.

Bibliography

Twitchell, James B., *Forbidden Partners: The Incest Taboo in Modern Culture*. New York: Columbia University Press, 1987.

Vogelsberger, Hartwig A., 'The Loves of Lord Byron – Byron's Sexual Ambivalence', in *The Eternal Pilgrim*. Newsletter of the Austrian Byron Society, vol. 9 (1987).

Voignier-Marshall, Jacqueline (ed.), *The Byron Society in Australia, 1977 Newsletter*. Sydney, 1977.

Waddams, S. M., *Law, Politics and the Church of England: The Career of Stephen Lushington 1782–1873*. Cambridge: Cambridge University Press, 1992.

Walker, Richard, *Regency Portraits*, vol. i. London: National Portrait Gallery, 1985.

Walker, Violet W. (revised and completed by Margaret J. Howell), *The House of Byron: A History of the Family from the Norman Conquest 1066–1988*. London: Quiller Press, 1988.

Walmsley, D. M., *Anton Mesmer*. London: Robert Hale, 1967.

Walvin, James, *English Urban Life 1776–1851*. London: Hutchinson and Co., 1984.

Ward, Herman M., *Byron and the Magazines*. Salzburg: Universität Salzburg, 1973.

Watson, George (ed.), *The New Cambridge Bibliography of English Literature*. Cambridge: Cambridge University Press, 1969.

Watt, Robert, *Bibliotheca Britannica; or a General Index of British and Foreign Literature*. Edinburgh and London: Archibald Constable and Co., and Longman, Hurst, Rees, Orme, Brown and Green, 1824.

Wentworth, Lord, *Lady Noel Byron and the Leighs: Some Authentic Records and Certain Circumstances in the Lives of Augusta Leigh and Others of her Family, that Concerned Anne Isabella, Lady Byron, in the Course of Forty Years after her Separation*. Strictly private. London: printed for the descendants of Lord and Lady Byron by William Clowes and Sons, 1887. [No publication of the contents of this volume may take place without authorisation in writing from Lord Wentworth or Lady Noel Byron's other representatives. Thirty-six copies only have been printed, of which this is number 20.]

White, R. J., *The Age of George III*. London: Heinemann, 1968.

Wilson, Colin, *The Misfits: A Study of Sexual Outsiders*. London: Grafton, 1988.

Wilson, Frances (ed.), *Byromania: Portraits of the Artist in Nineteenth- and Twentieth-Century Culture*. London: Macmillan, 1999.

Wilson, Harriette, *Memoirs of Herself and Others*, preface by James Laver. London: Peter Davies, 1929.

Wisdom, Joseph, *The A to Z of Regency London* (introduction by Paul Laxton). Kent: Harry Margary in association with the London Guildhall Library, 1985.

Woolf, Virginia (Andrew McNeillie, ed.), *The Essays of Virginia Woolf*. vol. III, 1919–1924, and vol. IV, 1925–1928. London: The Hogarth Press, 1988 and 1994.

Woolf, Virginia, *Great Writers: Virginia Woolf* (Jane Dunn, ed.). London: Aurum, 1994.

Ziegler, Philip, *Melbourne: A Biography of William Lamb, 2nd Viscount Melbourne*. London: Collins, 1976.

ACKNOWLEDGEMENTS

Thanks, firstly, to the Earl of Lytton and his literary representatives at Laurence Pollinger Limited for permission to read and quote from Lady Byron's massive archive of papers, the Lovelace Papers, on deposit at the Bodleian Library, the University of Oxford, and to the librarians in Room 132 at the Bodleian, Colin Harris and Nicola Keenan. Also to the librarians in the British Library, the Gennadius Library in Athens, the National Library of Australia, and the Fisher Library at the University of Sydney.

To Michael Duffy for everything that started this book and to Gail MacCallum for everything that finished it. To *The Bulletin* – particularly Max Walsh, Paul Bailey and Kathy Bail – for giving me time away from one job to work on the other one. And to Max Suich, a catalyst for the right places and the right times.

To all the people who gave me spaces to work in – Marilyn and Les Hay, Sophie Cole and Ross Warren, Wendy Cohen, Jen Rosenberg and Gary Scholes, Stewart Luke, Martin Kinnane, Richard Neylon, Lisa Upton. To Helen Suich who found things for me in London when I wasn't. To all the people who read drafts and pieces of drafts (particularly Lisa Andersen), and asked questions and said it would finish – here it is.

Thanks, too, to Steve Offner, who sharpens my words.